BEYOND THE ORDINARY

BEYOND THE ORDINARY

Dr. Philip Ayers

XULON PRESS

Xulon Press
2301 Lucien Way #415
Maitland, FL 32751
407.339.4217
www.xulonpress.com

© 2017 by Dr. Philip Ayers

Edited by Xulon Press.

All rights reserved solely by the author. The author guarantees all contents are original and do not infringe upon the legal rights of any other person or work. No part of this book may be reproduced in any form without the permission of the author. The views expressed in this book are not necessarily those of the publisher.

Unless otherwise indicated, Scripture quotations taken from the English Standard Version (ESV). Copyright © 2001 by Crossway, a publishing ministry of Good News Publishers. Used by permission. All rights reserved.

Printed in the United States of America.

ISBN-13: 9781545614938

DEDICATION

I DEDICATE THIS BOOK TO MY WIFE, LOIS AYERS, WHO has stood by me and our ministry for twenty-eight wonderful years; she knows all my faults and still loves me. Jesus Christ, together with Lois, helps me to live **beyond the ordinary** stresses, hurts, joy, and triumphs of ministry.

My greatest appreciation goes to Rev. Bonita Durham, who was so gracious to read this work through watchful eyes. Her suggestions greatly enhanced the presentation of the lives of the disciples. It was her encouragement that motivated me to complete this book.

FOREWORD

MY FRIEND, DR. PHIL AYERS, HAS ADDRESSED AN issue that has plagued our American church culture for far too long–complacency. *Beyond the Ordinary* calls every born-again, power-filled believer, to live lives that are extraordinary with encouragement found in the life examples of the twelve disciples. By revealing the *Beyond the Ordinary* lives of the disciples; all Christ-Followers are reminded that the same power that compelled these original twelve to high levels of service is the same power available to each of us.

Following the life examples of these twelve men; may we all purpose to live with such a sense of urgency, passion and power, motivated by the kind of love that can change this dark world. I am very thankful for *Beyond the Ordinary,* as the American church needs to be shaken and awakened to be free of the complacency and mediocrity that has silenced and disabled too many for far too long! May this book be that tool that causes many to revisit their level of service and take the steps needed to have lives marked as *Beyond the Ordinary*!

Thomas McCracken
Founder of CommUNITY Church
Author of *Being the Believing*

A CHALLENGE FROM THE AUTHOR

PAUL, PETER, JAMES AND JOHN ZEBEDEE, ANDREW, Nathanael, James Alphaeus, Thomas, Matthew, Philip, Thaddaeus, Simon the Zealot and Judas Iscariot were the chosen ones of Jesus Christ. Their lives are featured in this book. They inspire Christians to reject a defeatist mindset through settling for a lesser role in serving Christ. Each disciple chose to serve Christ to the utmost of their ability. They would make human mistakes along the way, but they never forsook their commitment to serve to the fullest. Their challenge to all believers in Jesus Christ is to extend their vision of service to a level outside of normal thinking.

Beyond the Ordinary is a challenge for you to reach above your upmost vision of service to Jesus Christ. It is not enough to serve Christ; Jesus desires you to serve beyond the norm. He wants you to change your world for Him. This mindset is foreign to the current thinking of the world that promotes the attitude of "receiving something for nothing or success is owed to me." You will find your attitude toward servanthood as you study through the lives of the apostles. One of them may mirror your thinking and stand out in your mind. It is this one that could guide you to acceptance of your divine destiny in Jesus.

The life of each apostle is narrated in story form. An attempt is made to portray their lives through intellectual and traditional information gathered from the summaries of many resources. There are characterizations of each apostle based on the environment of their times and social practices, such as cultural and ethnic prejudices that dictated certain mindsets which lead to predictable behaviors. A decision to look behind the lines of many resources and evaluations from many Bible scholars is used to create the family, employment and religious backgrounds of each apostle to bring their lives to the written page. Since we did not live during their lifetime, certain assumptions need to be exercised; no author's description of the apostles can be declared as absolute. There will always be critical argumentation about these presumptions, but these do not change the basic theme of this book, which is serving Jesus **beyond the ordinary**.

Each apostle of Jesus had a specific and defining moment when their attitude toward themselves and others changed. This is factual and observed in Scripture. Each chose to move **beyond the ordinary** principles of success, such as: risk taking, remaining true to oneself, community and religious obligations and passion. Each one chose to leave their careers and ideology to step out on extraordinary faith to reach the lost for Jesus. Scripture shows that the miraculous and creative power of Jesus Christ, the same creative power used by God to speak the world into existence, changed their thinking about their possibilities and propelled their ministry to a supernatural level. They would ascend to phenomenal accomplishments for the cause of Christianity.

David Brainerd, an American missionary to the Native Americans, said, "As long as I see anything to be done for God, life is worth having; but O how vain and unworthy it is to live for any lower end!"[1] Charles Spurgeon, an English Baptist preacher, said "If we give God service it must be because He gives us grace. We work for Him because He works in us."[2] Jesus implants on the soul of each Christian, a gut-wrenching impression of being used mightily by God. So, what event or encounter would make the difference in a Christian's thoughts that would raise their service for Christ to extraordinary heights, **beyond the ordinary**, and therefore, avoid a guilt-ridden life of mediocrity?

Every Christian can obtain this position in servanthood, based on God's grace, even in the face of opposition coming from human

---

[1] Brainerd, David. (n.d.) AZQuotes.com

[2] Spurgeon, Charles. Christianquotes.info

or spiritual assault, and can reach the summit of their service to Jesus Christ. You can make the same choices and commitments to serve Christ. It may take a change in your attitude and faith that God can bring to fruition His plan for you. God will bring you to a "crossroad" in your life. Will you recognize this intersection in your life when it presents itself? Will you travel the road to a life ***beyond the ordinary*** or the road of a detached awareness of the potential you possess in Jesus Christ? God prefers to do great things through you. Believe it and act upon it!

TABLE OF CONTENTS

Introduction xv

Chapter One–The Apostle Paul, a Giant of a Man,
    Goes Beyond the Ordinary 1
Chapter Two–The Apostle Peter, the Fisherman,
    Goes Beyond the Ordinary 26
Chapter Three–The Apostle Andrew, the Quiet One,
    Goes Beyond the Ordinary 43
Chapter Four–The Apostle James, the Fiery One,
    Goes Beyond the Ordinary 55
Chapter Five–The Apostle John, the Beloved Disciple,
    Goes Beyond the Ordinary 68
Chapter Six–The Apostle Nathanael, a Good Man,
    Goes Beyond the Ordinary 80
Chapter Seven–The Apostle Philip, a Pessimist,
    Goes Beyond the Ordinary 89
Chapter Eight–The Apostle Matthew, the Tax Collector,
    Goes Beyond the Ordinary 99
Chapter Nine–The Apostle Thomas, a Questioner,
    Goes Beyond the Ordinary 108
Chapter Ten–The Apostle James Alphaeus, a Mama's Boy,
    Goes Beyond the Ordinary 120
Chapter Eleven–The Apostle Thaddaeus, the Big Hearted,
    Goes Beyond the Ordinary 135
Chapter Twelve–The Apostle Simon Zealot, an Assassin,
    Goes Beyond the Ordinary 146
Chapter Thirteen–The Apostle Judas Iscariot, a Traitor,
    Goes Beyond the Ordinary 159
Chapter Fourteen–Beyond the Ordinary Summary 185

Bibliography for Advanced Study 195
Dr. Phil Ayers Bio 201

INTRODUCTION

HAVE YOU EVER WONDER WHY SOME PEOPLE accept Jesus Christ as their Savior, but never advance to a high level of service? When they come to a "fork in the road" in their commitment to serve; they choose the road of ease, avoiding the necessary change in their servanthood that would advance them *beyond the ordinary*. It seems that people would desire to advance in the faith, to become a difference-maker in the lives of others, but there is no desire. Many believers in Christ reach high levels of service, becoming world known for their achievements, yet some never serve, and others serve half-heartedly. This suggests that the atonement of Christ is not enough to bring success in the lives of all believers. Some might argue that Christ is prejudiced towards some and uninterested in others, but that would be totally contrary to the nature of Christ. There is another factor that answers the dilemma.

The answer to the question is found through an examination of the lives of the Apostle Paul and the twelve disciples. Each one of them had a distinct moment in their life that moved them to an unwavering and totally committed life of service. Each one had two profound encounters with Christ that changed them. The first was the fullness of the salvation experience and the second was a life-changing encounter with Christ that redirected their opportunity for success in ministry. This was their defining moment!

The second encounter had nothing to add to any major doctrinal argument found in theological debates, such as the "born again" experience or the "second blessing," sometimes referred to as the "baptism of the Holy Spirit." Nor did it involve the lifelong battle between the "old sin nature and the new nature." (I John 3:1-16, 1 Cor. 2:13 ESV) Instead, it was the result of a major life crisis, a crisis of extreme importance that elevated the believer to the extreme height of service, which is the theme of this book. The outcome of this encounter is witnessed in the spread of Christianity in their culture and throughout the known world, and is the reason that some Christians become frontrunners in the faith.

Every believer in Christ will come to a point in their life where a decision must be made to continue in mediocrity or accept the challenge of faith that explodes them to a dynamic walk with Jesus. He exposes them to circumstances that cannot be ignored; a cross-road of no return. This challenge of faith is available for every believer to experience. Somewhere, and at a definite time in your life, you too will come face-to-face with this challenge to remain in your former behavioral pattern of servanthood, or move **beyond the ordinary** of serving Jesus at a mediocre level of success. Your walk with Christ will change should you decide to accept the challenge.

The challenge which I speak about is not salvation. It is not an encounter with the acquiring of the Holy Spirit in one's life. However, this encounter cannot happen until a person is saved and indwelled by the Holy Spirit. Salvation is the first step to a meaningful relationship with Christ. The Bible is clear that a person is lost until the "born again" experience takes place. (John 3:1-6) "Lost" is a condition brought about by the sin nature of the human being. It means a person is lost from God; eternally separated from the presence of God.

Humans lost their right to a relationship with God, because they inherited the penalties of disobedience, innate in them from the first man and woman, Adam and Eve. (Gen. 3) When Adam and Eve disobeyed God in the Garden of Eden, a terrible inheritance was passed to all mankind—lostness. The beautiful relationship and fellowship between God and human beings ended. Now, something must take place to restore mankind. God required a sacrifice be made to restore that family division caused by sin. Ultimately, that sacrifice would be His Only Son, Jesus Christ. One must be "born again."

Being "born again" means a person is saved or pardoned from the judgment of God, which originated from the original sin debt caused by the actions of Adam and Eve in the Garden of Eden. A person is given a new life and a new nature through the rebirth. (2 Cor. 5:17) This rebirth takes place when a person chooses to turn from their innate sin, admit their sinful acts and accept the forgiveness of sin provided by Jesus Christ through the fulfilling of the Gospel: the death, burial, and resurrection of Christ on the third day. (I Cor. 15:1-4) God's anger toward mankind is satisfied through the shed blood of Jesus Christ on the cross of Calvary when a person asks for God's forgiveness. (Rom. 10:13, 10:8-10) A true act of belief on the part of a sinner triggers the grace of God on their behalf and they are placed into the family of God, forever. (Eph. 2:8-10)

Humans are then allotted the opportunities of a faith walk with Jesus. This faith walk is enabled by the indwelling of the Holy Spirit in the life of a believer. It involves the never-ending fight between the flesh and the spirit that of the innate sin nature of the flesh against the new spiritual nature given to a person at the rebirth. A believer in Jesus Christ has the assurance of the Holy Spirit that the war is won and their destiny is settled, a Heavenly home upon their death. (I John 5:13; John 14:1-7) It is the work of the Holy Spirit to set aside a believer for the safety and service of that person. (Eph. 1:13; 4:30) The believer has the awareness that their purpose in life is to surrender their desires over to the desires of God, and even during all the battles with the flesh and the challenges of being obedient to God; a greater path of service can be reached.

The believer is granted help to accomplish all that God has planned for them, using spiritual gifts. These gifts are given to the believer for the twofold purpose of winning other people to faith in Christ and acquiring the fulfillment of their mission in this present life. (Jer. 29:11-12; Rom. 12:6-8; I Cor. 12:8-10; I Pet. 4:11) It is during the exercise of this twofold purpose that a believer reaches the intersection of no return; a mile marker in life. One way will lead to a life and service of useless mediocrity, and the other way will take the believer to the mountain top of their purpose for living. (Exod. 34:2) All Christians should seek to travel this road, the road ***beyond the ordinary,*** *a* life of serving Jesus Christ.

Chapter One

THE APOSTLE PAUL, A GIANT OF A MAN, GOES BEYOND THE ORDINARY

The Apostle Paul was a devout and motivated Jew, with strong traditional ties to the Sanhedrin, but he would have to change his attitude toward servanthood if he was to go beyond the ordinary.

ARE PEOPLE THE PRODUCT OF THEIR ANCESTRY, environment, culture and intellectual endeavors? Do these qualifiers doom a person to failure or success in future Christian service? Does God command certain outcomes in the life of a person? Do believers in Christ have an advantage over non-believers, or can anyone, regardless of faith in God, achieve the upmost in the servanthood of God? Will faith in Jesus Christ solve the life problems faced by Christians or will they labor in life like non-believers while working toward a goal?

The answers to these questions have been argued through the centuries by theologians and philosophers. The fact remains that whatever the influence these answers may have on the life of an individual, there is more to the success of Christian service than what lies within meaningful debates of wise scholars. There is an unexplainable inner-peace that accompanies extraordinary servanthood.

The life of the Apostle Paul lends answers to these questions. He had good genes, a profitable family environment, a culture ripe for change and the best advantages education could offer; yet he found he would come to a crisis in ministry that would forever change his destiny. God would help him accomplish his calling in life, but Paul had to choose his path; to go **beyond the ordinary** accomplishments in service, to acquire the inner-peace that eluded him in his Judaic service and his early walk with Christ.

Saul of Tarsus, later known as the Apostle Paul, was born in AD 2 in the city of Tarsus, a Mediterranean coastal city that was mainly pagan at the time of his birth. (Acts 9:11; 22:3) It was located at the corner of the country of modern day Turkey where Asia Minor met Syria north of Israel. Commerce was thriving with the wharves on the Cydnus River bustling with trade. The city served as a learning center, and was compared to the cities of Alexander and Athens. It was no ordinary place to live, and impressed young Paul with its reputation, so much so that he returned there after his training in Jerusalem, once to become a master teacher in the synagogue and later after his conversion to Christianity. (Acts 9:30; 11:25) Paul's family was strongly connected to the Pharisaic traditions and zeal, later making Tarsus a target for evangelism of a newly converted religious zealot, such as Paul. His aggressive ministry style was drawn there.

Tarsus was well-known for making a certain kind of felt cloth from the wool of shaggy black goats, and it is very possible that Paul learned his tent making skills at Tarsus. Paul, once a Christian, did spend eight years there, learning and engaging the false religious beliefs of its citizens, until Barnabas recruited him to go to the Syrian Antioch.

Young Paul would move to Jerusalem in AD 12, and would face major life changes from that of Tarsus. He would stay with his nephew, the son of one of his sisters while there. (Acts. 23:15) The remainder of his family; Andronicus, Jason, Sosipater, Lucius and Junia, stayed in and around Tarsus. He would never lose his Roman citizenship granted to him as a birthright of Tarsus origin.

His father, a Pharisee himself, wanted his son to receive the best possible education that only teachers from Jerusalem could give. He attended the school of Gamaliel, where he learned the Stoic philosophy of Athenodorus, Zero, Antipater and Nestor. (Acts 7:58-60; 22:20)[3] The Stoic philosophy taught a constant practice and training that included logic; Socratic dialogue and self-dialogue contemplation of death, training one's attention to remain in the present moment, and daily reflection on everyday problems and possible solutions. All subjects of interest that he would later use in winning the lost to Christianity.

Paul would emerge from this influence with a life style of aggressive and constant courage, but bathed in ill-informed wisdom, temperance and justice. These qualities would be remolded into powerful evangelism during his walk with Christ. This is clear when examining his dialect with the converted Stoics in Athens, as he taught these new converts the word of God. (Acts 17:16-18)

Paul, while studying in Jerusalem, went from exposure to pagan rituals in Tarsus to practicing the purest of Judaism, from eating forbidden Jewish dietary catfish to enjoying the finest of Jerusalem food, and from drinking poor water to consuming hot wine diluted with sea water. His pastimes changed from being exposed to gladiatorial fights with lions and tigers to reading poetry, oftentimes quoting Epimenides of Crete and Aratus of Cilicia. (Titus 1:12; Acts 17:28) He was exposed to classical literature, philosophy, and ethics. He also became fluent in Hebrew and Konia Greek, while contemplating the temptations of an immoral society verses the strict Pharisaical laws, not unlike the challenges faced by the youth of our society. (I Tim. 1:15)

Paul was being challenged by many conflicting customs, differing environments, intellectual insights and styles of living that would influence him in his most important decision of all– accepting Christ and being the communicator of the Gospel to the Gentile population. (Rom. 1:5; 11:13; Gal. 2:8) He would be prepared by God to change the religious world, if he chose to believe in Christ.

The early life of Paul offered the benefits of a good family, yet not without turmoil. This turmoil would remain with him until he

---

[3] Attridge, Harold W.; Hata, Gohei, eds. <u>Eusebius, Christianity, and Judaism</u>. Detroit MI: Wayne State Univ. Press, 1992.

finally made a change in his thinking, a change that came years later.[4] His father was a member of the ruling class of religious leaders, known as the Pharisees, meaning his family was heavily influenced by differing conflicts among this ruling class of religious men. This is evident in the behavior of Paul once he became a man and a member of this religious political party. He would develop very self-righteous and segregated habits.

Paul's life was infested by turmoil. Part of the turmoil surrounding Paul was the actions of the Sanhedrin; a group of judges appointed by God to command religious behavior from the Jewish people. The Sanhedrin made up of the Pharisees and Sadducees never agreed on anything, except killing Christ. They fought over social and religious conflicts among the Jews, and were constantly at odds with the Romans authorities. Their actions caused unrest and fear among the people as they went about their daily activities. The arguments between these religious leaders were a constant point of contention and were even disputed within the homes of Jews.

The Sadducees were heavily concentrated in the Hellenization of the culture, while the Pharisees vividly opposed the movement. Their stance caused cultural divisions between the Hellenized Jews and Aramaic-speaking Israelites in Jerusalem that brought a language barrier into the affairs of the Jews and Christianity. The Hellenists were Christian Jews who spoke in Greek, and the Hebrews were Christian Jews who spoke in Aramaic. Paul, because of his extensive education, understood both dialects and could communicate with both parties.

The Sanhedrin had no answer for this unsettled atmosphere. The people were even more confused by their religious leaders who argued the existence or non-existence of a resurrection of the dead. Paul would hear these arguments between his father and his opponents, and was drawn into the fray. He weighted the Hellenist argument against the resurrection of the dead, even though he

---

[4] Maccoby, Hyam. The Mythmaker: Paul and the Invention of Christianity. New York, NY: Harper & Row, 1986.
Dunn, James D.G. Jesus, Paul, and the Gospels. Grand Rapids, MI: Wm. B. Eerdmans, 2011.

claimed to be a Pharisee, and decided there was a resurrection. These resurrection issues were always on the table, and the people never had solid ground to base their faith upon until Paul entered the gospel ministry and declared there was a resurrection for all who accepted Christ as Savior. Paul had a determined opinion on these issues, and declared later that there was neither Jew nor Greek, bond or free, male or female; for you are all one in Christ, and everyone who was saved would be resurrected. (Acts 23:6; 9:29; Gal. 3:28) He would defend this truth as vigorously as he had Judaism.

Many such disputes hounded Paul. He was a devout Pharisee and angered many religious factions in the Judean region. The more conservative Jewish Hellenist, for example, threatened his life. These serious issues steered Paul into a certain argumentative and prejudiced mindset that helped him in his defense of Judaism, but would not aid him in his Christian service. Not until he had a major adjustment in his thinking and preaching. He ruled from a stubborn mindset governed by a strong-willed belief system that made it nearly impossible to reach **beyond the ordinary** ineffective approaches to ministry. This mindset displeased God and upset Paul's happiness in ministry. God worked through this unrest caused by Paul's inaccurate view of proper ministry to bring him to a God-directed ministry.

Individuals, such as the Apostle Paul, can be subject to a nurturing family, outstanding education, a wonderful environment and every beneficial opportunity, but it does not mean they are suited for what God has in mind for their future service to Jesus. The best of intentions, parents who love their children, teachers who push for excellence, a religion full of attributes of goodness, or circumstances of the best possible outcomes, do not guaranteed that people, such as Paul, will choose service tactics that are virtuous and unprejudiced toward others of perceived lesser character or disagreeing ideas. Paul served God Jehovah with ill-advised tactics of service, and could have been a hindrance to true faith in God. However, a merciful God can use all these factors to bring an individual to a crisis of decision, a decision to change the outcome of past attempts at serving others, and so it was with the Apostle Paul.

The actual journey of the Apostle Paul's walk with Christ starts with a terrible decision on his behalf. He hated and spurned all challenges to his beloved faith in Judaism. It was the decision to allow Stephen, a follower of Christ, to be murdered in AD 32 by the Jewish companions of Paul. This decision was grounded in his jaded expectations of right and wrong, even though that decision broke every principle of Judaism. (Acts 6 & 7)[5] Paul was blinded by Satan to his motives for attacking Christianity, because he allowed himself to wear blinders to the claims made by Stephen against the corruption of the ruling religious leaders, such as temple corruption. The priests were belittling and robbing the peasants of their opportunity to offer a sacrificial lamb for the forgiveness of their sins by declaring their offering as unfit. (I Tim. 1:13-16; II Cor. 4:4; John 2:11-12)

Stephen was a Hellenizes Syrian-Cilician Jew, who had been converted to Christ while staying in Jerusalem. He was a deacon of the church in Jerusalem and was assaulted for giving money to help the poor. Giving to help the less fortunate was an acceptable act by the church, but because the church was growing so fast, some of the poor had been over looked, especially the Hellenistic widows. Stephen was a godly man, but not seasoned in the social disputes of his day, even though he walked daily under the control of the Holy Spirit; something that probably irritated Paul. There is no doubt that Stephen had the fullness of the Spirit, but being a young believer, he lacked the fullness of a mature believer with many years of service, so he exasperated the religious establishment. It is obvious from his willingness to die for the cause of Christ that he was totally submissive and dependent on Jesus. Again, a virtue that Paul, who was submissive to no one, had to learn. Stephen was living a consistent life, and was a consecrated servant of Jesus. Paul would learn an inconsistent life will never aid in his service for Christ to the lost. (Rom. 7:7-25)

---

[5] Ehrman, Bart. Peter, Paul, and Mary Magdalene: The Followers of Jesus in History and Legend. Oxford University Press, USA, 2006.

Stephen would show a great willingness to serve tables, and to bring his message to the Hellenistic Jews from the Synagogue of the Freedmen. (Acts 7:10, 22) He learned humility from Christ's death on the Cross, and Stephen, by humbling himself to the Holy Spirit, realized the totality of the wisdom in the message from the Cross. It was a message of faith and trust in the sovereignty of God who called Abraham out of a pagan country and insured the completion of the Abrahamic covenant.[6] He preached that Christ gave a New Covenant to save His chosen people, despite their rebellious and sinful actions.

The humility of Stephen offended Paul, who was a proud man, so Paul would not allow this message to go unchallenged and responded by overseeing Stephen's death. Ironically, later Paul would defend this message of salvation and die in the service of its cause. Paul learned the hard lesson that the sovereignty of God means God knows in advance who will serve Him and by what means God will use to bring this truth to fruition. Then every believer must either decide to accept God's divine discernment for their ministry or be controlled by the senseless wisdom of the world. Stephen was serving God exactly as God had decided for him.

The Jewish leaders of the Freedmen cult, consisting of the Cyrenians and Alexandrians, and the members from Cilicia and Asia, were horrified by the message of Stephen that Jesus Christ was the Son of God, who came to deliver sinners from the penalty of sin. Paul was one of these Jewish leaders and vehemently opposed every spoken word of Stephen. The more Stephen expounded on Jesus as the end of the law of righteousness for those who believe and that He was superior to Moses, the heavier the debate became. Eventually, the Jews brought in witnesses to falsely accuse Stephen of preaching against the Law and the temple. They stirred up the local citizens, finally bringing him before the Sanhedrin. Once there, they accused him of teaching that Jesus would destroy the Jewish temple and the ways of Moses.

Paul was there during the mockery of this courageous man, and said nothing to defend him, because he did not understand

---

[6] Langton, Daniel R. The Apostle Paul in the Jewish Imagination. Cambridge, UK: Cambridge University Press, 2010.

the truth of Christ. Stephen proved that God's messenger can be bold, unwavering, powerful, yet humble, and Paul could not handle him. The men that stoned Stephen laid their cloaks at his feet. He and the other Jews did not know God in a personal way and they had not experienced the forgiveness of sin that Stephen had embraced, because they only had the empty religion of self-righteousness and pride. Many times, in Paul's future, his mind would go back to these memories, because he would find himself in front of accusing men bearing false testimony to his ministry. Men accused Paul of not telling the entire redemptive process, that a person must earn their salvation through submitting the Law of Moses, good deeds and baptism. (Acts 21:27-40)

Stephens' show of the grace of God towards poor people and his blistering sermon brought death to him, yet he only showed grace to his executioners as they stoned him to death; a miraculous show of divine constraint. He asked God to forgive his persecutors as they threw stones to crush his body, instead of performing a delivering miracle on his behalf. (Acts 6:8; 15:12) Paul and the religious men saw the angelic countenance of Stephen as he died that day. Perhaps his countenance mimicked the face of Moses, after being in the presence of God on Mount Sinai, since Stephen had proclaimed Christ as better than Moses or possibly portrayed the glory of God seen on the Mount of Transfiguration. (Exod. 34:29; Matt. 17:1-13) Paul saw this glory and it was a first step for his coming to know the Savior, the Lord Jesus Christ, even though he would stubbornly attempt to persecute the Christians for some time to come. (Acts 8) Many converts who either witnessed this death or heard of it were scattered aboard and came to Antioch to preach the words of Christ to non-believers. (Acts 8:4-5; 11:19)

The Apostle Paul, in AD 34, met Christ on the road to Damascus, less than two years after the death of Stephen. (Acts 9:1-31; 22:1-22; 26:12-18) He had caused terror in the Christian movement and was one of the most feared men of his time, yet he would become a missionary, evangelist, leader, thinker, statesman and lover of souls, writing most of the New Testament. His is a story of reframing his birth right, Roman citizenship and destructive circumstances, all of which stood for everything opposed to kindness, forgiveness and love shown through the Christian movement. Paul, until this time, had gauged his actions on prestige, authority coming from being a Pharisee, personal abilities stemming from his education, and his desires to advance the teachings of Judaism, based on what he had learned while interacting with his chosen life style of self-exultation. (Phil. 3:4-6)

Paul testified that one day, while traveling 130-miles from Jerusalem to Damascus to make havoc of the Christian church and to incarcerate or kill Christians; his defense of Judaism would dramatically change to that of following Christ. (Acts 8:3) There is no doubt he was saved on that day, but his pilgrimage with Christ would come to need a major attitude adjustment. Everything in his pre-conversion life, his motivation to succeed in his own strength and understanding of the happenings around him, needed to change. His adjustment would come years later!

Damascus was a city of about a hundred and fifty thousand people, and at least twenty thousand were Jews. Christianity had established a foothold in this community, and Paul knew the Christians continued to meet in the synagogues, so he sought them out. These Christians, in the mind of Paul, were defaming the nature and character of God and the very foundations of Judaism. Their heresy consumed his every moment, and their slaughter was his passion. He was determined to stop this movement with the permission of the high priest, and this was his reason for traveling the long distance to Damascus, but he never planned to meet Jesus Christ, the very person the Christians followed.

It was the plan of Paul to bring these offenders of Judaism back to Jerusalem for trial, and he enlisted many people to help with this mission. Their journey carried them through Samaria, where a great revival was happening under the evangelist Philip, and then Peter and John. The gospel was spreading like wildfire infuriating Paul, but he stayed to his plan of stopping the Christian movement in Damascus. Six days into the seven-day journey from Jerusalem to Damascus, at noon time, an astonishing encounter with the supernatural took place; Jesus showed Himself to Paul. Paul was knocked from his donkey and blinded by the glorious light of the Christ. Paul's accompanists were thrown to the ground, hearing a noise, but not seeing Christ. (Acts 9:22; 26:14; I Cor. 15:18) Slowly the others stood, but Paul remained dazed on the ground, in the dirt, listening to the words of Jesus.

Instantly, Paul's mind flashed back to the face and words of Stephen, and he heard Jesus ask him why he was intending to persecute Him. He asked the Lord in bewilderment, "Who are you, Lord?" Jesus answered, "I am Jesus of Nazareth, whom you are persecuting. It is hard to kick against the goads." Jesus said it would take the piercing of nails attached to the end of a stick, a goad, to change Paul's demeanor. (Judg. 3:21)

Jesus rebuked Paul for his sinful actions and confronted him with knowing he was doing wrong. Jesus forced him to see the error of his threatening and killing believers, the difficulty that comes with opposing God, and the weight of a guilty conscience. (Eph. 2:1-10) Jesus made him see the masked fear he faced was admitting Christ was truth.

Paul, without any hesitation, asked Jesus what He wanted him to do. Jesus told him to go into the city and wait to be told his mission in life. Paul opened his eyes but could not see, so the others led him into the city to the house of Judas. Ananias, a disciple of Jesus, was appointed by God to find him and lift his blindness. Paul, over the next several days, had time to think about the words of Jesus and Ananias, who would tell him he was to be the apostle to the Gentile people, and then he was baptized. Paul was saved and the church found rest for a moment in time. (Acts 9:8-19, 31)

Paul would immediately start to preach the gospel in the synagogues, but this did not mean he was fully prepared to accept all that had happened in his life to that point; it may have been a hindrance. (Acts 9:20) He had a lot of baggage concerning his past murderous affairs. Paul fell in love with Jesus, much like he loved Judaism. However, it is evident that his aggressive schemes to impact people did not improve, even though God could use them, and it is obvious Jesus continued to deal with Paul's past and present style of service. (II Corinthians 5:16-21; Romans 7)

God loves unconditionally and forgives completely, no longer remembering sin once it is repented and confessed, but believers hold on to their ways of doing things. Believers compartmentalize the actions of love. Jumping into instant ministry, as Paul did, could prevent a believer from hearing the full council of God, and for Paul; he thought his relentless service would earn God's favor. However, it is remaining in past accomplishments and failures that must change if a believer is to reach the apex of their love relationship and service to Christ. The entire life of Paul, to this moment in his life, was controlled by his self-will and ambition to succeed in ministry, doing what he wanted to do, but this is not the way of Christ. Submission and surrender is God's way to succeeding in His purpose for reaching the prize that is placed before a believer. (Philippians 3:12-16; Colossians 3)

Paul would learn that first comes grace through faith, followed by works. (Ephesians 2:8-10) He would be introduced to this truth as he traveled around the countryside preaching a gospel of good news and salvation by grace, yet attempting to serve apart from the grace that saves. He labored for an understanding of how to embrace the gospel through the eyes of a servant. Paul would come to know it is a good thing to accomplish great things for Jesus because it helps others, but never at the expense of communing with Jesus.

He traveled to Arabia, the location of Mount Sinai, and back to Damascus, ultimately finding himself three years later in Jerusalem. He met with James and Peter for fifteen days before departing, and would not return there for fourteen years. (Galatians 1:13-24; 4:24-25) Paul would make his peace about the gospel message being preached to the Gentile people and accepted his role in God's plan for his life. (Galatians 1:11-16) He would settle the issue of his salvation, making mention of it four times in his writing to the churches.[7] He discerned that salvation was an ongoing work of grace: being saved from the judgment, temptation, exercise and presence of sin. (II Timothy 1:9; I Timothy 1:15; Titus 5:5; I Corinthians 15:1-2; Romans 13:11) Paul would become settled in his thinking, ready to preach the gospel and reach the apex of his service opportunity. The Holy Spirit led the church to ordain Barnabas to find Paul, bring him to Antioch and start their gospel

---

[7] Towns, Elmer. Theology for Today. Dubuque, IO: Kendal/Hunt Publishing Company, 1989.

ministry. (Acts 11:26) Later, he and Paul would bring offerings from the churches they founded to the famine stricken church in Jerusalem.

It was God who put the Apostle Paul into ministry. (I Timothy 1:12-16) Paul was sold out to Christ from the very beginning of his walk with Him, unlike many believers who never truly commit everything to Jesus. Paul was sold out to serve, but had to learn how to leave his will behind. He meant every word when he said, "Lord, what will you have me to do?" (Acts 22:10) The challenge was not in whether Jesus was his Lord, but by what manner he was to fully obey Him in servanthood. This would be a growth process that brought God's will and Paul's will together as one; it took time and some mistakes on Paul's part. Paul got it right sometimes, such as following the leading of the Holy Spirit into Macedonia, and he missed it sometimes, such as his fight with Barnabas and his rejection of young Mark. (Acts 15:36-41; 16:6-10) Paul would miss Barnabas and labored in his soul over losing a good friend and ministry partner. Any believer would be beside themselves. He made those errors in ministry because he approached service from the wrong direction.

Another wrong direction in Paul's service to Jesus was his dispute with Peter's decision to stop eating with Gentile believers or sharing the Lord's Supper with them. Paul felt that Peter feared the followers of James, who thought his association with Gentiles would bring harm to the church in Jerusalem at the hands of the Jewish nationalists. Nevertheless, this heated church crisis was a testimony to everyone's national pride and racial ties. This seemed to contradict Paul's view of himself as being all things to all people that he might win some to faith in Jesus, since Peter was accused of the same basic thing. Paul was a strong defender of the gospel being preached to all people with the same energy as he showed when defending Judaism earlier in his life. His cause was just, but his method was harsh. (Galatians 2:11-21) Paul accomplished his purpose, but at the expense of uneasiness in his soul.

Perhaps the most pressing issue in ministry faced by the Apostle Paul would be the misunderstanding over the debate about women not having leadership roles in the church, known as women usurping men's authority. He was attacked for believing God had a hierarchy for leadership which presumably disallowed women to hold positions of authority over men. In fact, he was understood as saying women were to be silent in church, and only speak at home, causing the Hellenist women to stand against the idea of women having no rights, no education and no roles in society except for childbearing. (I Timothy 2:8-15; I Corinthians 14:33-36) The task of solving this issue was laid upon Paul. Paul had to reconcile the knowledge, perspectives, convictions, character and skill of all concerned in settling these conflicts. He solved the debate but at great distress to his mental health. (Romans 12:1-5; II Corinthians 10:3-5)

The Apostle Paul was straightforward in his directives to the church. He was unbending in his opinions; such attitudes haunted him because of his expectations placed on others while living with his own inabilities to fulfill his self-expectations placed on his ministry. He faced an uneasiness in his service and it bled over into his strong approach to solving the women issues.

Paul was of a background where the culture extremely limited the women in their behavior and responsibilities. Married and unmarried women could not leave their homes without their father's or husband's permission. Remember, Paul's father was a Pharisee and upheld this practice, not allowing his wife to leave the home without his blessing. Women had little or no authority over men or their choices in any matter, including who they could not speak to, especially strangers, nor could they ever be unveiled in public, or testify in court. Basically, they had no rights and were the property of men.

Women were barely better off than slaves, and oftentimes treated worse than beasts of burden. Paul disagreed with this harsh treatment of women, but his inflexibility on this and other issues locked him into a rigid approach to solutions by others associated with him. He found it very difficult to break with his demanding demeanor. Again, Paul's battle between grace and obligation limited his connectedness to Jesus in his service. He understood grace as a part of the salvation process, but he could not apply it to service. Service was something he must do on his own efforts apart from grace.

Paul's dilemma maintained a hold on him even while he pioneered a change in cultural thinking about education, especially with women's education. Perhaps the most restrictive condition for women was they could not be educated. Earlier, no doubt the Apostle Paul learned and followed these beliefs, until he became a Christian, and God inundated him to a better understanding of the value of women. However, Paul had to communicate this to a very prejudiced people, and this debate brought much controversy to his ministry and agony in his heart.

The religious crowd expected him to agree with them on this and every issue. Jesus pressured him within his heart to follow his conscience. Strangely, in the middle of this controversy, Paul began to climb out of his mysterious unhappiness in ministry, to start the journey of going **beyond the ordinary**!

The controversy continued. Some women had broken the subordinate role of women, and had advanced to leadership roles, such as acquiring an education and gaining wealth. This was a change in society that met with great opposition from those who highly held to the traditions of the patriarchal system of keeping women, as they would say, from destroying the purity of Judaism, but these women were beginning to have a voice in business and politics. Again, the pressure placed on Paul to solve this issue was enormous, and he would not satisfy everyone by his position on the matter. It seems that Paul did not think the traditional role of women to be totally negative, as is seen in his writings, and he did think his directives were not demeaning to women, but he was emotionally touched by the affair. Imagine trying to please the demands of men and women coming out of a Jewish, Hellenistic and Roman culture!

This unsettled atmosphere over gender roles within the church kept Paul's joy unsettled within his soul. Turmoil within him lingered because his philosophy on receiving happiness was centered in successful service which abated him in this debate. He felt extreme pressure to solve these painful stances between the genders. The circumstance seemed to change from moment to moment. Coupled with the conflict over the role of women in the church was the attitude of maintaining a Godly appearance and presence in public and private; the displays of actions and worship.

Some women were drawing attention to themselves, as were certain men, in pursuit of their selfish desires and passions. The Apostle Paul reacted to this display of self-indulgence by instructing everyone to reverently worship God and not themselves, to not flaunt their sexuality, wealth, or ignorant behaviors, and to show a proper shame about them. Paul wanted all people to express genuine love for God, reverence for His holiness and self-control of their passions, actions and desires. Most importantly, he insisted that all people, especially women, be privy to education, something withheld from women in the past. He knew education leveled the playing field, and insured equality in spiritual privileges, rights, blessings and promises for men and women. (I Corinthians 11:1-16; 14:26-34-35; II Corinthians 13:7-10; Galatians 3:28) Except in the Church at Corinth, where great anarchy through false teaching was taking place, he said there was no difference between people in Christian communities; all are equal.

However, he stood firm in teaching and insisting that God set up the rule within the church. Paul never worried about political correctness or universal human rights, even though he was learning to gently act with kindness, but this warring between the genders had to prey on his mind, as his memories drifted in and out of past Jewish customs and current Christian practice. His desire to please God in his leadership role and discover the inner-peace he sought through serving Jesus continued to push him to a moment of crisis, to a critical decision to let go of his abilities and surrender to those of Jesus.

Jesus uses all things for his purposes, in this case, to bring Paul to a stalemate in his theory of grace being totally separated from works. Remember, Paul believed salvation was solely a work of God through grace, but peace within the soul came because of personal works. So, another great controversial conflict arose in Paul's ministry. It was between James and Paul over grace verses works. (James 2:14-26) This disagreement was nearer to the internal argument within Paul's soul. The omniscience of

Jesus brought these two men together to force Paul to face his greatest enemy, himself. It was a doctrinal debate that was misunderstood then and still is today. (Romans 9:32) It was not that Paul and James were spiritual enemies, as some insisted, but they approached Christian salvation and service with Jesus from two different directions, although both doctrinal positions ended at the same place. It is easy to study the stances of each nowadays, because we can see the whole picture, but it was not so at that time in the two men's lives. People took sides, putting them at odds with each other.

Paul believed a non-believer is saved by the grace of God through faith and nothing else, while James believed that faith, of which Paul speaks, without proof of righteous works was meaningless in the sight of God. Paul taught that faith is complete trust in and obedience to Jesus Christ and works are outward ritual acts and following a code to attain merit. (Romans 3: 23; 6:12-23; Ephesians 2:8-10) James taught that faith is belief in Christ, the resurrection and salvation with works being spontaneous acts of love that come from inward faith. James sought service as an outward expression of grace which nurtured peace, and Paul pursued service as a justification for grace which fueled happiness. Both men needed to understand that it is God who justifies grace and service in the lives of his servants. Jesus authored the faith of both men. (James 2:19) Faith in Jesus brings peace, joy and happiness, and each one must live by his faith! (Galatians 2:15-16; 3:11)

Each one labored over the other's argument, and suffered greatly for the position they supported. Neither man could waver, because they felt so strongly about their relationship to Christ, and probably regretted the language tossed toward each other. Good men of God never are pleased over heated disagreements for the sake of the Lord, and many nights are spent in prayer begging God for peaceful, yet correct conclusions. The correct service for which both men strived to obtain suffered while they solved their differences. Both men longed for peace!

The Apostle Paul suffered at the hands of others because of his aggressive pursuit of the lost. (Acts 9:29; 13:50; 14:19; 16:22; 22:22; II Corinthians 4:9; 11:24) Many religious leaders and teachers questioned the techniques and mannerisms of Paul. Many were offended by his evangelistic style of going into the local synagogues to preach Christ to the unbelievers, both men and women. They believed this action stripped the local synagogue of its members, and was viewed as an inflammatory reach on the part of Paul into their sanctuary. Sometimes, the synagogues would find it very difficult to remain open for worship because its members had left, leaving it in financial and social ruin, and oftentimes without leadership.

The members that remained saw Paul as a proselyte, who only cared about his fame and building the Christian church. They claimed he used his knowledge of their Jewish customs, practices and scriptures to capture the imagination and curiosity of the Jewish population, making them easy prey for his theology. Many criticized his former position as a Pharisee which was perceived as giving him an unfair advance over the local priest, which caused an unsettled environment in these communities, yet Paul continued this strategy throughout his career. (II Corinthians 11:23-26)

Satan, through a type of metaphorical "thorn in the flesh," ordained a demon to hound Paul with ever-increasing pressure to keep the church free of false teachers. The Devil presents opposing forces and temptations to disbelieve the sufficiency of Christ in ministry controversies, to slow or defeat the Christian worker and movement. Paul faced this opposition daily. (II Corinthians 11:28; 12:7-9) Paul needed to be assured by Jesus that his approach to ministry was correct, and not just an ordinary tactic used to force change in the hearers of his message. Jesus would help Paul realize that when heavy pressure is brought to bear upon his servanthood he reverted to his former ways of dealing with it, that which came natural to him. He drew upon his preconceived notion of what is right or wrong and acted quickly and decisively. The problem for him and any servant is that habit does not always please Jesus and may not offer the joy of which Jesus would bestow on all who sought His ministry plan.

Any Christian ministry brings conflict of ideas: theology, differences of opinion brought about from being exposed to different environments, family customs, ethics, race, religious training and personal experiences in life. The Apostle Paul was subject to these same challenges and undoubtedly had to live with the choices he made, as he dwelt with them. He, by his own testimony, was not always happy with his behavior throughout these experiences. It is not unusual for everyone to be unhappy with certain behaviors or outcomes from decisions made under fire or even in the best of circumstances, especially well-meaning Christians, and to say accepting Christ as Savior eliminates this truth is unfair and incorrect.

The Apostle Paul was a saved man, and fully devoted to the Lord Christ he loved, yet he knew he needed more devotion to Christ, that he might be able to live with his conscience and his servanthood. He knew something was missing in his service with Christ, and whatever it was, it caused him great anguish of soul. (Romans 7) He had the Holy Spirit indwelling him, and he had the acceptance of the call of Christ on his life, yet he was miserable. Paul needed something to change his attitude about what coincides happiness with ministry, to go **beyond the ordinary** unfolding of ministry as a producer of inner-peace. So, ***what made the difference in his life that raised his service to extraordinary heights instead of casting him down to despair in ministry?***

The Apostle Paul discovered that within his soul, his inner-peace was hampered and it influenced his outward actions because of this, not unlike many Christians. He was trying to define his servanthood by the level of peace within his soul, or lack thereof. He delighted in God's law in his inner-being, and did not mind doing exactly what God ordered, but his inability to be perfect in his thoughts, words and actions hounded him constantly, to the point of near insanity. His difference in attitude came when he realized it is all about Christ's wisdom and power to offer him peace that really counts in life; not his dos and don'ts of serving Jesus.

He realized his purpose was to have fellowship and peace with Jesus, and in doing so, he would accomplish his calling to the Gentile world. The peace he longed for, a peaceful heart while facing the trials associated with winning the lost, had eluded him for years, because he saw peace as the avoidance of harm, trouble and unrest, when it is the exact opposite. (Philippians 4:7) Every conflict and decision he was involved in to this point in his life was designed by Jesus to bring him to a profound truth in serving Jesus. This truth is acting in obedience to the purpose of Jesus in ministry and it is different for every servant, not to gain peace from self-oriented service results. His servanthood for Christ brought him to this final stage in life, and is the reason for his personal testimony of Romans 7. Peace does come from any work or person other than a personal and intimate relationship with Jesus Christ!

He acquired the peace Jesus spoke of and promised to all believers; "My peace I leave you; My peace I give to you; not as the world gives do I give to you." (John 14:27) Just imagine his thoughts and memories about his conflict with James over their works and grace debate, when Jesus confronted him with his dilemma over peace being freely given. Think about his longing for peace and finding out peace that passes his own understanding is not associated with worldly philosophy or human endeavors, and realizing he had operated in much of his ministry being bound by the same, entangled between the two worlds of grace and works.

Paul writes of this in Romans 7, describing the war within himself, trying to find contentment in ministry confronted with opposition to the gospel, his own feelings of competitiveness to be the best in service for Christ, and his conquest for peace from his emotional battles occurring deep within his soul over his self-imposed standards of service; peace of which he would find. (Philippians 4:10-13) He came to accept whatever came his way each day in service to Jesus, his failures and successes. (Philippians 4:11-13) Paul realized that speaking with Jesus was far more rewarding than checking off the things on his daily list to complete. He learned to not bring tomorrow's woes into today. (Matthew 6:34)

The Apostle Paul was a very complex man, driven to excellence by his ambitious endeavors to serve God. His entire life had been one of succeeding on his own merits, which robbed him of the very peace he sought in Jesus. He sensed there was something more he could do in pleasing Jesus, but the outer walls of his self-righteousness and self-deception must fall. He learned that joy is not found in finishing something on a list. Paul came to live by faith. (Romans 1:17) Work would never make him a better person. Finally, he would acknowledge his weakness in the flesh, and self-dependence on the benefits of a reputation that would not stand in the presence of Christ. He would decide to turn his ministry over to Jesus and step **beyond the ordinary** attempts at reconciling ministry and personal accomplishments. His righteousness is in Jesus Christ only.

It must have been devastating for Paul to admit the things he wanted to say but did not, and the things he did not want to say he communicated. Even though he was successful in writing fourteen books of the New Testament, and preached to hundreds. To admit that the things he wanted to do he did not, and the things he desired to do, he failed at accomplishing is gut wrenching to a servant of Paul's caliber; to not understand himself is unthinkable. (Romans 7:15-25) Paul's words describe the most depressing and hopeless realities of his life, but he had the good sense to reach outside of his reasoning to a more powerful source; Jesus Christ. Paul, unlike many believers, confessed his inability to live that righteous life and ministry he desperately sought.

It was discouraging to Paul to not be able to bring the extreme standards of his former training in Judaism and stoic principles to his new life of humility in Christ. His mind told him to depend on God's gracious provisions for living righteously and serving in obedience to Jesus, but he found this practice to be nearly impossible without shedding his own motivation. Paul was a driven person and accustomed to doing things his way. So, how does one perform in Christian service to such a high level of ecstasy without being in total control and self-determined? How does a person not surrender to a life of mediocrity under such paradoxical pressure? How does one choose to live in peace with life choices and a ministry ordained by someone else, Jesus Christ?

So again, what makes the difference in someone's choices that raise them to extraordinary heights in life and servanthood or cast them down to unbearable depths of despair? The Apostle Paul found the answer, at this specific time and place in his life, when he exposed his weakness of ministry planning to submit to God's provision for ministry, and found the "peace of grace" came as a reward of this sacrifice. His entire life had brought him to this destination. (Romans 3:10-13; 7:7-13) Paul saw that battling the temptations of sin and serving God are two separate battle fields, and if he mixed them he only suffered agony. God's grace was sufficient for the stress of the temptations in his life, and the Holy Spirit would lead in the arena of servanthood. It is war fought on two separate battlefields.

Paul identified with the agony of defeat; his lowest point in life. He came to grips with the marvelous truth that the Cross of Christ offers deliverance from the self-dictated restraints placed on his life and guarantees the righteousness God promised to believers. Paul finally saw with spiritual eyes that Jesus wanted to expose his errant two-fold approach to living. One errant approach was not understanding that both the law of God in his mind, and sin in his body, was a real phenomenon. This could only be overcome by the indwelling Holy Spirit in his life.

The other was seeking inner-peace through a determined mindset, to be great in serving Jesus to capture the happiness that eluded his life, and to appease all his wrong approaches to defeat the first errant approach. (Matthew 6:22) His overwhelming sense of despair for the analyzation of his life is diffused in one great statement of faith, and when he considered this, his heart and mind connected. The Holy Spirit touched him. (Hebrews 4:12) He emphatically declared, "I thank God—through Jesus Christ our Lord! So then, with the mind I myself serve the law of God, but with the flesh the law of sin. There is therefore now no condemnation to those who are in Christ Jesus, who do not walk according to the flesh, but according to the Spirit." (Romans 7:25-8:1) **Paul gave up on his ability to do anything of importance for Jesus Christ, and let go of his needed expectations for himself as his source of joy**. He saw Christ wanted his very existence to be about serving God in extreme measures, **beyond the ordinary**, amid all circumstances, great and small, with the only purpose being to win the lost to Jesus. It was a defining moment in his life!

The irony of Paul's journey to this point is that he was so near to all he longed for in faith when he received Jesus Christ as his Savior, but was quickly thrown into evangelism by his own choices, initiating the long travel to lasting peace. His experiential peace was hidden by honest pursuits of the lost. Paul's life could be summarized by imagining someone who is paralyzed from the neck down, who wants to pick up an item off the floor.[8] This person can mentally pick it up, but not physically, and so it is with Paul, or any Christian, who desires to serve Christ with body, soul and spirit, but serving in the absence of inner-peace, will camp in the flesh alone to achieve success, not by faith in God.

Paul should have experienced the same peace that Christ exhibited. Jesus had his own personal peace, a deep inner-peace that stilled his heart during every possible circumstance, mockers, haters, traitors and killers. He possessed an unnatural calm during the worst of his persecution, even while dying on the Cross. It was this peace that the Apostle Peter preached, yet needed, and Jesus freely gives through the ministry of the Holy Spirit to all who will slow down enough to appropriate it. (Acts 10:36; II Thessalonians 3:16; Galatians 5:22; John 16:14) This is the peace that now undergirds the throne of Paul's thinking and life commitments. It is a peace not based on circumstances, like the world's peace stemming from pleasure seeking and avoidance of pain. This peace does not make sense, so it is sometimes missed by egoistic Christians, and misunderstood on the human level. (Philippians 4:7)

This was the peace that Paul had missed in the beginning of his walk with Christ. Peace that deals with the past mistakes that tortures a believer day-in and day-out, a peace that eliminates unsatisfied desires of a sinful heart, a peace that offers hope for the future, regardless of the unknown events of the next hour, a peace that solidifies the forgiveness of past sins and empowers the believer to overcome the trials in life, by knowing there is an eternal reward awaiting the faithful; every lasting life. (John 3:16)

Remember, Paul felt he could not experience inner-peace while his work was unfinished, but really, the inner-peace he sought comes from knowing Jesus and is not based entirely on serving Jesus. Followers of Christ can claim the peace that Jesus gives from the beginning of their friendship with Him. Jesus said He gives this peace to all who lay hold of it, regardless of teachings

---

[8] Murphy-O'Connor, Jerome. Paul the Letter-Writer: His World, His Options, His Skills. Collegeville, MN: Liturgical Press, 1995.

to the contrary or errant trust in Christ. (John 14:27) Troubling affairs in life come from past lies based in fear of the unknown, and are based on unwarranted anxieties caused by not concentrating of a beloved Savior. (Matthew 6:34)

Paul learned it is best to not worry about the past or the future, or the success of ministry, because both are under the sovereignty of God; nor did he have to feel guilty for being happy. Paul learned that God is a heavenly umpire of sorts, who is totally capable of controlling all the decisions in life required of a Christian, and the bench mark is the peace of Christ and a supernatural ministry. (Colossians 3:15) So, if a decision must be made and a believer feels at peace with the decision after speaking with Jesus, then go for it, even when it makes no logical sense. Just be ready, be willing, be happy, and be available to move **beyond the ordinary** attitude of many Christians walking around in a stupor! (Ephesians 5:16)

The Apostle Paul was beheaded AD 68 by the Romans, under Emperor Nero.[9] He was denied crucifixion because he was a freeman of Rome by birth.[10] The Roman historian, Eusebius, recorded his death shortly after much of Rome was burned. Christ had predicted Paul would suffer for his faith, and he was ready to give his life for the cause of Christianity. (Acts 9:16; 21:13)

---

[9] Eusebius (1989). <u>The History of the Church from Christ to Constantine</u>. G.A. Williamson, trans. New York: Dorset Press.

[10] Fox, John. <u>Foxe's Book of Martyrs</u>. Crosswalk, 2007.

Moving Beyond the Ordinary

1. Detail your life before Christ. Modern-day Christians face many dilemmas and mixed emotions stemming from their background. They simply do not have the foundation for untangling the mess that follows them into their Christian pilgrimage; their unpacked baggage. What were your defining circumstances: family traditions, religious background, home environment, education, major challenges to your faith walk with Christ and relationships with others? Do any of these details still define who you are as a person? How would compare your life to the life of the Apostle Paul?
2. Explain, in detail, your acceptance of Jesus Christ as your Savior.
3. Have you found peace with God? Socrates said, "An examined life is not worth living," (Plato's Apology), and that most people are "sleep walkers." Many Christians do not understand their own being; they are confused about who they are, where they are headed, and what to do if they get there. They never find a true direction for their life and God's purpose for them in His service, so they spent most their lives out of sorts with God, and unhappy. They remain in the uneasiness of disharmony with their family, friends, co-workers and other church members, leaving them with no peace. Identify your purpose in life, and explain why you are not a "sleep walker."
4. How would you define your walk with Christ? Is it meaningful, and is it making a difference in other people's lives on a regular basis? What motivates you to serve Christ? Are you a happy person?
5. Sin separates you from feeling at peace with God, and halts communication with Him. How long do you allow sin to reign in your life? Does your understanding of the presence of sin or righteousness have any bearing on your answer? Are there things you would like to change about your life? Would you classify your life as mundane or reaching for the

upmost in Christian service? Use illustrations from Paul's life to identify with your experiences.
6. Stephen prayed for God to forgive his murderers as they stoned him, and Paul, after Romans 7:25-8:1, embraced the peace he found, even during the many assaults faced in ministry. He was robbed, beaten, left for dead, arraigned before rulers, ship wrecked, hungry and thirsty, faced countless dangers in the sea and among his own people, falsely accused of uncommitted crimes, and beheaded for his faith in Jesus Christ. He suffered under the pressures of caring for the church, yet he was victorious in spreading the good news that Jesus saves, and all because he knew of the peace of the Savior. (Acts 7:60; II Corinthians 11:24-29; 4:8-11, 16-18) Do you know that peace, and would it stand up to the attacks, such as these men faced for their faith? (Isaiah 26:3)
7. Have you experienced a specific time and place in your walk with Christ, apart from your conversion, where you decided to move beyond the ordinary? (Philippians 4:4; Colossians 3:15) Paul found it when he saw with his eyes, his inner-soul that does not lie, what Jesus and Paul calls the eyes of enlightenment. (Matthew 13:16-17; Ephesians 1:18) What brought you to that encounter with Christ? Describe it. If you have not reached the plateau of only seeking Christ, are you ready to reach for the heavenlies?

Chapter Two

THE APOSTLE PETER, THE FISHERMAN, GOES BEYOND THE ORDINARY

*The Apostle Peter was impulsive and non-thinking which kept him from intimacy with Jesus for a long time. He would have to change his approach to life, if he was to go **beyond the ordinary**!*

THE APOSTLE PETER WAS BORN ABOUT 1 BC AND was originally named Simon. (John 21:15) He was from a town which Jesus condemned on the western side of the Sea of Galilee, named Bethsaida; a town extending to both sides of the Sea of Galilee, but he later moved to Capernaum. (Luke 5:10; 10:13-14) He is pictured in paintings as a slender, tall man with a pale complexion. He had a short, thick and curled beard with very thin eyebrows and dark eyes. He was a very domineering individual from the fishing trade, not unlike the typical fisherman. He was a married man and a successful fisherman by trade, as was his father, Jona, and his brother, Andrew, and their partners James and John. (Matthew 8:14)

Fishing was a very difficult and rough occupation and life, demanding a fisherman to be physically fit, fearless, and robust and determined to overcome the financial challenges of owning and maintaining fishing boats and gear, and conquering the natural elements of the sea, all which Peter achieved.[11] Peter was impulsive, argumentative and spoke without first thinking, often causing him great difficulty, especially after he met Jesus and became a disciple. (John 18:15-27) He was coarse, despicable and many times undressed, used crude language and suffered from mood swings, vacillating between humbleness, great anger, loyalty and love; a very complex person. (Matthew 26:74; Luke 22:33; John 18:10; 21:7; 21:15-17) Peter, once in ministry, tended to fall back upon his old way of doing things, a way which caused him to need a major change in which he approached ministry. (John 21:3) He would have to decide to move **beyond the ordinary way** of relating to and serving Jesus, if he was to become the outspoken one for Jesus.

Peter, as with Paul, would have been heavily influenced by his family, environment, customs, current events and religious views of the time in which he lived. A person's place of residence has a way of entangling all the elements of their background, and depending on an individual's response, it affects their behavior and choices in life, which was true in the lives of the apostles Paul, Peter, and the other disciples. The City of Capernaum, on the northern shore of the Sea of Galilee, where he lived and had his business, offered many challenges to his everyday life style, even though the first-century Roman historian, Pliny, called it one of the beautiful towns on the Sea of Galilee.[12] It was very close in proximity to his birth place of Bethsaida, and it would serve as a possible sanctuary town for Peter after his betrayal of Christ. (John 2)

Capernaum was a large Galilean fishing city, a busy trading center, the most crowded district in Israel, and afforded Peter many choices. It lay on the road between Damascus and Caesarea on the Mediterranean Sea, and between Tyre and Egypt, making it a leading stopover for caravans and a center for collecting customs taxes. (Matthew 9:9) It was a town of mixed population containing both Syrian Gentiles and Jews, which challenged Peter's acceptance of non-Jewish and pagan religions. Peter, by confession was

---

[11] Isaac Lambertsen, The Lives of the Holy Apostles, Holy Apostles Convent Press, Buena Vista, CO, 1990.

[12] Wasson, Donald L. "Pliny the Elder." *Ancient History Encyclopedia*. Ancient History Encyclopedia, 12 Jun 2014. Web. 14 Sep 2017.

a sinful man, a follower of John the Baptist, but lived in expectation of a coming Messiah, and most of his society seemed to oppose that thought. (Luke 5:6-8) The citizens of the region were spiritually blind, and Jesus criticized them for their lack of faith, even though Jesus spent many days in the area. (Mark 6:45; John 1:44; 12:21)

Peter's house was a simple one with coarse walls, a roof of earth and straw and several rooms clustered around two open courtyards. The courtyards were the most extensive part of the house, consisting of a circular furnace made of refractory earth with grain mills and a stairway to the roof where he could see the streets below. The floors were made of cobbled stones with the walls made of coarse basalt blocks. It had low windows through which sunlight entered the dwelling. It was reflective of his success as a fisherman and yet, was a striking testimony to his humility and care of his family. Peter's home, no doubt, would be visited by Jesus, and was a place of great emotion and friendship shared between the two men. (Mark 1:1; Matthew 8:14)

The atmosphere in Palestine, when Peter reached his adult life, was one of great tension and animosity toward the Roman occupation. The only hope for Israel was for the Messiah to come and defeat the Romans, and Peter would attempt to force the hand of Jesus to bring this to pass.[13] He was constantly asking Jesus when He would put an end to the Roman madness. Peter's first encounter with Jesus was motivated by his desire for Jesus to restore the Kingdom of Israel, and he was ready to see it through, but this was not the mission Jesus came to fulfill. He came to save mankind from their sin. (Mark 1:15; Acts 1:6; Luke 19:10) Peter's home affairs, more importantly, showed he could eventually be trusted by the Savior to care about the future church.

The synagogue of Capernaum was a magnificent white walled basalt building that sat on the highest point in the city, facing the Sea of Galilee. When time permitted, Peter and his family would visit there to receive word from the chief rabbi. Peter would hear the reading of the book of the Law, the prophets and Psalms,

---

[13] Jensen, Irving. <u>Jensen's Survey of the New Testament</u>. Chicago, IL: Moody Press, 1981.

and would worship God. The synagogue was the most important part of the Jewish people's relationship to God, and served as a place for prayer, a school house and a courtroom. (Mark 1:21) It is possible that Peter went to school in this synagogue. Inside the synagogue were benches on three sides of a worship room, on which the prominent, visiting priests and Levites sat, a small platform from which speakers would teach, and a seven-branched candlestick standing on the platform. The commoners sat on the dirt floors, and so, Peter probably sat on the floor, as the teacher of the day sat on the Moses Seat. (Matthew 23:6) The blowing of the ram's horn announced the beginning of the Sabbath service and the people before entering the worship service would wash in the Mikveh, a ceremonial wash basin used as a symbolic cleansing of their sin.[14] This did not satisfy the longing for a change Peter felt he needed in his heart, a change for which the teaching of Judaism could not satisfy, the mundane practice of an empty Jewish religion. Tormented by the circumstances around and the emptiness of a sinful heart, Peter was ready to meet Jesus. Peter must have remembered this each time he heard Jesus speak, cure a demon-possessed man, heal a man with palsy and restore life to the daughter of one of the synagogue's rulers. (John 6:25-59; Mark 5:22; Luke 4:33; 7:1-10; 8:41)

Peter's life was a steady routine of fishing all night and repairing the nets all day. The day Peter met Jesus started like many of his days with him, and his brother, Andrew, cleaning their fishing nets after a long night of fishing. It was hard and boring work, untangling the seaweed and sticks from the netting, and mending the many tears in the net, as to not let the next day's catch escape.[15] Peter's boat was anchored to the shore, a common practice, so the freshly mended nets could be thrown into the water to wash off the final debris, for better storage. Jesus approached him, followed by a very large crowd of people. The crowd moved closer and closer to Jesus, forcing Him to take drastic measures to avoid getting wet from the incoming waves off the Sea of Galilee. He

---

[14] EL Sukenik. *Ancient Synagogues of Palestine and Greece*, (London, 1934).

[15] Batten, Alicia J. "Fishing Economy in the Sea of Galilee", n.p. [cited 14 Sep 2017]

asked Peter to row his boat out into the water so he could use it as a platform from which to speak to the gathering crowd; everywhere Jesus went a crowd gathered. Peter, who heard Jesus' compelling message in Judea and had been told by his brother that Jesus was the Christ, even though tired from the nights fishing, agreed and they put out into the deeper water. (John 1:28, 40-41) Jesus taught the crowd and Peter listened intently, hanging on every word, and thinking to himself, "Could this be the Christ?"

When Jesus finished talking, he asked Peter to row further into the deep and to put out his freshly cleaned nets. Peter, being very outspoken, was agitated and questioned Jesus, explaining he had already fished the previous night with no success. Peter complied and what happened next was spectacular. Peter's net was filled with so many fish, that he yelled to his partners on shore, John and James, to row out to help haul the catch into the boat, nearly causing his boat and his partner's boat to sink. The four men were frightened and did not know what to say or what might happen next. This caused Peter to confess to Jesus that he was a sinful man and asked Jesus to leave, but Jesus astonished him by calling him by a new name, Cephas, and by telling Peter to follow Him, and He would make him a fisher of men. (Luke 5:1-11; John 1:42) Immediately, Peter accepted Christ's invitation, put down his trade and followed Him.

Peter's conversion to faith in Jesus Christ as the Messiah was his first step to fulfilling the purpose of God for his life. Jesus told him He wanted him to be the fisher of men, and for Peter to act upon that calling, he would need to change his attitude and desires. He would be challenged, broken and molded by Jesus before he would be ready to move to higher ground in ministry, to break away from the ordinary way of serving Christ. (John 21:15-19) Peter demonstrated his faith and insights many times, but he also showed weakness of his will, and capacity to deny Jesus when under pressure from the enemy. These were learned behaviors dictated to him by the surroundings in which he lived: family, environment, religious and cultural pressures and his hatred of the Roman occupation. Judaism had left him empty; religious leaders had lied and manipulated him and his fellow Jews, destroyed their confidence in mankind, and now he would follow a different kind of leadership. It would be a difficult pilgrimage as he learned to trust and lean on another man, even when that man was Jesus, one that would take him through many different trials and temptations of his own making.

Peter's first year with Jesus starts in a very unusual way. Jesus re-names him, changing his name from Simon to Peter, meaning a "rock." (Mark 3:16; Luke 6:14; John 1:42) Jesus raised the bar in Peter's life and expectations of the future. He was exalted from being a fisherman with no religious status to be the potential leader of the Christian world.[16] Jesus tells him the church will be built on his name. (Matthew 16:18) The mental adjustment and new-found prestige was extensive for Peter to contemplate. He still had to learn humility and his proper place in the unfolding of history, and it came by way of experimentation. He would make great statements of faith by declaring Christ to be deity, the Holy One of God and the only one through which eternal life could be granted, but then deny Jesus by telling Him what was expected of Him by His followers; to set up the new kingdom on earth for the Jews instead of dying. (John 6:68-69; Mark 8:31-33; Matthew 16:21-22)

Peter was privy to the first miracles in the ministry of Christ at his own home when Jesus healed his mother-in-law of a fever. Jesus took her by her hand and instantly she was healed, and she immediately fixed a meal for them. (Mark 1:29-31) The show of empathy by Jesus re-affirmed Peter's loyalty and care of his family, and proved Jesus was truly interested in him. Later, Peter witnessed the unheard of, the raising of a little girl from the dead at the home of a local ruler. The ruler came to Jesus and requested He come to help his daughter, a great example of faith on his part, one that impressed Peter, who was a bit upset over a ruler approaching Jesus. Along the way to the ruler's house, a sick woman touched the garment of Jesus and was healed. Peter heard Him say her faith had made her well. Jesus, the ruler, Peter, the other disciples and a large crowd reached the place where the girl died. The flute players, which was customary for mourning, and a noisy gathering

---

[16] Wuellner, Wilhelm H. <u>The Meaning of Fishers of Men</u>. Louisville, KY: Westminster Press, 1967.

was already there. Jesus was criticized for asking them to move out of way, so he could take the dead girls hand. She arose from the dead the very moment Jesus touched her. (Matthew 9:18-26) First, his mother-in-law is healed, then an unknown woman is healed and now a dead little girl is brought back to life, all by the touch of Jesus. Three people from differing backgrounds and relationships and yet Jesus shows no prejudice, amazing.

Peter was bewildered by the supernatural power of Jesus and wondered how he would ever perform this way. Would he ever perform such miracles with the mercy and grace that Jesus exposes to all that met Him? He certainly did not learn the full measure of the examples of Jesus until after he was bathed by this same mercy and grace on the shore of the Sea of Galilee after the resurrection of Jesus. In fact, he would have many encounters with Jesus that demonstrated the exact opposite of spiritual things, such as his entertaining the argument of the other disciples over who would sit next to Jesus in His kingdom. (Matthew 18:1-5)

The Apostle Peter's first year in ministry would end with Jesus taking authority over nature, such as His walking on water. (Matthew 14:28-29; John 6:19-20) This should have been a life-changing experience for Peter, but again, he did not realize the implications of the miracle. Peter was a man of the sea, and his fishing and sailing should have made him very sensitive to the realities of nature. Men simply do not walk on water and especially not on angry waves with a strong blowing wind. The disciples had left Jesus and set sail across the Sea of Galilee to Gennesaret when a storm arose, causing the men to panic for fear of drowning. Jesus appeared in the distance coming to them walking on the water, but they imagined Him to be a ghost, which was customary thinking for those days when something of the supernatural was happening, an event out of the realm of natural laws.

They began to cry out in fear, but Jesus denounced their fear by encouraging them with words of cheer. Peter immediately spoke with indecision and lack of recognition of Christ, but paradoxically asked that he may come to Jesus, and Jesus invited him to come. Peter stepped out of the boat and started for Jesus when the wind picked up. It frightened Peter and he began to sink into the waves, calling out to Jesus to save him. Jesus took him by his hand, and asked him why he doubted Him. Immediately they were safe in the boat and the storm ceased at the command of Jesus. The men worshiped Jesus and proclaimed Him to be the "Son of God." Once again, Peter had acted foolishly by not maintaining his focus on Jesus and was corrected by Jesus, leaving him with a sense of failure stemming from his poor act of faith. (Matthew 14:30-33) Peter could have moved to a higher level of obedience, but he remained in his ordinary stance of mediocre abilities.

The next two years of following Jesus would prove to be lost opportunities for the Apostle Peter to grow into a mature relationship with Jesus. Peter would have successes and failures, proving a need to change in his approach to serving Jesus and the future church. This period of his life started with Jesus announcing the local church would be built on Peter's authority. (Matthew 16:18) Jesus refers to him as a rock on which the gates of hell will not prevail. This was a great prediction by Jesus, and Peter should have understood it had to mean that he was given a great job to accomplish; one that should have greatly humbled him. Instead, Peter rebuked and denied Jesus as his source of inspiration and strength to stand against Satan.

Peter would not accept that Jesus was the foundation for the church and salvation for all who would repent and accept forgiveness of their sins, based on His death, burial and resurrection on the third day. (Romans 5:6-11) Jesus told Peter he was acting like a helper of Satan by his spoken words and attitude toward the plan of God. The stubbornness of Peter blinded his mind to the reality that Jesus must die at the hands of the elders, chief priests and scribes. (Matthew 16:23) Peter set himself up for a big denial of Christ. He did not heed the message of Jesus, to deny his desires and dictates, to totally give his life over to Jesus and accept the future death of his Master. Instead, he insisted on Jesus establishing an earthly kingdom that would over throw Rome. Peter would remain on track to deny his Lord. Peter needed help!

An astonishing event took place on the top of the Mount of Transfiguration. (Matthew 17:1-3; Mark 9:2-3; Luke 9:29-32) Peter, James and John would climb the mountain with Jesus, and witness the transfiguring of the body of Jesus into a glorious one. His face shone like the sun and his clothes became as white as the light, another supernatural phenomenon taking place in the presence of Peter. Then, Moses and Elijah appeared, and talked with Jesus. Peter, spellbound for fear, yet being the impulsive one, had to speak, so he called to Jesus if he and the others might build Jesus, Moses and Elijah a tabernacle in which to dwell. Suddenly a bright cloud fell on them, and God intervened from Heaven telling them that Jesus was His Son, pleasing to Him and they needed to listen to what He says. Peter and the others collapsed to the ground in great fear, hearing God speak, but not seeing Him. Jesus touched them, helped them to their feet and just as He had done on the Sea of Galilee encouraged them to not be afraid. They were alone with Jesus. The glory cloud, Moses and Elijah were gone, and Jesus led them down the mountain, instructing them along the way not to speak of what just happened until after the resurrection.

Peter needed to know more, to make sense of what transpired high on that mountain because it was his nature to question Jesus, just not listen to His answers. It was a serious flaw that had to be eradicated before he could reach the apex of ministry. He asked Jesus if Elijah had to come before the Messiah, as he had been taught by the priests, so Jesus explained that the message of Elijah came through the preaching of John the Baptist, but the message was not received. They murdered John, and so it would be with Jesus. Jesus had attempted to give Peter a glance of eternity, a spiritual lesson to internalize his belief in Jesus as the Messiah, the Son of God, who was there to offer all people salvation. This could have been the end of Peter's insistence on doing things his way, to recognize he was to preach the same message Jesus was fulfilling, but he did not listen. He still had no change of heart.

Peter had to have his spirit broken before he would move **beyond his ordinary** approach to serving Jesus, something that would devastate him. It was the third year of their time together, and Jesus had brought Peter through each event of their friendship to equip him with wisdom to succeed in ministry, but Peter repeated a dangerous cycle of moving forward and then falling back to his old way of doing things. Jesus spoke to him with prophetic words–three times he would deny that he knew Jesus, and he would not be faithful when the time came for Christ to be crucified. (Matthew 26:34-35; Mark 14:30-31; Luke 22:34; John 13:38) He gave Peter another supernatural sign that he would deny Him three times before a rooster would crow, yet another show of the authority of Jesus over creation. Peter's response was ignorant. He would never deny Jesus!

The fateful time of Peter's final lesson began in the Garden of Gethsemane on the night of the arrest of Jesus. The disciples had a last meal with Jesus in an upper room and had ventured out onto the Mount of Olives to pray. (Matthew 26:40-51; Mark 14:37-47; Luke 22:45-46; John 18:10) This peaceful place overlooked Jerusalem and was the place of many prayer meetings during Jesus' visits to Jerusalem. Jesus asked Peter, John and James to go with Him to the center of the garden to pray, while the other disciples stayed closer to the entrance. Jesus went to a more secluded place to pray, and upon returning to the three; He found them sleeping. This was the most challenging time in the life of Jesus, as He sought assurance from His Heavenly Father that dying on a cross was in the eternal plan. He sweat tears drops of blood, as He agonized over the will of the Father, and Peter should have been there for Him if he had learned the real reason for Jesus coming to earth; to put an end to the wrath of God toward sinners and offer salvation to them.

Peter could have learned that strength to obey God comes by way of prayer, not the sword that he pulled when the arresting soldiers, with Judas, came to take Jesus. He just made things worse by cutting off the ear of Malchus, who was the servant of the high priest, which forced Jesus to heal it. Peter should have heard Jesus say that the answer he looked for was not in violence, but in obeying the plan of God; not in boasts of grandeur, but in submission to God. The actions of Peter on that night were as demeaning to Jesus as the kiss of Judas, his betrayer. The others would flee, leaving Jesus alone with these malicious soldiers, and Peter would follow Jesus at a distance, which symbolically and ironically pictured his entire walk with Jesus. Peter's words and works kept him from truly knowing the heart of Jesus.

The denial of Jesus by Peter would come in a public setting, centered around the camp fire of the haters of Christ. (Matthew 26:69-75; Mark 14:66-72; John18:16-27) This was appropriate because Peter had boasted publicly about his trustworthiness in the cause of Jesus, and he needed to be humiliated. A young girl would call Peter out, as he warmed himself by the courtyard fire of the enemies of Jesus, and declare that he was a follower of this Jesus who was on trial before Caiaphas, the high priest. Peter denied his relationship to Jesus, and moved to the gate of the courtyard, where another young girl challenged his relationship with Jesus. Once again, he denied knowing Jesus, but when the crowd accused him of walking with Jesus, he cursed and swore he never knew Him. Suddenly a rooster crowed, and Peter broke down in tears and ran. He ended up in an upper room behind locked doors, a bewildered and deplorable excuse for a Christian. (Mark 14:15)

Peter undoubtedly would hear of the crucifixion of Jesus on the cross, but the next actual word of the condition of Jesus would come from the women followers of Jesus; the very ones looked down upon by the men. Remember the controversy that the Apostle Paul had over the role of women in the church and their appearance in public places? Yet they were more willing, by caring for Jesus, to face persecution from the Romans and Jews than the men followers of Jesus, adding to the confusion in Peter's heart over his own future with Christ.

It is hard to imagine what was going through the mind of Peter, when Mary Magdalene pounded on the door and bolted into the room, exclaiming that she had seen Jesus and He had risen from the dead. Neither Peter, nor any other of the disciples made this declaration, but a woman. (Matthew 28:9-10) Did this mean Jesus had changed His mind and a woman would start the church, not Peter, who Jesus said would do this? Peter and John, needing answers, ran to the tomb of Jesus and found it empty as Mary had said. (Luke 24:12; John 20:3) Still, Peter had not fully realized that Jesus had to rise from the dead, so he returned to their place of hiding. The disciples, being engulfed with great fear, remained in hiding, while Jerusalem was overcome with confusion caused by dead bodies of the saints rising from the graves, the earth quaking, and the Jews and Romans trying to restore some sense of control.

Jesus would visit the hiding place of the disciples and women on two occasions, and He offered words of encouragement to them, but He seemed to ignore Peter, leaving him to his own thinking about the future. Peter decided to return to the sea and fishing, where he would once again meet Jesus. (John 21:1-19) He had come full circle in his calling to follow Jesus, and it seemed he had failed at fulfilling his call to be fishers of men. He had been privileged to see many miracles, wonders and signs: the healing of the sick, casting out of demons, authority over the natural laws that govern the universe, the glorification of Jesus, the raising of the dead, and the resurrection of Jesus, but to no avail. If he was to fulfill what Jesus had said of him, there must be a change in his relationship to Christ, by moving **beyond the ordinary** practice of following Jesus at a distance, which he had done in words and works. He must come close to Jesus, by letting Jesus speak through him; he must choose to deny himself. (Matthew 16:24; 26:58; John 21:19)

Peter and six other disciples had gone fishing on the Sea of Galilee, and exactly like the evening before he decided to follow Jesus three years earlier, they had caught nothing. Jesus called to them from the shoreline and told them to cast their nets off the right side of the boat, and just like before, the catch of fish was overwhelming. John, recognizing the Lord, told Peter and he jumped into the water and swam to shore. The others rowed to shore and with Peter's help landed the fresh catch of fish, and joined Jesus in a breakfast that He had already prepared. None of them spoke, including Peter, for fear of being renounced for returning to their fish trade, but Peter had already showed he was ready to listen to Jesus by helping the others haul the fish to shore, an act of serving, and by his total silence before Jesus. Peter was finally ready to change his behavior, to have a lasting difference take place in his life, so Jesus took him aside and asked him three soul searching questions. (John 21:15-19)

Jesus began His questioning of Peter by calling him by his former name, Simon, Son of Jonah. He hoped this was not the last encounter he would have with Jesus, if he failed with his answers, because Jesus called him by his former name. He listened intently as Jesus asked him if he loved Him. Peter could not help remembering his feeling of shame and sorrow when his eyes met Jesus' eyes after he had denied Him in the courtyard of Caiaphas. Now, he was face to face with his Lord, searching the eyes of Jesus and sensing Jesus penetrating his soul.

Peter answered the first question of Jesus with, "Yes, Lord, You know that I love you," and Jesus told him to, "Feed My lambs." Jesus asked a second time if Peter loved him, and Peter answered with the same declaration. Jesus told him to, "Feed My sheep." The third-time Jesus asked him if he loved Him, Peter broke down and cried, saying, "Lord, You know all things and You know that I love you." Peter, with that one true acknowledgement of the sovereignty of Jesus to know all things, heard Jesus say, "Feed my sheep." He understood Jesus was saying that he would care for the souls of men, and assist them to mature from infants to adults in faith. Peter realized Jesus would help him in this work, even to the time of his death. (I Peter 2:2) Peter, in a moment, had the last three years of his life flash before his eyes. He saw that Jesus had brought him from the faith of a child, or what Jesus called a lamb, to a full-grown adult, or sheep, who would constantly need the Savior's support. He heard Jesus repeat His original call for him to, "Follow Me."[17] His heart was immersed in the love of Jesus, and no more would the focus be on Peter, no more would he lead an unexceptional life of service. Peter moved **beyond the ordinary**. It was his defining moment!

Later, the Apostle Peter would be instrumental in leading the disciples to choose a replacement for Judas Iscariot, who had hung himself in response to the gospel of Christ. (Acts 1:16-26) This was the first evidence that Jesus had given him authority to lead the church, and that he had been anointed with the Holy Spirit of God. His sound leadership would guide the church through its enormous growth, and many challenges that lay ahead of it.

Peter would move on to great accomplishments for Christ. Earlier in his walk with Jesus, he had opportunities to speak and a

---

[17] Ryle, Charles Caldwell. Basic Theology. Chicago, IL: Moody Press, 1999.

chance to heal the sick and cast out demons, but failed, as did the other disciples. (Acts 1:16-26; 2:14-36; 3:6-8; 4:3; 4:18; Mark 6:30) Now, he would preach with authority, heal the sick on many occasions and oppose the Sadducees and Roman leaders. (Acts 4:18) The Sadducees, a division within the Jewish Sanhedrin, disbelieved the resurrection of the dead, which Peter proclaimed loudly and clearly, and attempted to silence Peter, but their continued opposition never stopped him from preaching. Peter acts with great boldness in confronting a husband and wife for lying about property, and would take severe steps within the church to insure its integrity. (Acts 5:3-9) They would drop dead in his presence because of their mockery of the Holy Spirit. He travels throughout the Roman occupied lands, teaching and encouraging the believers in Christ. He shows his understanding that Jesus was working through him, not him through Jesus, by raising a little girl from the dead, and Peter remained humble and shows no boasting in his own strength. (Acts 9:40) His self-centered attitude had totally changed.

The Apostle Peter crossed the boundaries of discrimination and prejudices when he preached the Gospel of Christ to all people. He went to preach in Samaria, to a race hated by the Jews, and to the Romans, who all Jews despised. (Acts 8:14) Peter brought the Gospel message to the house of Cornelius, a Roman centurion, while traveling through Caesarea. This created a stir among the believers back in the church in Jerusalem, and forced Peter to defend the Gospel before that church. Remember, he had to argue his actions with the Apostle Paul. (Galatians 2:11) He, also, visited the home of Lydda, a woman and minister of the message of Jesus. (Acts 9:32)

Peter endured imprisonment when Herod, the grandson of Herod the Great and nephew of Herod the Tetrarch, thought he could find favor with the religious establishment in Palestine and the Roman consul by fueling corruption. Herod was the choice of the Romans to rule the Jews living in the region. Herod had put to death James, the brother of John, by the sword, and he wanted to cause more trouble for the church in any possible way. His actions brought him new found popularity with the Jews empowering him to attack Peter, and imprisoning him as an attempt to uproot the

Christian movement. God interceded on Peter's behalf by sending an angel to release Peter, and Peter continued to speak for Christ. Herod would later die at the hands of an angel, his intestines eaten by worms. (Acts 12:1-8)

The choice of the Apostle Peter to live **beyond the ordinary** carried him to the summit of ministry, and he, like the Apostle Paul, preached in Rome. Peter, in AD 64, would be crucified upside down, because he felt unworthy to die the same way as Jesus. (John 21:16, 19) Tradition says his wife was crucified first, and it is said that Peter told her, "Remember the Lord."[18] He was put to death in Rome under Emperor Nero Augustus Caesar, and became the impeccability of the omniscience of Christ. Peter did not quit and his ministry glorified God.

---

[18] BiblePath.com, 6921 D Carnation St, Richmond, VA 23225

Moving Beyond the Ordinary

1. Chapter One and this chapter correlate the many dilemmas and mixed emotions stemming from the background of the Apostles Paul and Peter. These two men displayed they did not have the foundation for untangling the mess that followed them into their Christian pilgrimage. Each one had to overcome their family traditions, religious background, home environment, education and major challenges to their faith. These were defining circumstances in their lives. The Apostle Peter came from a hardy and unlearned back ground, while Paul came from a privileged and educated background. Their back grounds occasionally crossed paths. Both men, for example, were members of a local synagogue. Are there any similarities in your background that identify with both men? Or do your background experiences only relate to that of Peter? What are these defining circumstances? Do any of these details still define who you are as a person? How would compare your life to the life of the Apostle Peter?
2. What are your major challenges to your faith walk? Be specific.
3. Finding consistency with God is a very important component of serving Jesus. Aristotle said, "Men acquire a particular quality by constantly acting in a particular way."[19] Some Christians never learn to act in a predictable and beneficial way. They do not learn from their mistakes, and they accept lesser rewards from living in ignorance of what could be by living a life beyond the ordinary. They simply accept an ordinary and non-exceptionable life. They never find God's purpose for them in His service, so they spent most their lives practicing unfruitful habits, traditions and the desires of others. Happiness escapes them. They never really connect with God. Identify the consistencies or inconsistencies in your life, and explain what examples

---

[19] Vaugh, Lewis. <u>Doing Ethics</u>. New York, NY: W.W. Norton & Company, 2017.

from the life of Peter could strengthen your efforts to overcome them.
4. The Apostle Peter had an up-and-down walk with Jesus. Many times, he responded impulsively and erroneously to the teachings of Jesus. When things did not go his way, he denied Christ, quit ministry and returned to fishing. What failures and successes, like Peter, can you use to grow into spiritual maturity? Can you relate to him? Explain.
5. Dr. Ayers believes that whatever it takes to cause a man to quit is the measuring rod of that man's character. What do you believe was Peter's cause for his denial of Christ, his sin? Did the denial of Christ prove or disprove the character of Peter? Explain. What is your measuring rod for character?
6. How can the testimony of Peter's moving **beyond the ordinary** inspire you to reach for the summit of your service and love for Jesus Christ?

Chapter Three

THE APOSTLE ANDREW, THE QUIET ONE, GOES BEYOND THE ORDINARY

*The Apostle Andrew saw himself as the unknown member of his family and left out of everything, and if he were to go **beyond the ordinary**, he would need to re-evaluate his self-worth.*

THE APOSTLE ANDREW WAS BORN AT BETHSAIDA on the Sea of Galilee in AD 1. He was the son of Jonah, older brother of the Apostle Simon Peter, had three sisters and was a cousin to Jesus Christ. He moved to Capernaum with his brother and took up the fishing trade. He, like Peter, had met Jesus earlier, but was not totally committed until later when he left his home and trade to follow Jesus. He was one of the closest to Jesus, and was always named along with the first four disciples: Peter, John and James. Andrew led Peter to Christ, and was a witness to the public ministry of Jesus, the Last Supper, the risen Christ, and the Ascension. He received the gifts of the Holy Spirit at Pentecost, helped strengthen the church during its early persecution and exercised his faith throughout Palestine. (John 1:35-44; 6:8; 12:20-22; Matthew 4:18-20; 10:2-4; Mark 1:6, 17-18, 21, 29; 13:3; Luke 6:14-16)

Andrew, before he followed Jesus, was a disciple of John the Baptist, who heavily influenced his thinking and action. John the

Baptist preached a message of repentance as a source for forgiveness of sins, and a strong demand for individuals to stop sinning. Jesus preached repentance, but always reinforced it with the acceptance of the gospel; His death, burial and resurrection for the forgiveness of sins. The message of Jesus was clear about the difference between repentance of so-called righteous works, taught by the Jewish religious leaders, and the changed heart made through faith in Christ, as the result of being born again.[20] Jesus said the spiritual rebirth of an individual came by faith in Him only, and was the way for entrance into Heaven.

The Holy Spirit would provide the insight to spread this word once Christ died. It was obvious that Jesus had all authority to claim this, since He did rise from the dead. John the Baptist came to proclaim the coming Messiah and Jesus was the Messiah. (John 1:29-30) Andrew would have to decide what and how he would preach the coming Kingdom of God, repentance with an emphasis on works or repentance through grace by faith. Repentance through a change in personal acts brought on by the old sin nature, as John the Baptist preached and the Pharisees alluded to, was the ordinary way of relating to God, but to move **beyond this ordinary** message would take courage and commitment by Andrew. It would take an influential event in his life to catapult him into the main stream of evangelism that was employed by John the Baptist and his younger sibling, Peter.

Andrew was accustomed to hearing John the Baptist vehemently denounce the Pharisees, and preach a message of self-denial and self-examination; whereas Jesus taught self-control and submission to the Holy Spirit as the way to righteousness, a classic reflection of the old and new natures of humankind. These two approaches to bring people to God were very different and reflected the personality of both men: Jesus and John the Baptist. Andrew's brother, Peter, was an "in-your-face" man, much like John the Baptist, so it is amazing that Andrew did not emulate those two, yet the Scripture is silent on this possibility. Andrew, when compared to Peter, was a subdued individual who took the

---

[20] Jeffrey, David Lyle. <u>Fishers of Men: A Dictionary of Biblical Tradition in English Literature</u>. Grand Rapids, MI: W.B. Eerdmans, 1992.

behind-the-scenes approach to life. These three men were different in character and temperament, but each was very complimentary of each other. John the Baptist and Peter were boisterous and Andrew laid back. Andrew, early in his ministry, was effective behind the scenes, but this approach would not be effective as the church spread beyond their homeland. (John 12:22; Mark 10:13-14)

There is no mention in Scripture or history of Andrew having a wife or home of his own, so he probably lived with Peter's family. His background was like that of Peter and the rest of his family, so he was exposed to the ups-and-downs of his environment. Perhaps his acquiescence began in this arrangement where he was the oldest by birth, but lived the role of the younger, yet devotedly loved his brother, Peter. This also may be the reason he levitated to John the Baptist, since John and Peter were so closely related in behavior. The oldest is usually the leader in a family, but in this household the second born controlled the direction and atmosphere of things. Remember the exposition about Peter; he always took charge. It would have been very easy for Andrew to pursue a man outside of the family, such as John the Baptist, for a role model that would not create a family rivalry, or a comparison of brothers, and who was preaching a message of expectation of a coming Messiah, which the family of Andrew was hoping would soon happen.

The authenticity of John the Baptist drew Andrew to the Jordon River where John was preaching. Maybe he saw in John a man he wished to become, a man full of fire and driven to change his world; a role model outside of the home. He saw in John a different kind of man, with a different kind of background. John's father, Zacharias, was a priest and his mother, Elizabeth, was an aunt to Mary, the mother of Jesus, making John a cousin of Jesus. (Luke 1:36) He was the preacher of his day, AD 29, and drew curious crowds seeking to hear from God and desiring to be baptized. John dressed in wild-looking clothes made of camel hair and a leather belt around his waist, lived in the desert wilderness, ate locust with honey, was the talk of his times, and drew people from every region: Judea, Perea and Samaria. John the Baptist knew his main mission was to identify and baptize Jesus, and he never wavered from that call on his life, not even in the face of imprisonment and death at the hand of Herold Antipas. (John 1:32-34)

Andrew would not be this kind of radical messenger, but John so impressed Andrew that Andrew never quit bringing people to Jesus, even amidst the constant threats of persecution and death that hounded the disciples. Andrew would come out of his shell of self-denial of his abilities to become a bold witness to the saving message of Christ.

The Apostle Andrew would learn from John the Baptist about the coming Messiah. Andrew, like Peter, was trained in the prophets and law, while attending meetings in their synagogue. He learned what the priests wanted the local attendees to hear, a message that kept the hearers in Judaic opposition and under control of the priests, but John had a different approach of presenting the Messiah. John was taught by his father and mother, who were only interested in his full mental and spiritual awareness and sensitivity to a coming Messiah, unlike the local synagogue priests, who were only interested in financial gain, manipulation of the Jews and pleasing their Roman counterparts. (Matthew 21:12)

John the Baptist was sure of the coming Messiah, because of the wickedness of Rome, the evil doings of Herod Antipas and the impotency of Judaism. Andrew embraced this view and joined him in believing the kingdom of Heaven was at hand, and this reinforced the resolve of Andrew in the impending end of the age. The only things challenging Andrew was his shyness, his inability to break free of just being the brother of Peter and the lack of authority this imposed on him.

John the Baptist, a Nazarite from birth, was seen by the Jews as a sanctified and holy man, with the same respect given to the high priest of Judaism. (Luke 1:13-17) The Nazarites were men of great heritage and service to God, such as Samson and the prophet Samuel. (Numbers 6:1-21; Romans 12:1-2; 2 Timothy 1:9) They took vows of abstinence from intoxicating drinks, grape juice or raisins, to let their hair grow, to refrain from touching the dead and to live a very secluded and restrained life. During this time, John patterned his life after the Jewish prophet, Elijah, and adopted his dress and lifestyle of living, but after years of pursuing this rigorous lifestyle, he branched out to a more open and drastic approach to proclaiming repentance from sins. Andrew listened and followed the teachings of John, and though he would not become a great public orator until after the death, burial and resurrection of Jesus, he would persuade men of their need for a Savior with the same intensity as John, his mentor. Andrew would become a great missionary once he decided to move to the forefront of those proclaiming Christ, and to move **beyond the ordinary** view of himself as not being a gifted leader.

Jesus would bring Andrew to his point of decision only after He was sure Andrew was ready to step into God's chosen role for him. The journey began with Andrew telling Peter he had identified the Messiah, the one they had longed for over the years. Andrew, in his earlier walk with Jesus, was the one who was always bringing someone to meet Jesus: family, friends, Jews, Gentiles or acquaintances. (John 1:41) No doubt he was a courageous man, willing to accept ridicule and rejection, even if it came from family; Peter in this case. He was willing to work for a younger brother who, because of his personality, was very demanding. He did not see himself as someone who could change his circumstances, nor was he willing to demand more respect. He was alright with his personal disappointment of others always taking the lead, and them receiving the praise for his efforts. Yet, he saw a need to approach Peter, who was tired and irritated after a long night of unsuccessful fishing. Perhaps this was not the best time to push Jesus on Peter, but, for Andrew, it was the first step of becoming the man that God would use to increase the church. (John 1:1-5, 14)

Remember, from our study about Peter, he and Andrew had already interacted with Jesus, and now Andrew pressured him to follow Jesus. The enthusiasm of Andrew was contagious. He had seen Christ baptized in the Jordan River by John the Baptist, and heard God speak from Heaven, and he was compiled to tell his brother about it. (Matthew 3:17) Experiencing this phenomenon was life altering for Andrew and many of those present at the time. Andrew's heart knitted in unity and companionship with Christ.

Imagine that life altering day. It started like any other day, but the experience of that day burned into the mind of Andrew, and he would never forget it. It was a normal day, with John the Baptist preaching his typical message of the necessity to receive baptism for the remission of sins and denouncing the corruption of their day, when Jesus came walking along the Jordan River. Jesus was seeking to be baptized by John. Andrew was cautiously excited at the diversity of the crowd gathered to hear John preach—a crowd filled with Jews, Sadducees and Pharisees, tax collectors and soldiers. (Luke 3:1-22) Then the most amazing thing happened. John declared Jesus to be the Lamb of God. Andrew heard John the Baptist ask for reassurance from Jesus to baptize Him, and then he saw John submerse Jesus into the water in baptism. His heart leaped within his chest when the heavens folded back as Jesus came up out the water. He gazed in wonderment as the Spirit of God lighted on Jesus in the likeness of a dove and heard God exclaim, "You are My Beloved Son; in You I am well pleased." (Luke 3:22) Some scenes and words make a lasting impression on an individual, and this is what happened to Andrew. He would never doubt that Jesus was who He claimed to be, while at the same time he was astonished at the hostility of the Sadducees and Pharisees. It was his first taste of conflict over Christ, his first eyewitness to the power of God, so their reaction meant nothing to him. He went immediately to share with Peter all that he had witnessed. Peter committed to follow Christ, and Andrew rejoiced!

The life of Andrew was reshaped quickly. He was the first disciple to follow Jesus, and Jesus had a special place for him among His chosen twelve. He was named with the first four disciples, but did not have the same access to Jesus as the others. Peter, James and John were always the leaders of the other disciples. This stage of Andrew's life was characterized by being over shadowed by others, including the two men he valued most, his brother and John the Baptist. It is obvious he put on the masquerade of accepting this plight, but coming from a family of fiery men, it is doubted that this were his real feelings. Perhaps, he longed to be recognized for his talents, and to receive some credit for his work. There is some of this longing in every individual's life. He would get his chance to shine, but only when he was ready by God's standards.

Jesus knew several very important qualities of Andrew's personality that would work in his favor. He knew that Andrew was a man of faith, and very willing to obey his Master. He knew Andrew was not prejudiced by seeing his willingness to share his faith with a family member, which is the hardest of all witnessing tasks, and Jesus was pleased with the humility by which Andrew lived his life. These qualities were exactly why Jesus, in His omniscience, called him first. Peter was much too aggressive early in his ministry to be effective in reaching others with the good news of Jesus Christ. Andrew was an example of working to please God and not men, a believer who could be trained and slowly graduate to the front of the class. (Ephesians 6:6) Andrew had a deep desire to bring others to Him. He must learn that to be seen and treated as a silent laborer was not a sign of a second-class servant for Jesus. His willingness to be that individual placed him in position to move **beyond the ordinary** thoughts of a lesser servant.

The lesson that Andrew must learn and embrace took place very early in his walk with Jesus. It happened in the house of the mother-in-law of Peter. She was very sick, as we learned while investigating the life of Peter. The amazing thing to understand about her healing is her response to Jesus. She was a servant who did not expect to be recognized by Jesus as someone who was extraordinary or privileged more than the next individual. She could have interpreted her healing as propelling her to the most favored of women. After all, she was the mother-in-law of the soon to be most famous disciple, plus some of the women of her times were seeking fame, and this could have been the start of a strong presence with them.

Instead, she saw her healing as an opportunity to serve Jesus. This gave encouragement to Andrew and helped him see his position in life can be beneficial to others, and it was a crucial step in his acceptance of his place in the kingdom of God. It was all right to be forever known as the brother of Peter.

The Scripture is silent about the work of Andrew until he is instrumental in assisting Jesus with feeding a great multitude of people. (John 6:15) The setting took place on a grassy mountainside off the coast of the Sea of Tiberias, near the town of Bethsaida, during the time of the Passover. The disciples had rejoined Jesus after a day of witnessing. Jesus and his disciples went up the mountain to rest, but as was customary, but a great crowd of people had gathered to listen to Him. It was late and the crowd was hungry, so Jesus asked Philip where they could buy some food for them to eat. Philip answered that they did not have enough money to buy that many people a meal, about 20,000 bystanders. That is the moment Andrew, still being referred to as Peter's brother, spoke up with a solution, "There is a boy here who has five barley loaves and two fish, but what are they among so many?" Jesus took the food, blessed it in prayer, broke the food into pieces and gave them to the disciples to give to the people. Everyone ate until they were filled, and there were twelve baskets of food left over. (Matthew 14:13-21)

The moment of decision came for Andrew to move beyond his characterization of his walk with Jesus, the agony of being second best and unimportant. He decided to move to higher expectations for himself in the service of the Lord. It happened when he realized that he and the crowd were satisfied by this miracle of the loving care of Jesus for all people. Andrew realized the loving care of Jesus for him was all he needed. Andrew found solace in his position in ministry, and stepped **beyond the ordinary**. (Mark 6:42; Luke 9:17) It was his defining moment!

Andrew grew and was comforted by several things of great significance that took place in the way Jesus used the disciples, and opened his eyes to the truth that his inhibiting self-appraisal was the source of his agony. First, Jesus did not call on one of the inner-circle men to perform this miracle. Second, Jesus involved Philip, a person who liked bringing people to Jesus, and whose nature Andrew could identify with and understand. Third, Jesus used the seemingly worthless lunch and faith of a little boy, who is never named, as the bedrock for this miracle. Andrew realized that names and status mean nothing to Jesus, only total surrender to Him. Plus, He asked all the disciples to feed all the people, not a select few. Andrew saw for the first time that everyone is important to accomplish the massive task of doing service, of caring for others. He moved **beyond his ordinary** self-imposed limitations that robbed his joy and fulfillment in knowing Jesus. The future door was open for Andrew to sit on the throne judging the tribes of Israel. (Matthew 19:28 Matthew 19:28)

Andrew had always done the right things, but he had not allowed his thought life to think in harmony with his deeds. His entire life changed when he came face-to-face with this reality, and chose to never let his mind go there again, he put on the mind of Christ. (I Corinthians 2:16; Philippians 2:5) His thought life would be seasoned by focusing on the words of Jesus, refusing to dwell on his circumstances, and bathing in the love of Jesus for himself and others. (Philippians 2:4-14; Romans 8:6; 12:2; Hebrews 8:10) He had learned the secret of the Apostle Paul, to live in contentment with all things. (I Timothy 6:6-8) He, like Paul, prioritized his thoughts on achieving the mindset of godliness, not material gain, and the vision of the eternal, not the temporal satisfaction of personal achievements. There was no room in the mind for anxiety, creed and unhappiness when the focus of thought is on Christ. Andrew would have no more wrestling matches with God or with himself over emotions caused by fruitless dreams for a self-made destiny.

The truth of Andrew's profound change is solidified on two occasions in his future. One is seen through the joint effort of evangelism with the Apostle Philip, and the other through a revelation revealing conversation with Jesus. (John 12:20-26) The Apostle Andrew reached a pinnacle in his relationship with Jesus when he was granted influence within the inner-circle. (Mark 13:1-4) He not only continued to bring people into the care of Jesus, but he could engage Jesus in very serious questions about the future of the kingdom of God. Each of these events warrants explanations.

The Apostle Philip, on the first occasion, brought certain Greeks who wanted to meet Jesus to Andrew to question Him about Jesus. (John 12:20-50) Philip came to Andrew because he was closer to Jesus, and Philip had seen Jesus seemly ignoring Gentiles. (Matthew 15:21-28) Together, he and Philip went to Jesus and He received them into His presence. Jesus cleared the air by explaining His message was basically intended for the house of Israel, but anyone who comes to Jesus with a humble heart will be accepted. (Romans 1:16) These Greeks, who were in Jerusalem to observe the Passover, had obviously converted to Judaism, so they could follow Jesus.

Jesus continues by acknowledging that He must die, the same as a seed must be planted in the ground to become a plant, and that His servants must die to their wants to be considered for advanced work **beyond the ordinary** expectation a master has for his servant. Just as important as the theme of their conversation, is the way it mirrors exactly what had happened to Andrew. Jesus explains that an individual must die to self, as Andrew did, before any good deeds can produce meaningful results, such as a lasting change of attitude in an individual. Jesus declared that an individual must surrender their desires to the desire of God if their love is to reflect an unconditional acceptance of their and others role in serving Jesus. True honor will come to the individual who truly loves the work done by all servants of the Lord Jesus. (John 12:23-24) Jesus is the only teacher who could share such a profound double message regarding the paths of servanthood. A productive person must accentuate God's work and true honor comes to those who care for others in the work of God, the kind of care that brings others to Christ to accept Him as Lord and savior. The way Andrew arrived at acceptance of his position was the greater plan of God.

The other evidence of Andrew's deepening relationship with Jesus is witnessed in a private meeting on the Mount of Olives with Jesus and the inner circle: Peter, James and John. They asked Jesus, on this occasion, what He meant about the buildings in Jerusalem being upheaved and the temple being destroyed? Jesus describes the end times for them in a very detailed manner. He said many will come to claim His deity, there will be wars and rumors of wars, nations and kingdoms will rise against each other and earthquakes and famines will increase. He continued to warn the disciples that governments and religious organizations would capture them, beat and put them on trial, but they were not to worry, because the Holy Spirit would give them words to say.

He prophesied that families will split and the disciples would be hated. Worst of all these happenings would be when the Antichrist takes control of the temple, and no one will be safe when this comes to pass. Pregnant women and nursing infants will be better off dead unless God shortens the days. Great tribulation will rock creation, stars will fall from heaven, and then, Christ will return. (Mark 13:1-27) This instruction was only for the closet disciples to hear, and now, Andrew was privy to the conversation.

History reveals that the Apostle Andrew never forgot his rightful place in the service for the Lord Jesus.[21] He had grown in faith by the end of his life, forsook his earlier lack of enthusiasm stemming from a wrong mindset and refused to accept any flattery expressed toward his ministry. His final words in life solidify this truth. Andrew journeyed to Armenia, Asia Minor, Macedonia and Greece.

Church historian, Eusebuis, records that Aigeatis, the governor of Patros, Greece, was enraged by Andrew's preaching, and had him tried before the tribunal in his attempt to stop the Christian faith. Andrew refused to obey the orders of the tribunal to cease preaching Christ. He truly cared for people, and Aigeatis had him crucified. The last recorded words of Andrew testify to his ascent **beyond the ordinary** recordings of individual service for Christ, "Accept me, O Christ Jesus, who I saw, who I love, and in whom I am; accept my spirit in peace in your realm."[22] Andrew knew it was not ever about him, but Christ!

---

[21] Fox, John. Foxe's Book of Martyrs. 2007.

[22] Eusebius (1989). The History of the Church from Christ to Constantine. G.A. Williamson, trans. New York: Dorset Press.

Moving Beyond the Ordinary

1. Andrew was a subdued individual when compared the Peter, and took the behind-the-scenes approach to life. He is typical of a sibling who is overshadowed by a dominant brother or sister. This can cause a harsh rivalry between family members. Is this the situation in your family dynamics between you and your siblings, you and your wife, between your children or grandchildren? How is the best way to resolve these circumstances?
2. The authenticity of John the Baptist drew Andrew to the Jordon River where John was preaching. Maybe he saw in John a man he wished to become, a man full of fire and driven to change his world; a role model outside of the home. This was well and good, but Andrew needed to learn about caring for people more than developing an aggressive attitude. Have you encountered such role models, and what were their agendas? Did their influence change your characterization of yourself and how so?
3. Andrew was willing to work for his younger brother, who because of his personality, was very demanding. Andrew did not see himself as someone who could change his circumstances, nor was he willing to demand more respect. He was alright with the disappointment of others taking the lead, and receiving the praise for his efforts. Yet, he still led Peter to Jesus. Is this your attitude and is it typical of your behavior? If not, would you be willing to change? How might Jesus help you in your efforts?
4. The way Andrew arrived at acceptance of his position was the greater plan of God! He was allowed access to the inner-circle meetings with Jesus and the others. Andrew was a man of patience and submission to God's desire for his life and ministry. Could this be said of your life and ministry?
5. What about the life of Andrew has changed your behavior and acceptance of your circumstances? Be specific.

Chapter Four

THE APOSTLE JAMES, SON OF ZEBEDEE, GOES BEYOND THE ORDINARY

*The Apostle James had a fiery temper and would have to manage it, if he was to **go beyond the ordinary**!*

THE APOSTLE JAMES, THE OLDER OF THE SONS OF Zebedee and Salome, whom Jesus nicknamed a "Son of Thunder," was thirty-years-old when he became an apostle. He was sometimes called "James the Greater" to help identify him from several other James' in the early church: James, son of Alphaeus, and James the Just. James and his brother, John, share the name "Sons of Thunder," and are in the circle of honor among the apostles. He was a man with a fiery temper and Jesus had to challenge this emotion, at the very core of his upheaval, if James was to be used in the Christian ministry. "Hotheads" cause hurt and division, not growth. Christ would bring him to a point of decision that would keep him grounded in his anger and of no use to Jesus, or would move him ***beyond the ordinary***, walk with Jesus. James would accept the challenge to harness his emotions and become a great force in the early church. He was a pillar of the church, even though his outspoken boldness to preach the gospel of Christ and his denouncing of the evils of King Herod led to his martyrdom.[23]

James was a temperamental and inconsistent man with seemingly two expressions, extreme anger or quiet calmness, each triggered by emotional upheavals, his anger being prevalent, and especially when his righteous indignation kicked in. His righteous evaluation of himself always justified his actions, and excused them away as necessary to accomplish his desires. It was this attitude in James that Jesus must re-mold, if he was to be effective and persuasive as a public speaker. James, the opposite of Andrew, who had intimacy problems, had no trouble speaking to Jesus. He, at times, could express himself in a calm manner to others, but when he was explosive he ruined the opportunity for effective conversation. This loss of dialectic control destroyed any opportunity to see both sides of controversial issues, such as the response to those who rejected his message. His actions greatly hindered his ability to grasp the concept of the message of Jesus to the non-believing Jews and Gentiles.

James, like his brother John and friend, Peter, lived in the areas of Capernaum and Bethsaida, and fished for a living. James, as with the Apostle Paul, would be heavily influenced by his environment, customs, current events and religious views of the time in which he lived.[24] James' father was a businessman, his mother was one of the pious women who helped supply the ministry of Jesus; his brother John, personally knew the Jewish high priest. They attended synagogue worship and were not poor people. His father did not dissuade James from following Jesus, and his mother, one of the followers of Jesus from the outset of His ministry, had no doubt whatsoever that Jesus was the Messiah. Her love for Jesus is witnessed by her willingness to go, with tear filled eyes, to the Cross to watch Jesus die, and then to the tomb of Jesus to anoint his body. She helped share the good news of His resurrection with the other disciples, and seemed to be in complete harmony with

---

[23] Halton, Thomas Patrick. <u>On Illustrious Men, The Fathers of the Church</u>. CUA Press, 1999.

[24] Robertson, J.C. <u>Sketches of Church History: The Age of the Apostles</u>. New York, NY: Crosswalk Publishing Company, 2001.

Christ. His parents' influence is seen in his devotion, vision and joyousness through his writings, and yet, James still had an explosive demeanor despite good parentage.

James' upbringing included no rabbinical training, and he was basically viewed as unlearned and without an official position among the Jews, both of which gave him no foundation to build a strong character or to promote change in his actions. Judaism had no empowering influence on his faith, so it is more likely that James' anger may have been a product of this background. His analogy of an immoral society, a failed Judaist religion and his inability to change it lingered in his mind. These entangling situations affect attitude for different lengths of time, and oftentimes dictate thinking for a lifetime, without some sort of intervention.

Angry feelings often have a specific starting place, and it is truly a strong possibility that James' emotions were the product of his times.[25] The City of Capernaum, on the northern shore of the Sea of Galilee, where he lived and fished, offered many opportunities to expose his passionate, zealous and uncompromising outbursts. Remember, it was a large Galilean fishing city, busy trading center and the most crowded district in Israel. It lay on the road between Damascus and Caesarea on the Mediterranean Sea, and between Tyre and Egypt, making it a leading stopover for caravans and a center for collecting customs taxes. Its mixed population containing both Syrian Gentiles and Jews, which like his family, challenged his acceptance of non-Jewish and pagan religions, and was a breeding ground for arguments over possible solutions to the acceptance of multi-faceted cultures. He, like his mother, lived in expectation of a coming Messiah who would correct the evils of his day, religious literacy, immorality and philosophical debates over what is right and wrong behaviors. James, like all the disciples, was confused and frustrated because of the direction Jesus, their Messiah, would take once He began ministry, a direction that did not appease his strong impressions over Roman oppression and felony Judaism.

The re-shaping of the Apostle James started early after his call to become a "fisher of men." Jesus needed him to develop into a

---

[25] Ayers. Philip E. <u>When Anger Strikes</u>. www.XulonPress.com, 2016.

mature leader who could channel his thunderous temper toward the unjust religious bigots of his day. Angry tendencies seem to levitate toward hostile circumstances, and James was no exception. His training began at the temple in Jerusalem. James was elated when Jesus cleansed the temple, and probably interpreted the action as justification for his outbursts. Jesus, shortly after beginning His ministry, entered the temple in Jerusalem during Passover, and drove the money changers out of the temple with a whip of cords. (Matthew 27:24-50) He poured out the money and turned over the tables declaring that His Father's house was not a house of merchandise. The fiery person that James was, found pleasure in this event, and it fit his ideology, convincing him that his righteous indignation protected the holiness of God. Directly opposing this event was the lack of anger shown by Jesus when the weeping crowds around the dead daughter of Jairus criticized him for resurrecting her. (Mark 5:35-43) This had to have raised James' blood pressure, and caused confusion in his mind, as to why Jesus did not angrily react to the crowd like He did in the temple. The problem with the behavior of James was he did not know when to explode and when to negotiate. Jesus would have to taper the zeal of James.

The work of Jesus on the behalf of James was successful. He would clear the Jerusalem temple a second time, and after three years of following Jesus, James would understand the second temple cleansing as more than the righteous indignation of Jesus. (Luke 19:45-46)

He recognized that God's house was a place of worship, a place to preach the gospel, not a place for thieves to rob people or for him to pick a fight. James would connect the earlier revelation of Jesus, that He was the true temple of God to the angry emotions of Jesus toward those who tried to destroy the things of God. James heard Jesus reveal that He was the true temple that if torn down, would be raised in three days, a reference to the future gospel account. (John 2:19; Matthew 24:2; I Corinthians 3:16) Jesus came to fulfill the work of God on the Cross, in the grave and in the resurrection, and James accepted this truth.

The second cleansing greatly influenced James. The temple priests convinced the peasants that their lambs were flawed animals. Jesus exposed the temple priests who took advantage of the peasants by charging exorbitant prices for substandard sacrificial animals. These evil Jews manipulated and commercialized the commands of God to offer pure, spotless lambs from their own flocks, during Passover, as an offering for their sin. They tricked the unsuspecting Jews into believing God would reject their unclean sacrificial lamb, and needed a lamb sold at the temple to offer for God's forgiveness of their sin. James realized Christ was truly justified in His action against this abdominal act, but more important than this was his observation that Christ never lost focus of His mission to save the lost. He immediately witnessed this, as Jesus took care of the blind and lame, and taught that His house was a place of prayer. He recognized that the nature of Christ was one of compassion and calmness, as well as, controlled force to attack evil. James, too, must reach this apex of attitude and action. However, he still must walk through the refining fire of God's creative hand!

James' next exposure to the devotion of Jesus to His ministry takes place in the town of Sychar in Samaria. Samaria was a place of contention for Jews who hated the thought of a Samaritan. Jacob's well was in that area and Jesus and his disciples stopped there to rest. Jesus sent the disciples into the town to buy some food. While they were away He met an adulterous woman, who came to draw water at the well in the middle of day, which was unusual because that was the hottest part of the day. Most came early, in the coolness of morning, to draw their water.

Jesus asked her for a drink of water, and a conversation started that led to her believing He was the Messiah. The disciples returned from town and were amazed that He was speaking to a woman, and that she had believed Him to be the Christ. Evidently, none of them, including James, were impressed, because they did not question Jesus or her about what had happened. She left them and went into the town. When she returned, she brought the whole town with her to see Jesus. Meanwhile, the disciples were only concerned about feeding Jesus, so they missed the real opportunity which was to bring people to Him. Jesus continued to explain to the disciples that His purpose in life was to save people from their sins, and that all these people, who had come to see Him, needed to hear that message. Jesus stayed there in that place for two more days, and many people did receive Him as the Messiah, to the dismay of the James. (John 4:40)

James heard the analogy of Jesus about the fields appearing to be ripe for harvest, as the masses of people walking toward them took on the appearance of a wheat field blowing in the wind. Jesus made a comparison of a wheat field ready for harvest to that of a crowd swaying up-and-down as they walked. Jesus told them that a "sower" and a "reaper" were needed to harvest it, and anyone willing to work would rejoice together and have eternal rewards. The fact that Jesus said they all would rejoice together hounded James, because he and the disciples did not include Samaritans in their plans for the coming Kingdom of God. James would display his attitude after another trip into Samaria near the end of the public ministry of Jesus.

The Jews, a pure race, and Samaritans, who were Jews that intermarried with Gentiles and pagans, had a loathsome history, and James and the Jewish disciples were angry over the Samaritan's disdain for their heritage. The bad history grew more intense from year-to-year and surfaced in the argument over the best location to worship God. Was it Mount Gerizim, proposed by the Samaritans or Mount Zion, insisted on by the Jews? The hatred between the Jews and Samaritans was involved, fierce, long-standing and went as far back in history as the patriarchs. The ancestors of the Samaritans were placed into the land of Israel by the king of Assyria after he took the ten tribes into captivity and exiled them in Babylon. The Samaritans wanted to help when the Jews returned to Israel to rebuild the temple, but the Jews refused their help, and the two never reconciled. (Nehemiah 2:10-19; 4:1-3) Every Jew knew of the history where Jacob had given Joseph a well which was passed on to his sons, Ephraim and Manasseh, and James was very aware of this. (Genesis 33:19; 47:22; Joshua 24:32) This well, now located in Samaria, was Jacob's well where Jesus spoke to the woman.

Jacob's well and the land around became Samaritan land, and the Jews abhorred it, to the point that when traveling, they went around the land instead of going through it. All this animosity festered in the mind of James. So, when Jesus was approaching His final days before the crucifixion, and on the way down to Jerusalem, an eruption would take place. The shortest route from Galilee to Jerusalem was through the mountains of Samaria, so along the way Jesus sent disciples ahead of Him into a Samaritan village to find aid in the journey. Perhaps it was the same village where Jesus had stayed earlier, but nevertheless, the Samaritans refused to accept Jesus, possibly throwing stones at them and cursing them, bringing the buried rage out in James.

What a great difference between James, who wanted to hurt people, and Andrew, who cared about people and wanted to bring them to Jesus. He and John asked if they might be the ones to call fire from Heaven to decimate the unruly Samaritans. Remember, James was present at the Mount of Transfiguration, just days before this, and should have learned submission to God's will for Jesus through being exposed to Moses and Elijah's submissive behavior. Instead, he would appease his rage by attempting to institute Elijah's practice of calling fire from Heaven to consume the sacrifices and, then slaughtered the Baal priests who were enemies of God. (I Kings 18:38-40) After all, God thundered from heaven when He spoke, and James was a "Son of Thunder," so why not strike?

Remember also, James saw Jesus angrily cleanse the temple. James, in his reasoning was justified to think he should strike these ignorant Samaritans. Jesus, instead of sending fire, taught James a lesson in sensitivity, a lesson about sharing the gospel with all people, including the enemies of Christianity. Jesus wanted servants who were passionate, zealous, dynamic and strong but not insensitive; otherwise service germinates hatred and cruelty. James listened, but he still did not accept the challenge of change that would move him **beyond the ordinary** responses of an emotionally unstable person when encounter by adversity, but he was moving closer!

Jesus told James he did not understand the severity of the words he was using and the evil spirit, a spirit of animosity, those words depicted. (Luke 9:55) James put his slant, his interpretations on of all the conversations of Jesus. He, for example, was deeply moved by the words of Jesus that had stopped the temple guards in their steps. (John 7:45-46) James saw this as the war power of the Messiah, a spirit of rivalry, but Jesus meant it as a way to continue His work. Then James had recently heard Jesus teach the story of the behavior of some workers of a land owner who were hired in the morning and were upset over being paid the same wage as those hired near the end of the work day. (Matthew 20:1-16) Jesus taught that the will of God must be accepted no matter what the circumstances or someone's interpretation of those circumstances. He tells them the first will be last and the last first in God's kingdom. This reasoning of Jesus did not make sense to an explosive person like James, who thought he had a corner on justice. James was probably braced for a stiff rebuttal from Jesus, but Jesus softened His rebuke of James' fiery request, and abnormal behavior to this point in his life. James could have been in serious trouble with Jesus, but the kindness of Jesus had the effect of planting a seed of change in James' interpretations, which struck at the heart of James' overbearing, uncompromising, task-oriented, angry attitude.

One more major event was used by Jesus to bring James to his change of heart. (Matthew 20:20-28) This event would infuriate the other disciples, but it struck James in a different way. James and John approached Jesus to request a special place in the kingdom. They wanted to sit at His right hand. Jesus, now in ministry, was thinking and preparing His spirit to go to the Cross, but James was wondering who would reign in the kingdom after the work of Jesus was done. James and John pulled all punches by bringing their mother into the fray. The three of them tried to convince Jesus that their plans would be best for all the other disciples. Jesus pushed her aside and addressed them directly. Jesus froze them in their places when He told them they would not reach prominence through selfish requests, but through practicing devotion and commitment to the cause of Christ. Jesus impressed upon James that He never shows favoritism, but He does reward those who love Him enough to suffer both self-denial and physical death. This knocked down James' last defense against denying his hateful attitudes and his unpredictable rage. It was strange, but somehow James realized he was comfortable with the idea of dying for Christ, but not because of an angry outburst or vicious act. James moved from seeing Jesus as the Messiah, who would change the oppression of the Jews to a loving Savior!

Jesus does not blast them for their request for pre-eminence among the other disciples or their selfish ambition for using their mother to ask for this request, but He does test their love for Him. Jesus' mind was on the Cross, and James must go beyond his ordinary thoughts of forcing Jesus to perform according to his likening. (Mark 10:32-34) He must trust Jesus as his Savior. James was not always so demanding, and this shows he had some high standards which did not involve his "hot-headedness." He realized there were more ideas than his when wishing Jesus would choose another way of saving the Jewish nation. (II Corinthians 5:17) Still, James had been slow to comprehend Jesus' teaching, but now he got it. Jesus must die on the Cross, and he was to tell everyone about it through a sympathetic message. It finally clicked with James that Jesus loved the small and great: rich and poor, healthy and sick, believers and non-believers, friend and foe with a sympathetic affection, and so James must be level-headed in his approach allowing the love of Jesus to shine through him. James finally heard the words of Jesus, and they propelled him ***beyond the ordinary*** understanding of the teachings of Jesus. Jesus did not come, born of a virgin, just to grant any desire that people may ask. James embraced the idea that nothing good comes from pushing a personal agenda, in his case, through an angry spirit. It was his defining moment!

The change in the actions and decisions of James is obvious from this point until his martyrdom. He had committed to control his temper, bridle his tongue, redirect his zeal, eliminate revenge and become an instrument of God. James's new service for Christ was a testimony of courage, sensitivity and passion that earned him the right to drink the cup of death at the hand of Herod. The cup of death that Jesus metaphorically spoke about earlier in the training of James. (Mark 10:38)

The new-found attitude of James is seen at the arrest of Jesus outside the Garden of Gethsemane. If ever the temper of James would have exploded, it would have been then. Not only did one of the disciples, Judas Iscariot, betray Jesus, but Peter encouraged rebellion when he attacked the servant of the high priest. (Matthew 26:47-56) James, before his change and had he known the meaning behind the actions of Judas Iscariot, would have flogged Judas when he saw him kiss Jesus with the kiss of death. James was a man of loyalty, and especially to Jesus, who had set him free of the guilt and shame of former actions. He certainly would come to the side of Peter when Peter pulled his sword and cut off Malchus' ear. This was the action he had longed for throughout his walk with Jesus, but James did not act. James identified with the words of Jesus to remain focused on the mission of spreading the good news of the gospel, instead of the cry of war. (James 1:1-3) James did not strike against the arresting mob that came to take Jesus away to be put on trial. He chose to flee the scene with the other disciples, not because he was a coward, but because he realized he would have a better opportunity later to speak for Christ, not spill the blood of those who knew no better. (Mark 14:48-52; Luke 22:52-54)

Later, there is more evidence of the change and maturity in James at the Council of Jerusalem, a conference of the apostles. His leadership demonstrates the power that comes from a new direction in one's thinking, a separation from the old way of reasoning.[26] The council, consisting of the heavy hitters in the church, Paul, Peter and Barnabas, met to direct the Gentile believers in the observation of the Mosaic Law of the Jews. The church in Jerusalem decided the Gentile Christian converts were not obligated to keep most of the Law of Moses, including the rules dictating the circumcision of males. The church did order these new believers to cease from eating blood, meat containing blood, and meat of animals used in fornication and idolatry. (Acts 11:1-18, 15) James agrees with Paul and says these believers should not have to

---

[26] Longenecker, Richard N., ed. Frank E. Gaebelein. <u>The Acts of the Apostles, The Expositors Bible Commentary</u>. Grand Rapids, MI: Zondervan Books, 1981.

prove themselves. He did not want to make it too difficult for the unbelievers to follow Jesus in salvation. What a change in James! He would have disagreed to this entire discussion prior to his move to a higher plane of understanding of the love of Christ. He had truly moved **"beyond the ordinary."** Now, he was the leader of the church in Jerusalem, and had the respect of the other leaders and all believers. (Acts 12:17)

James' very words in the Book of James to the church illustrate his deep understanding of the teachings of Jesus. James, led by the Holy Spirit, urges all followers of Christ to act like children of God. His language is so strong that he nearly commands Christians to pursue a life of holiness, allowing no excuses for not measuring up to this expectation. He wanted all believers to evidence their faith, and not merely talk about it. James relates this desire by referring to himself as a slave to Christ, coming from his gratefulness to Jesus' longsuffering toward him; he owed Jesus his life.

His book testifies to his use of harmful words, before he decided to change his attitude, of saying one thing and then not following through with his claims. James forbade this form of hypocrisy because it mirrored his failed way of serving. James gives honest and penetrating instructions to run from wickedness, playing favorites, unclean language, foolish wisdom and useless work. Instead, concentrate on a life of faith seasoned with Godly wisdom, helping the needy and orphans, and sharing the gospel message. His writing offers to believers, who stumble for lack of repentance or acknowledging the need for forgiveness, helpful guidelines to overcome weaknesses and reach for better ground from which to serve; like Jesus did for him.

There is one more proof of the change in James, and it was his approach to the opposition of a rapidly spreading church. James, in just fourteen years from the ascension of Christ into Heaven, became the outspoken apostle for Jesus and against the evil of Herod. The impressive thing about James was that he spoke in relentless boldness, yet not in repulsive anger. When King Herod committed to stop the church movement, he first killed James, because James was so important to the church that to let him live would undoubtedly prolong the church. (Acts 12:1-3)

It was said of James that he courageously led his executioner to Christ before the sword fell upon his neck.[27] The executioner fell at the feet of James, repented of his sins and begged to be pardoned by James for his part in the execution. James raised him to his feet, embraced and kissed him and offered him peace in the forgiveness of his sins. The executioner immediately proclaimed Christ as his Savior and was beheaded with James. Herod had James beheaded, the same fate that befell John the Baptist, but this would not hinder the church from growing throughout the known world.

Amazingly, the Apostle James had become somewhat like the Apostle Andrew, bringing people to Jesus, even while going to his death. A sign of a great leader is when their work continues at breakneck speed after their death. When God needed someone to stabilize the church against Herod's furious attack on the church, God chose James, not the great preacher, Peter. James had this distinguished honor bestowed on him. James had wanted prestige, Jesus gave him a cup. (Matthew 26:39) James wanted prestige but became a bondservant. He desired to lead with great power and authority, and Jesus gave him a sword. James had become a true measure of a servant who was willing to die for Jesus!

---

[27] Fox, John. Foxe's Book of Martyrs. 2007.

Beyond the Ordinary

1. The Apostle James was a fiery servant of Jesus until his change. Christ had to soften him through several years of trials and temptations. How do you feel that God changed James? How is God molding your attitude? What is the characteristic of your attitude that needs changing for you to move beyond an ordinary walk with Jesus?
2. Anger can be a good or bad emotion. James had a specific problem with wrongful anger. Godly anger can be a force for good, as Ephesians 4:26-27 instructs. Do you have an anger challenge? Was there a definite time when your anger became a controlling force to manipulate others and your circumstances? How do you think Jesus might change this attitude in you, and when will this happen for you? Can you identify a definite time in James' background where his permanent anger may have started? Perhaps it began amidst his family dynamics, environment, culture or religion? What and where was the stopping point for his uncontrollable anger?
3. James had several major encounters with Jesus that showed he approached people in a negative and hurtful way. His anger stopped his ability to serve Jesus. What are these encounters? Do any of them remind you of similar circumstances in your life?
4. The writings of James emphasize the necessity of believers in Christ to live per the dictates of their faith. Do your actions reflect your faith in Jesus? This question is faced by all who follow Jesus. Everyone would like a walk with Jesus that promotes genuineness and effectiveness in our witness for Him, but we have gaps in that walk that nullify our desire to serve with dignity. What are your "faith gaps?"
5. The early life of James mirrors a life that was out of touch with the true purpose of Jesus for James' future ministry. What areas of your life would need to be cleaned up so that you might fulfill your purpose in ministry and move beyond the ordinary?

Chapter Five

THE APOSTLE JOHN, THE BELOVED DISCIPLE, GOES BEYOND THE ORDINARY

The Apostle John had the reputation of being a "hothead", a "Son of Thunder", yet he self-proclaimed himself as the "beloved disciple" of Jesus. Really?

THE APOSTLE JOHN AND HIS BROTHER, JAMES, were called "Sons of Thunder" by Jesus Christ, yet these men were vastly different in personalities. James was a "hothead" by habit, but John was somewhat guilty by association with him. John, in the beginning of his relationship with Jesus, wanted to be sure he was included with the special ones of the discipleship, and to live up to Jesus' characterization of him and James. (John 19:16, 20:2, 21:7, 20) The best way to accomplish this, in his reasoning, was to be like his brother. It can be observed that John's strong desire to be like James and one of the Lord's favorites drove his thoughts and actions, until he learned it would be better to be known as the "beloved disciple," but this status must be earned by sincere submission to the service of Jesus. He would move **beyond the ordinary** association in relationships, once he learned of true love, the love he so boldly exclaimed in his writing at every opportunity. (John 3:16)

The Apostle John differed from James in his pre-Christ life in one major way; John allowed himself to be exposed to rabbinical hierarchy. (John 18:15-17) He was a Palestinian Jew and was interested in the prophecy of the coming Messiah, which his association with John the Baptist reinforced. John was exposed to the same conditions as James: family dynamics, customs, environment, home town and occupation. He, unlike James, was more acquainted with the religious leaders of his day. (John 18:15-17) Nonnus, a Greek poet and historian, spoke of John as the one who sold fish to the rabbis and priests, and was acknowledged by the high priest.[28] John surrounded himself with the most influential ones in the missionary team of Jesus, such as Peter, who he became a close companion with in missions. They prayed together and performed miracles, and confronted the Sanhedrin in fierce debates. (Acts 4:1, 22; 8:14-15)

John could be overly aggressive, bold and confident in his dealings with people, much like his brother, and unrelenting in his fight against the heresies in the church. (Acts 4:19) He was explosive, like his brother, yet on the other hand, could be humble and gentle. (John 21:20, 23-24; Luke 9:54) It was this inconsistent attitude that leaned more toward angry responses to people and circumstances that was dwelt with by Jesus. John misconstrued love as a wedge to separate him from the common associates of Jesus, and insure that he would have the personal endorsement of Jesus to rule over others. It was his misunderstanding and wrong application of love that must change!

John was bigoted and driven to protect the interests and integrity of Jesus, and it was this attitude of John that made Jesus insist that others could work for Him; such as those who cast out demons in His name. (Mark 9:38) John forbade strangers to work in Jesus name. (Mark 9:38-41) His intolerance, vindictiveness and selfish ambition got him into trouble. Remember, John and James infuriated the other disciples by asking if they might hold the seats of authority in the coming kingdom of Christ. (Mark 10:35-41) John had many mistakes and had sinned in his life and he would learn to handle these through prayers of repentance and confession. This is seen through his expansive and personal teaching

---

[28] Robertson, J.C. Sketches of Church History, The Age of the Apostles. Crosswalk, 2007.

about forgiveness in his writings. (I John 1:8-9) Jesus tamed John's zeal, narrow mindedness and misdirected violence by drawing him into a deep personal relationship with Himself. Jesus harnessed John's love.

The change in John's pilgrimage with Jesus and, later with the church was ongoing throughout his walk with Jesus. It started when he was twenty-four, the youngest of the disciples, and ended when he died in AD 85 at the age of one-hundred years. He remained unmarried throughout his life. It did not take long for Jesus and the others to realize he was the youngest of the Zebedee family and was accustomed to being spoiled, yet Jesus recognized in him a great capacity to love others. (John 2:1-12; 4:46-54; 5:1-15; 6:1-21; 9:1-12; 11:1-43)

John was there when Jesus turned the water in six stone ceremonial water pots to wine. Jesus, to the amazement John, the master of the feast and the other disciples, defied the natural laws of the universe when He changed one substance to a completely different one, water to wine. This was the start of many miracles performed by Jesus. He would walk on water, heal a blind man, feed thousands of people from a small lunch of a little boy and raise several from the dead, including His good friend Lazarus. There was no sickness that Jesus could not heal, including the lame, paralyzed, leprosy and demon possessed. John saw Jesus walk through angry crowds and not be seen or harmed by them. He witnessed all these things and would write about them in great detail, but the most transforming influence on John was the nature in which Jesus loved people.

The reputation of Jesus was spreading throughout the Galilean countryside. People were talking about this amazing healer and the unique message of hope in a new kingdom. Some loved it and others hated it. It had been four hundred years since anyone had heard or seen such unbelievable displays of miracles, and the entire ministry of Jesus contradicted the teachings of the Jewish leaders. One of those leaders, Jairus, a Synagogue ruler, had a sick daughter, and he searched for Jesus to come to her rescue. Jesus had left Jairus' area and gone across the Sea of Galilee to preach in another place. Jairus did not find him until Jesus was returning from His venture. Jairus found Jesus among a large crowd and fell on his knees begging Jesus to come to his dying twelve-year-old daughter and lay hands of healing on her. This was a desperate move, but desperate times demand desperate action, and he was willing to cross the establishment, forget that he had status in the synagogue, and was accustomed to ordering others around—now he was helpless.

The Apostle John witnessed the great love of Jesus as He healed her. John saw true compassion for a hurting man and an innocent little girl. He saw Jesus cross the barrier of disdain that many had for this Jewish leader, and give mercy to this father, for Jesus felt his pain. John's sentimental side of his nature was touched, but he still did not fully grasp the unconditional and unbiased love of Jesus. (Mark 5:21-24; Matthew 14:14; 20:34; Hebrews 11:6)

The same love that would allow Jesus to heal a woman who touched His robe, as He made His way to the home of Jairus. Jesus showed unrestricted kindness and unbridled love.

The young girl died before Jesus arrived to heal her, but that did not hinder Jesus from raising her from the dead. John saw that Jesus had power over sickness and death, power displayed through the administering of unmerited, gracious, beneficial love. This sacrificial love does not come naturally, but this seed of love was planted in John and it would grow. John was forced to compare his conceited approach to love versus the love of Jesus that was only interested in benefiting others.

John's next exposure to Godly love would take place on the Mount of Transfiguration. (Matthew 17:1-8) Remember, Peter and James were present when this meeting took place and each was mightily impacted, but John would see another side of Jesus that they missed. John would interpret the words of God to mean Jesus would have a serious mission to accomplish that would require the greatest of all love, which was to voluntarily and sacrificially die for others. God said, "This is my beloved Son, with whom I am well pleased; listen to Him." (Matthew 17:5) John later refers to this when he wrote that Jesus was the Son of God and would die for all sinners that they may have eternal life, once they have repented and asked for forgiveness. (John 3:16)

Peter and James on the Mount of Transfiguration were engulfed in the temporary excitement of witnessing Moses and Elijah speaking with the glorified Jesus. John revered the eternal presence of the two prophets and the proof of everlasting life that their presence confirmed. He saw it as a display of divine love. The full magnitude of eternal life represented in the visit of Moses and Elijah did not manifest itself in his soul completely, but he understood enough to realize the seriousness of what God meant when He said, "Listen." God would sacrifice His Only Son, Jesus, on a cross because of His great love for mankind. John was subconsciously accepting that he must surrender his selfish motives for claiming to be the "beloved disciple" by giving his entire life to the unfolding message that Jesus saves sinners; his subconscious stirring must become his conscious thought.

John would write of a very defining moment in his transformation from a "Son of Thunder" to the "beloved disciple" while in the upper room at the last Passover meal with Jesus. (Matthew 26:1-29; Mark 14:12-25; Luke 22:7-20; John 13:1-38) Several events took place that challenged the reasoning of John's existence in ministry, and added new dimensions to his future practice of loving and serving others. Since Jesus was the most loving man anyone had met, John seized on Jesus' example of loving others to advance his agenda of getting closer to Jesus than the other disciples. Again remember, his brother and mother desired this and pushed for it.

Jesus chose to wash the disciple's feet, a menial slave job, to demonstrate his desire for them to drop the pretense of being humble and the seeking of an emanate position in the discipleship. Ultimately, Jesus urged them to practice a loving perspective toward each other, one of serving others, not being served. Jesus explained to them that He must wash them clean of their sinfulness or they would never be fit for Heaven, and implied they must do the same for those they serve. (John 13:8) Remember, Peter missed the original point of Jesus' teaching, but John toyed with a new dimension to this kind of true love, a true servant's heart will commit his entire soul to helping others. John was learning to serve Jesus so that he could serve others. However, he was not fully ready to commit to this idea.

    The Passover meal began with the disciples positioned along the table with John next to Jesus. (John 13:23) Jesus identified the traitor who would betray Him to the authorities during the meal in the upper room. This was a very distressing time, as each of the disciples questioned themselves if they might be the traitor. This vicious act depicted the exact opposite of the theme of washing of the feet because an act against the love of Christ was not only demeaning, it was detestable. Judas Iscariot would prove to be the traitor, but imagine the aguish in the hearts of the disciples, and especially in the heart of John, who had insisted that he loved Jesus beyond measure. Now the thought of a possible betrayal was heart wrenching to him and the others, particularly Peter, whom the Lord said would deny Him soon. John must have wondered how love would persist in such controversy. Yet, love would prevail through the New Covenant in the blood of Jesus, which Jesus announced. This covenant promoted the following of Jesus by loving one another and living by the power of the soon coming Holy Spirit. (Jeremiah 31:31-34; Hebrews 8:6-13; 9:15; Luke 22:20)

    Jesus prayed for the disciples, reminding them of His deep love for them and the resulting events to follow. He asked His Father to keep them from evil and to consecrate them by the truth, which is His Word. Afterwards, they left for the Garden of Gethsemane. (John 17:11-20) John came closer to understanding the words of Jesus that expressed His unending, unfailing love for them, even in His death. Jesus persisted in true unconditional love for them which meant going to the Cross. John's incentives to serve others began to change when he saw this vast and unconditional love for people which Jesus processed. Jesus had a supernatural strength to love friend and foe. Everything was unfolding in slow-motion for John. He was now ready to change, to go **beyond the ordinary** bounds of love and simple expressions of love to the extreme fecundity of loving others; expressions of love ranging from sharing a cup of water to dying on a cross. (Matthew 10:42; Luke 23:46)

    Two incidences grounded the Apostle John in true love; the charge to John from Jesus to care for the mother of Jesus and the restoration of the Apostle Peter to service. John had all the traits of authentic love swirling around inside of him, but something was missing. Something was needed to touch his heart, emotionally, that would insure his deeds would become the outcome of sacrificial, enduring love stemming from the right motives for his actions. The request of Jesus from the Cross to care for Mary was the missing link that bound together the loose ends of love's confusion within John's heart into a force to be reckoned with. (John 19:26-27) John no longer could keep buried his true self, his feelings of kindness, compassion and care for others when he heard the dying words of his Lord. His raw emotions flooded to the surface of his thought life, and manifested in his actions. Now, they must become permanent!

True love brings unheard of action, and John, overwhelmed by emotion, was on public display. John chose to be one of the disciples who were present at the Cross, just like he decided to be present at the trial of Jesus. (John 18:15) The scene from the Cross was gruesome. The image of the mangled body of Jesus nailed to the Cross burned into John's mind. His thoughts raced back-and-forth in his mind between a need to hate or love the persecutors of his dear loved one, Jesus. The answer came from the mouth of Jesus, "Behold the woman," referring to Jesus' mother. (John 19:27) Jesus spoke to John to focus on helping the poor in spirit, not the surrounding circumstances, not the Roman soldiers, priests or mockers. (Matthew 5:3; 27:27-31, 38-44) John was a changed man, and the proof of this is seen in John's reaction to the request of Jesus. (John 19:28-30) He would live **beyond the ordinary** weaknesses and confinement of human love from that moment. It was his defining moment!

John, who at an earlier time, had desired to hold a key position in the coming kingdom of God, learned true love obeys the desire of the Savior, and waits for the greater service positions. John listened to Jesus as He agonizingly instructed him to take care of Mary. John felt the pain of Jesus and those who stood watching Jesus bleed and die on the cross. He was salted with the maturity of Christ; as he witnessed Jesus voluntarily sacrifice Himself for others. John, who expected to see retaliation and words of anger from Jesus, only heard words of passion and love spoken by Christ. There were no words calling for rebellion or hatred expressed on that day from Jesus, even though many witnesses of the crucifixion mocked Jesus. Jesus truly loved all people! The concern of Jesus for His mother eternally impacted John, and tradition teaches that John never left Mary for ministry until she passed away.[29] This is a great change in attitude from a man who had previously called for fire to burn up those who rejected Jesus.

Then, there is the restoration of the Apostle Peter to ministry. Remember, Peter had denied Christ and returned to fishing. Jesus appears on the shore of the Sea of Galilee, after the resurrection, and beckoned for the disciples to cast their nets off the right side of the boat. The catch of fish was so enormous that they could not pull the fishing nets into the boat. John recognized that the person on the shore was Jesus. Peter, upon hearing this, put on his outer garment, jumped into the water and pushed to the shore, while the others rowed to shore with the catch of fish. Once there, they saw that Jesus had prepared a breakfast of fish and bread. Peter brought some of the freshly caught fish and they ate. (John 21:1-14)

Jesus took Peter aside and questioned his love for Him. John was near and was listening.[30] The conversation overheard by John between Peter and Jesus was forever itched in John's heart. You will recall that Jesus asked Peter three times if he loved Him. However, the questions had a different connotation each time. Jesus asked Peter if he loved him with a Godly love the first two times He questioned him, called agape love. John knew that Jesus was asking Peter if his love for Jesus was unconditional love, with no strings attached. John interpreted this to mean that Jesus was asking Peter if he was willing to give up all his earthly desires and treasurers, his self-made attitude and even his life for the advancement of the church. (John 21:19)

---

[29] Utley, Bob. The Study Bible Commentaries Series, New Testament. Bible.org, 2012.

[30] Kruse, Colin G. The Gospel According to John: An Introduction and Commentary. Grand Rapids, MI: Wm. B. Eerdmans, 2004.

John saw Peter's heart break when Jesus asked him the third time about the sincerity of his love. This time Jesus used the Greek verb meaning a love totally different than God's kind of love. Instead Jesus asks of a love shown to friends, called phileo love. John heard Jesus peel away Peter's flesh and cast it on the fires of sacrifice. (Proverbs 25:22; Romans 12:20) The pain was nearly unbearable for Peter, and it internally sheared John's conscience and heart. John envisioned the words of Jesus to apply to him also. Jesus commanded Peter to follow him, but John was summoned to obey Jesus' words as well. (John 21:15-19) Jesus would never have to ask John if he loved Him.

These moments between Jesus and Peter were precious, and when Peter realized John was within hearing of the conversation, he rebuked John for robbing him of his time with Jesus. However, Jesus quickly reminds Peter that the only one he needs to worry about is himself. Jesus tells Peter to stay focused on the business at hand, sharing the gospel and building the church. John needed to hear the same rebuttal from Jesus, because he had tended to expect more favoritism from Jesus than the others. John's thoughts are eternalized as he accepts the importance of love not being about prestige, position, but sacrificial.

The scene between Jesus and Peter was never forgotten by John. He always remembered the tender expressions of love shown to Peter by Jesus, as Jesus compassionately restored Peter to service. John moved **beyond the ordinary** opportunities to share temporary love, those opportunities that merely stem out of a deep affectionate love for someone else. John imprisoned himself with steadfast love that endured the test of time and fellowship in the gospel. (Philippians 1:5)

The further change in John is witnessed by those who read his writings. John believed that the work of Jesus was finished, as Jesus proclaimed from the Cross. (John 19:30) John gives a vivid account of the empty tomb of Jesus. He and Peter ran to the tomb after Mary Magdalene reported to the disciples that the tomb was empty. He and Peter saw the grave wrappings of Jesus neatly placed in the tomb, pondered the idea of a missing Jesus, and returned to their dwelling. Mary told them that the angels said

Jesus had risen and would go before them to Galilee, which John and the others accepted as truth. John acted so quickly by running to the tomb, because he was longing to see Jesus, and therefore, he was blessed to be the one to first recognize Jesus at the Sea.

John's love was rewarded by Jesus many years later.[31] Jesus appeared to John in a vision while John was exiled on the Isle of Patmos, because of his unwavering love and service for Jesus.[32] He had become a pillar in the church, endorsing the Apostle Paul by acknowledging God's grace was upon him, and powerfully influencing the churches in Samaria, Jerusalem, Galilee and Ephesus. (Revelation 1:9-10; Galatians 2:9) John partnered with Peter to minister throughout the Judean territory, was there at the healing of the lame man at Solomon's Porch, endured imprisonment with Peter, preached in Samaria with him and unashamedly preached a gospel message free from entanglements with the Jewish Law. (Acts 3:1; 4:13; 8:14) Now, Jesus would give him the prophecy of the coming future of the church and end times, the apocalypse.

Truly, the Apostle John had reached his summit of service in the army of God. John's life ended in a characterization of implicit trust in Jesus, a dedication to loving others, and a steadfast love for Christ. Jesus inspired John to write about forgiveness and acceptance that is found only through the grace of God.[33] He became a man of loving service rather than ruling authority, a man who lived **"beyond the ordinary!"**

---

[31] Metzger, Bruce. <u>An Introduction to the Apocrypha</u>. New York, NY: Oxford, 1957.

[32] Fox, John. <u>Foxe's Book of Martyrs</u>, 2007.

[33] O'Day, Gail R. <u>Introduction to the Gospel of John in New Revised Standard Translation of the Bible</u>. Abingdon Press, Nashville, 2003

Beyond the Ordinary

1. John, in the beginning of his relationship with Jesus, wanted to be sure he was included with the special ones of the discipleship, and to live up to Jesus' characterization of him and James. The best way to accomplish this, in his reasoning, was to be like his brother. Have there been times in your life when you depended on relationships for reasons other than noble, and occasions to cheat or manipulate situations to gain notoriety or a reputation that does not represent the true you? What would you do to be included in the popular crowd?
2. John could be overly aggressive, bold and confident in his dealings with people, much like his brother, James, and unrelenting in his fight against the heresies in the church. He was explosive, like his brother, yet on the other hand, could be humble and gentle. Does your attitude in life have two sides; one that is calm and compassionate and another that is angry and hateful? How does the life of John mirror your zeal for good versus evil? What would you like Jesus to change about yourself?
3. John was forced to compare his conceited approach to love versus the love of Jesus that was only interested in benefiting others. What is your definition of love? Does it match that of Jesus, and what attitude in you does it produce? What would it take to force you to change your thinking? Would benefiting others motivate you to share Jesus love?
4. Jesus prays for the disciples, reminding them of His deep love for them and the resulting events to follow. He asks His Father to keep them from evil and to consecrate them by the truth, which is His Word. Do you ask God to reveal to you the truth of His word for your circumstances in life, and how to change the negative results into positive ones?
5. John saw Peter's heart break when Jesus asked him the third time about the sincerity of his love, except this time Jesus used the Greek verb meaning a love totally different than God's kind of love, a love shown to friends. Would you

describe your love for yourself and others as sacrificial love or manipulative love? What would it take to change your devotion to Jesus and others?
6. John moved **beyond the ordinary** opportunities to serve, opportunities stemming merely out of a deep affectionate love for someone else. Do you desire to go beyond the ordinary love relationships in your life? What are the things that hold you from experiencing the full joy and peace of God's love? Are you willing to give up those things that would hinder your love for Christ and others?
7. How do the life experiences of John impact your life?

Chapter Six

THE APOSTLE NATHANAEL, A GOOD MAN, GOES BEYOND THE ORDINARY

The Apostle Nathanael was a true Israelite, knowing the prophecy of the coming Messiah, but blindly not embracing Him.

THE APOSTLE NATHANAEL'S GIVEN NAME WAS Nathanael, son of Tolmai, after his father, Tolmai, and it is most likely that he was from the sect called Tolmaians. This sect was devoted to the study of the Scriptures, and explains why he was so well versed in the Messiah prophecy. Tradition says he was the youngest of seven, was unmarried and the sole support for his aged parents.[34] Nathanael, once he became a follower of Jesus at the young age of twenty-five, acquired the use of the name Bartholomew. He was from the town of Cana in Galilee, and attended the same synagogue as Andrew, Peter, John and Philip. (John 1:43; 21:2) The Armenia Church claims him as their founder, and describes him as a man of medium height with curly hair that covered his ears. He had large eyes, a straight nose, a long beard and wore a white robe. He was a true seeker of God, and rested on the hope that the Messiah was soon to come. Nathanael, like

---

[34] Smith, William and Cheetham, Samuel. <u>A Dictionary of Christian Antiquities</u> (1875)

the other disciples, was a follower of John the Baptist, who was declaring the imminent coming of the Christ.[35]

The disciples lived in a time when the scribes, priests and most devout Jews were filled with hatred and prejudice against any suggestion of religious differences to Judaism, who fought with the Romans on social and racial differences and religious bias. Nathanael was a by-product of his times, a very prejudiced person, and his prejudice was reinforced by the elements of his home town; it robbed him of any ability to truly love others. Remember, Cana was a town within walking distance from Nazareth, the home town of Jesus. Nathanael's skepticism shows that there was a rivalry between Cana and Nazareth. He insisted that Nazareth had no social or religious influence in the region. (John 1:46) There were no important people living there, except for himself and his friends, and this had a social bearing on the prejudicial attitude of Nathanael, including his opinion of Jesus and his family. It was this attitude that caused the people to reject the message of an uneducated Galilean carpenter, non-typical religious preacher, such as Jesus, and it blinded them from the hearing the gospel message.

Nathanael believed the inhabitants of Nazareth were ignorant and unworthy of hearing from God, even though Nazareth was in a key location, on the main route for travelers traveling north to south, up the coastline of Israel or east to west. The town, in his estimation, was occupied by uneducated, rude and an extremely prejudiced Gentile populace. The Galileans looked down on the Nazarenes who spurned the Judeans who hated the Galileans and Nazarenes. It was viewed as a cultural disaster. Nathanael viewed Nazareth as evil and corrupt, and believed nothing good could come from there, even though he lived next door in Cana, an unsubstantial town. This kind of prejudice separates a person from any acts of love. His relationship with Jesus would cure him of this characterization flaw.

Traditionally, Nathanael was given the characterization, "without guile," based on the testimonial that Jesus originally said of him. (John 1:47) This seems to be a strange description to

---

[35] Tenney, Merrill C. New Testament Survey. Grand Rapids, MI: Wm. B. Eerdmans Publishing Company, 1961.

assign someone until you understand it vividly portrays the person. Scripture alludes to Nathanael as sincere and honest, yet ironically, he was very biased and proud of his family, home town and his reputation, which was a predictable observation based on his education in Judaism that promotes such pompous opinions. His one major hindrance to the success of his future service for Jesus was his pride. This pride manifested itself in his prejudice toward individuals in accordance with his opinions, and must change for Nathanael to carry on a rewarding ministry. His saving quality was his willingness to change, and to move **beyond the ordinary** attitude of being better than anyone else, segregated from underprivileged people and extremely opinionated in interpretation of the Law of Moses and the Prophets.

Nathanael was an astute student of the Old Testament, and his life was consumed in the study of Moses and the Prophets. He was undoubtedly the apostolic philosopher of the twelve apostles. (John 1:46, 49) He filtered every conversation and action through Scripture, and anyone wishing to befriend him had to associate a relationship with him based on Scripture. This is the reason Philip could so easily introduce Nathanael to Jesus. He told Nathanael he had found the man that Moses and the prophets wrote about coming. (John 1:45) Philip could have told Nathanael that he had witnessed the greatest miracles, but Nathanael would not have responded because he was looking for one thing and one thing only; the coming of the Messiah. Nathanael was living in a cocoon, yet this tunneled anticipation of a coming Savior kept him seriously centered on the business at hand of watching the eastern sky, since the Messiah would come from that direction. (Matthew 24:27)

The conversion account of the Apostle Nathanael to Christianity reveals the positive and flaws of his mentality. Philip came to Nathanael and told him he had found the Messiah of which Moses and the Prophets foretold. (John 1:45) Philip and Nathanael were friends and Philip sought him out, because Nathanael was a true Israelite and well-trained under the Rabbinical doctrine. Possibly, Philip was seeking reinforcement in his decision to accept and follow Jesus as the Messiah. Nathanael immediately challenged the invitation of Philip. (John 1:46) He could not accept the fact that Jesus came from the town of Nazareth. Rabbinical teaching held that the Messiah would come from Judea, the land of King David, so it was inconceivable that Jesus could be the one Nathanael was watching to come and establish the new kingdom. Surely, the Messiah would not come from the Galilean territory where Gentiles ruled. Nathanael was prejudiced against any reference to the Holy One of God being associated with any other race other than the Jewish race. He was sincere in his opinion but he was seriously wrong.[36]

Nathanael had one reasoning trait that was to his advantage. He was open to meaningful dialect. Maybe he was open to the excitement of Philip, or perhaps, he remembered the preaching of John the Baptist. He may have heard of the baptism of Jesus and was willing to entertain Philip's claim of finding the Messiah. Possibly, Nathanael went with Philip to renounce the testimony of Jesus. Nathanael was a devoted defender of the Scripture, and simply did not believe Jesus was the One, but the most important issue is that he went with Philip to see for himself, setting the stage for his change. (John 1:47)

Nathanael, deep within his soul, was a man who really wanted to help people in their quest for God. Jesus knew this about him, and was willing to invest time in his needed change to surrender his prejudice against anyone who promoted a faith in God which contradicted his understanding of prophecy. Nathanael was no different than any other religiously minded Jew, but he was blinded to the manifestation of the Messiah as being Jesus Christ. Defenses against false understandings of the Law of Moses or arguments against a needed encounter with the God of Israel was not the problem with Nathanael. However, his self-imposed awareness of God's purpose for his time in history was the problem. It is a sad man who has a heart for God, but acts in a hypocritical way to the truth of Scripture. Nathanael desired a Messiah that would reign and rule over God's creation and the nation of Israel in a physical manifestation, not a sacrificial lamb, as John the Baptist and

---

[36] Pearlman, Meyer. Through the Bible Book by Book – Part IV New Testament Epistles and Revelation. Springfield, MI: Gospel Publishing House, 1935.

prophecy declared. This type of spiritual blindness is known as a "veil of humanness", and needed to be removed from Nathanael's mind. He must not approach Jesus through human reasoning.[37]

Jesus removed the veil through one conversation with Nathanael. Nathanael heard Philip introduce Jesus as the son of Joseph from Nazareth, and this encounter appealed to Nathanael's human side. Nathanael was a spiritual man, but he also was human. He must forget the physical confinements of nature, and open his heart to the spiritual realm. Many people label others by the dictates of family, environments, customs, religion and last names. Nathanael heard with human ears, but Jesus quickly drew him into the supernatural arena of revelation, a revelation that only an omniscient God could know.

Prior to Nathanael's meeting with Jesus, he had been in meditation under a fig tree, probably near his house. Houses in the Galilean region were very small and it was difficult to have a private time in such close quarters. Families cooked, carried on their daily chores and shared the same one-room space together. The fig tree, because of its height and width, provided shade from the heat of the day and a private place to pray. When Jesus spoke to Nathanael for the first time, Jesus knew his name, his lineage and his physical location, and Jesus revealed this to Nathanael without hesitation or doubt. Jesus was omniscient God in the flesh and Nathanael recognized this truth immediately. (John 1:47-49)

Nathanael knew his own nature and that it needed redeeming, so in that moment, he chose to change his mind and approach to the deity of Jesus. He went from an intellectual awareness of the Messiah to a soul conversion. Nathanael, unlike any of the other disciples, who would struggle with their relationships with Jesus, went **beyond the ordinary** relationship with Jesus in his first meeting of Christ, and he was immediately open to the truth of God's word. It was his defining moment! Jesus did not have to expand Nathanael's education, physical experiences or spiritual understanding of God's Son to increase the potential of Nathanael's ministry. Nathanael's future ministry was instantly

---

[37] Campbell, Joseph. <u>Papers from the Eranos Yearbooks</u>. Princeton University Press, 1981.

guaranteed. No other disciple experienced the quickness of such a miraculous change.

The only thing left for Nathanael to take his rightful place in the discipleship was to submit to the authority of Jesus. Nathanael exclaimed that Jesus was the Son of God, and this was necessary for him to be born into the family of God, but he also said that Jesus was the King of Israel, indicating that Jesus would rule immediately from Jerusalem which was a belief that Jews insisted upon happening. Jesus corrected Nathanael with the prophetic announcement that Nathanael would see much greater things than the reign of a king. Jesus opened the spiritual eyes of Nathanael with an astonishing statement, "Nathanael would see Heaven open and the angels of God ascending and descending upon the Son of God." (John 1:50-51) Nathanael could have never envisioned going this far **beyond the ordinary** perception of one's purpose in ministry. His ministry would not be ordinary in any way. The statement of Jesus was a metaphoric revelation that Nathanael would see Heaven open to Jesus with supernatural revelation and power.

What does it mean to move **beyond the ordinary** in life and ministry circumstances? The changed lives of the Apostles Paul, Peter, James, John and Andrew have helped answer this question. Jesus used these men in unimaginable ways, ways that go above their most extreme imaginations. Now, the Apostle Nathanael would be used far above his richest desire. Jesus tells him that he would have a clearer vision of Godly truths and that he would explain them effectively to the masses, the angels and saints. (John 1:50-52; Genesis 28:10-22) Nathanael would be blessed by Jesus with divine understanding to the purpose of the miracles performed by Jesus–miracles from the turning of water to wine in Cana to the ascension of Jesus back into Heaven. Nathanael would know that Jesus was the absolute fulfillment of all prophecy, both the Abrahamic and Davidic covenants.

Jesus exposes Nathanael to the dream of Jacob and the ladder of which Moses spoke. He was introduced to a different dimension of Jacob's dream through the words of Jesus. Jacob's words that the Lord was in his presence took on new meaning to Nathanael because Jesus was the Lord and He was in the presence of Nathanael. (Genesis 28:16) He realized the dream was really about the Christ, as the God-man, who was God in Heaven, but man on earth, who would be the mediator between God and man, man's Savior. Nathanael appropriated the truth that authentic peace, which he and the others sought, comes from a relationship with Christ and not through a manly king who would rule over the masses. He unraveled the dream and reasoned the ladder was Jesus through which revelation would flow from God the Father to Christ through the Holy Spirit, a truth only a scholar of Scripture, such as Nathanael, might apprehend. Jesus revealed to Nathanael that He would be the conduit through which the deep things of God would be clarified to the others, and this confirmation was likened unto angels going from Heaven to Earth and back again.

Nathanael needed to know for certain that Jesus was the Messiah, so Jesus opened the Scripture to Nathanael, so any doubts would be dismissed from his mind. Nathanael, momentarily, was still thinking in political terms, a political messiah, when he declared that Jesus was the King of Israel, and this had to be resolved. Nathanael would appropriate the truth that Jesus was the sacrifice that would satisfy God's wrath toward the sinful rebellion of the nation of Israel against God's law. (John 1:49; Romans 3:25; I John 2:2)

Political prejudice would have no place in Nathanael's future because this prejudice is what caused Israel to reject Jesus. (Mark 6:4) So, Jesus referred to Himself as the "Son of God," a reference He would use often, and a fulfillment of the prophecy of Daniel, of which Nathanael knew. (Daniel 7:13) Israel's rebellion continued against Jesus, and was witnessed often. One such attack came on Jesus with the fruition of the Jews attempt to carry Jesus out of His home town of Nazareth and kill Him, simply for preaching that God anointed Him to deliver the people from their wickedness. (Luke 4:29)

The faith of Nathanael was solidified by the truth that Jesus had supernatural abilities, such as His revelation to Nathanael as to his presence under the fig tree, and that Jesus was the "Son of God" and "King of Israel." Nathanael, later in his walk with Jesus, would witness the deliverance of Jesus by the angels, and have the "Resurrection of Christ" verified by angels at the empty tomb. (Luke 2:8-20; 22:43; John 20:12) It is true that Nathanael, with the other disciples, abandoned Jesus on the Mount of Olives during the Passion Week, but it was not for fear of being arrested or murdered. (Mark 14:50) He knew that Jesus was doing exactly what the plan of God was for His life. He refused to attempt to alter the redemptive work of Christ by intervening in that plan. (Luke 24:46-49) Nathanael, like Jesus, trusted in a sovereign God. Indeed, Nathanael would see and do things **beyond the ordinary**; he would see that Jesus was the great "I am!" (John 1:50; Exodus 3:14; John 8:58)

The Apostle Nathanael died a martyr's death for Christ; the highest act of Godly respect. (John 15:13) Tradition says his father died just after Pentecost, at which time he became a missionary to India and Armenia. He converted Polymius, the king of Armenia, to Christianity. Polymius' brother ordered him to be flayed alive and crucified upside down in Albania after Nathanael refused to recant the gospel message.[38]

---

[38] Fox, John. Foxe's Book of Martyrs: Crosswalk, 2007.

Beyond the Ordinary

1. Nathanael lived in a society that was prejudicial. All sinful people have a temperamental nature that is prejudice. We all make prejudiced comments, draw prejudicial conclusions, and make prejudicial comparisons about certain people, classes, societies and religions. Would you say this is true of your attitude and nature? Name your prejudice. What are the ways in which they handicap your relationships with others and with Jesus?
2. The Apostle Philip realized the prejudice of Nathanael and brought him to meet Jesus because he believed Jesus could change Nathanael. Do you know other people who harbor prejudice? Are you willing to bring them to Jesus? Is your faith in Jesus strong enough to trust Him to remold your prejudiced friend? Why or why not? Are you willing, if your faith is weak in this area, to allow Jesus to change you?
3. What are the preconceived and unreasonable judgments or opinions that you see in the religious world around you? Do you see how prejudicial behavior, suspicion, fear, intolerance or hatred keeps people from accepting Jesus Christ as Savior and Lord?
4. Hidden prejudice is one of the worst kinds of sickness. It is harmful, depressing and detrimental to a joyous life. Do you allow for hidden prejudicial attitudes in your life? If you know they are there, why would you ignore them instead of confessing and repenting of them? Why would a person do this to oneself?
5. What about the life and testimony of the Apostle Nathanael impressed you the most and why? Be specific.

Chapter Seven

THE APOSTLE PHILIP, A PESSIMIST, GOES BEYOND THE ORDINARY

The Apostle Philip, the curious one, had faith enough in Jesus to believe His message of salvation, but did not fully understand its impact until after the Resurrection.

THE APOSTLE PHILIP HAS A UNIQUE STORY. HE grew up in the town of Bethsaida, the same home town of Peter, James, John and Andrew, which means he knew them. They attended the same synagogue and were exposed to the same religious opportunities. He was a Jew by birth, but had a Greek name, and no one knows the reason for this but his Jewish name is never mentioned. Tradition says he was the second borne of seven children, of a family of three boys and four girls, and he had the privilege of baptizing his family after the Resurrection of Christ.

Jesus saw that Philip took care of the physical needs of his family, providing for their care and safety.[39] Jesus knew that he was not overly energetic in his chores, but he was consistent in providing food for his family, and because of this heedfulness he could be the spokesman of the second four of the discipleship,

---

[39] Dr. Vladimir Antonov, Edition and Commentaries. Translated by Anton Teplyy, Dr. Mikhail Nikolenko and Hiero Noni, Antonov V.V., 2002.

which included Nathanael, Thomas, and Matthew. This was a trait that Jesus needed of His disciples to carry on His future ministry.

Remember, Andrew brought Peter to meet Jesus and John introduced James to Jesus, while Philip would bring Nathanael to the Lord, but Jesus, Himself sought Philip. This was a break from the normal routine of these men reaching each other, and it was done for a specific reason because Philip was a different kind of person from the other disciples. He needed tender encouragement and patient nurturing from Jesus if he was to grow into a powerful missionary of the gospel message. Philip was a persuasive public speaker and tenacious in anything he undertook, but he wore his emotions on his sleeve. Remember, he did answer Nathanael's complaints about Jesus by insisting that Nathanael come and see Jesus for himself, but he was slower to see the big picture than the others. One wrong move by Jesus in His molding Philip's need for toughness could dampen his ego and silence him forever.

Philip was the fifth disciple to be chosen by Jesus, and at the age of twenty-seven, still was curious about everything. He was much like a child in many ways.[40] He wanted to be shown everything and really did not care for sight unseen circumstances. His lack of imagination would prove to handicap his ability to reach **beyond the ordinary** day-to-day hustle and bustle of ministry and the commonplace drudgery of life. This mindset must change for him to fulfill his assigned task of stewarding the goods and provisions needed to sustain a daily ministry. Philip wanted things to run smoothly and without stress, both monetarily and routinely when acquiring the physical needs of the discipleship. Jesus would carefully and skillfully lead him into a dramatic change in his prosaic character that would mobilize his full potential, allowing for his exceptional methodical reliability and abstract mathematical talent.

The problem for Philip was his unimpressive dealings with life's circumstances and no vision for the future; he was simply a commonplace man with many questions. It was not that he was pessimistic. He just was not spiritual and could not see the miraculous

---

[40] Attwater, Donald and Catherine Rachel John. <u>The Penguin Dictionary of Saints</u>. 3rd edition. New York, NY: Penguin Books, 1993

possibilities of any given situation. The poor man had no spiritual bones in him. Jesus never wounded Philip's spirit by hurtful reprimands, but allowed Philip to ask his questions and learn about the vast wisdom of Jesus to answer every dilemma with the perfect solution, which Philip would come to see is something that only God could do.

How does one who is extremely intelligent change their unfruitful ambitions for the future, while being lack luster in motivation to take any meaningful initiative to climb out of the pitfalls of such lack of vision for the future? One does not, but God does. (II Corinthians 5:17) Can God really redirect the thinking of such a complex individual as Philip? The answer is, absolutely this is possible. Philip's change starts the same as any person willing to follow Jesus. He was saved! (John 3:1-16; Romans 10:13, 8-10)

Jesus, as earlier stated, took the initiative in the conversion of Philip. Philip was fishing with Peter and Andrew, one day after Jesus was announced as the "Lamb of God" by John the Baptist, and Peter and Andrew were saved, when he had his encounter with Jesus. (John 1:43) Jesus walked up to Philip and said, "Follow me." The transforming word of God is **beyond the ordinary** language of the common man, and it pierces the very heart of an individual. (Isaiah 55:11; Hebrew 4:12-13)

Nathanael experienced this. Jesus, being God in the flesh, the one who spoke all creation into existence, called Philip out from among an ordinary lifestyle of meaningless tasks. (John 1:1-4, 14; Genesis 1:1-3) Jesus seized on Philip's desire to find the Messiah, drew Philip to Himself, and Philip became a Christian. Now, he must follow through with his relationship and work with Jesus, which is something that many new converts never accomplish.

Philip had a shortcoming that Jesus addressed first in his training. He was not completely truthful in his evaluation of things and this surfaced in his testimony to Nathanael. Philip went to find Nathanael, so that he might take Nathanael to Jesus, but he revealed his self-triggered deception by saying he had found Jesus which was not true, Jesus had found him. (John 1:45) Philip must learn to honestly evaluate his motivations in life's choices if he were to move to higher ground in his service for Jesus, going beyond the restrictions to his ordinary reactions to life events. Self-deception, even those little white lies that mature over most of a person's life, are deeply rooted within that person's mind and are nearly impossible to uproot and replace with honest appraisals of one's thinking. Self-deception about what fuels reasoning feeds on itself and it will shut down any efforts to change one's perception of who they are and why they think and act in certain ways. It causes the fear of rejection or possible failure to tie an individual to a hitching post; much like a mighty horse is tied to a post and not allowed to run free. Jesus would free Philip from this blight on his mind. (Romans 12:1-3)

Philip would learn that his conversion was in line with the calling of Jesus, and he could be truthful about it, as was Jesus in everything. Philip was trained to share the absolute truth that Jesus came to give His greatest of creations, mankind, an opportunity to have the sin debt, that innateness to always sin because of the sin of Adam and Eve, forgiven. Jesus brought hope to humanity by offering eternal life in the presence of God, avoiding the everlasting separation from God which is insured to them, if this sin debt goes unforgiven. (Romans 6:23; Matthew 25:46) Philip's faith, over time, grew to truly appreciate the unfailing love of Jesus to save everyone who believed His message, and this became his motivation to aggressively preach the good news. Jesus saves those who call upon Him; one at a time! Bad habits are hard to break and would take time. Philip's training was not yet complete, but it was growing.

The next major event in Philip's transformation came at the feeding of the five thousand, after Philip had been with the discipleship for some time. (John 6:1-14) Philip had witnessed the gracious actions of Jesus through many occasions: the supernatural power of Jesus at the marriage at Cana, the evangelism of the Samaritan city of Sychar, the healing of many illnesses and casting out of demons, the Sermon on the Mount, the authority of Jesus over the natural elements, the way Jesus dealt with His rejection by the Jews and the beheading of John the Baptist. Philip had plenty of opportunities to see that Jesus was preeminent over all circumstances and everybody, but he still was hesitant to take a great step of faith. This did not stop Jesus from moving Philip to a life changing commitment.

Sometimes, the obvious is hidden from the consciousness of a person who is centered in the presence. This was the case in Philip's situation one afternoon on the grassy slopes situated on the northern end of the Sea of Galilee.[41] Jesus had preached, healed many sicknesses and cast out many demons from the nearly 20,000 people who were there, counting the men, women and children. It was late and Jesus was concerned that the crowd was hungry, so He asked Philip to feed them. The only problem was that Philip, you remember, who oversaw the necessary daily provisions, had not prepared for such an undertaking. He was not ready to feed so many people. If Philip had remembered that Jesus turned water to wine, this insurmountable challenge would have seemed easy. Trust Jesus to do a miracle!

Instead, Philip, unsatisfactory to the wishes of Jesus, gives Jesus a wrong answer, and responds with a mathematical evaluation. He explains to Jesus that two hundred pennyworths or two hundred day's wages, a penny a day, would not pay for this meal. Philip was frozen in place, he could not get beyond the request of Jesus to buy 7, 200 biscuits, which was the sum of paying one penny for thirty-six biscuits. They were not near a bakery and, if they were, to cook and distribute so many biscuits, at such a quick notice, would be unforeseen. What happened to the lesson from the water to wine miracle?

Philip saw the situation as impossible, no future vision of what could happen when God is introduced into the equation. (Matthew 19:26; Luke 18:27) Philip, even if he exaggerated the possibilities of feeding so many people, saw the situation as insurmountable. Andrew, however, saw the circumstance as a potential miracle in the making, which is the difference between successful ministry and mundane service to Jesus. Andrew sheepishly intervenes by offering Jesus with an alternative, a young boy's lunch of five barley biscuits and two small fish. Philip's heart must have jumped out of his chest when he heard this futuristic suggestion

---

[41] Mason, Steve. Josephus and the New Testament. Peabody, MA: Hendrickson Press, 1992.

by Andrew that Jesus could multiply this lunch into a feast. He must have thought that his failure to see miraculous possibilities would bring instant criticism from Jesus, but Jesus moves straight to the need at hand of feeding the people. Philip starts to realize that Jesus was consumed by ministry—past, present and future. Philip started to see the full picture, and his heart and mind were coming into focus of moving **beyond the ordinary** grip of seemingly impossibilities.

Jesus would order the disciples to sit the people down. He prayed and thanked God for the provision of this boy's lunch, broke the biscuits and fish into pieces and had the disciples give the food to the people. The people ate until they were full. Then, Jesus had the disciples collect twelve full baskets of remaining portions of food. Philip learned a valuable lesson in trying to use a commonsense approach to providing answers in situations that seem to have overcoming impossibilities. He saw the unfruitfulness of depending on material things to solve the conflicts of life. Now, he witnessed a bounty of food being left over from a barren beginning.

Jesus showed Philip that He would supply the needs of those who follow Him, even if those followers are not visionaries. However, Philip must saturate this truth into his soul, so that he could depend on the future guidance of Jesus for his ministry. Jesus plants this seed in Philip's thinking, but it would take more time to blossom. Jesus gave each of the twelve disciples a basket of food in testimony of the truth that He fulfills His promise to supply our every need. (John 6:13; Matthew 6:11; Philippians 4:19)

It was Passover and Philip was called upon to evangelize some God-fearing Greeks who were searching for Jesus. (John 12:20-26) This meeting took place after Jesus raised Lazarus, his good friend, from the dead. (John 11:1-44) The situation in ministry was growing more dangerous by the day. The chief priests and Pharisees were plotting to kill Jesus and Lazarus, because so many people believed in Jesus. (John 11:45-57; 12:9-19) These Greeks were practicing Judaism, but they had heard about the resurrection of Lazarus and wanted to meet with the miracle worker called

Jesus. They came to Philip because they perceived he was sympathetic to the Greek cause, due to his Greek name.

Philip had learned to share Jesus by this time, but he was still slow in accepting the divine mandate to trust Jesus with his life, especially under such local hostility. He, in his indecisiveness, set up a meeting between them and Andrew in hopes that Andrew would know what the reaction of Jesus would be if Gentiles were brought to Him for salvation. Remember, Philip, like the others, had reasoned that Jesus had come to set the Jews free from bondage, not the Gentiles. (Matthew 10:5-6) God's grace had not fully flourished in the mind of Philip.

Philip made a final decision to change his futuristic thinking. Philip would be forever changed by the meeting between the Greeks, Andrew and himself. Jesus tells them that their way of thinking and trusting Him for their eternal destiny rests on the next days ahead. Philip heard with spiritual ears, for the first time, that his whole world depended on Jesus ignoring His fleshly desire to live and fulfilling His death on the Cross. Jesus explains that He, and all who take up the Cross, must die to their desires and internalize the truth of eternal life. All followers of Jesus must be driven by the future hope of seeing Christ again, after His death and Resurrection, something that was foreign to Philip's ambitions and way of thinking.

Philip heard that true love sacrifices all dependence on earthly talents, physical stature or human reasoning, and will follow Jesus wherever, whenever and however He chooses. True Godly recognition comes from this mindset, and will be honored by God. (John 12:23-26) Philip made the decision to move **beyond the ordinary** way he had spent his entire life of analyzing the facts through human eyes, and ending up with nothing to show for it. Jesus supernaturally energized Philip's thinking capabilities. It was his defining moment!

Philip, three years later, proved his new outlook by drawing the other disciple's attention to the truth of the oneness of Jesus and God, the Father. Some would interpret this conversation that takes place between Philip and Jesus as proof of Philip's failure to change, but Indeed the opposite is true. (John 14:1-11) Jesus insures Philip and the other disciples that they will have a house in Heaven that is made by Jesus, and that Jesus will personally come to escort them to it. (John 14:1-3) The Apostle Thomas asks Jesus to reaffirm that they will know the way spoken of in this revelation, and Jesus tells them they already know this truth. Jesus further comforts them by reminding them that they know God, the Father, because they have seen God in Him. This is when Philip asks Jesus to show them the Father. (John 14:7)

Philip makes this declaration to solidify all that they had seen in Jesus, not to question the accuracy of what Jesus was sharing. (John 14:8) It was a bold statement by Philip to allow Jesus to offer affirmation of His success in teaching the disciples about the trinity of God: God the Father, God the Son and God the Holy Spirit. It shows Philip had changed his vision for the future, and that he was no longer impotent in the understanding of the redemption plan of God for humans. Jesus tells the others through His explanation to Philip, that they very well know the Father. Jesus, sarcastically and yet profoundly, says "Come on men, you know the truth of my oneness with the Father." (John 14:9) Jesus emphasizes that it is through this union that He could do the works that they had been a part of for three years.

Philip set the stage for Jesus to encourage the disciples to serve with vigor and perform greater works than Jesus had accomplished. (John 14:12-14) Jesus says their future work would be aided by the answer of prayers on their behalf. Philip would move on to greater heights in his service for Jesus, and he would push **beyond the ordinary**, far beyond what you could dream. He became a visionary!

Tradition teaches that Philip would be martyred after preaching for more than twenty years. He proclaimed the gospel of Christ in Scythia, southern Russia, and then, went to Asia Minor and worked in Laodicea and Colossae. It was in Hierapolis that Philip led the Roman proconsul's wife to Jesus, after healing her of a sickness. Her husband was infuriated by this and ordered the crucifixion of Philip. He was eighty-seven years old. Philip's final request was not to be wrapped in linen, as with Jesus, because he felt unworthy of such honor.[42]

So impressive was Philip's faith that his wife and daughter became witnessing Christians. His wife was said to have stood at the crucifixion of Philip, encouraging him to preach Jesus to his murderers, until she was silenced by being stoned to death. Their daughter, Leah, continued their work, and became the prophetess of Hierapolis.[43]

---

[42] Fox, John. Foxe's Book of Martyrs, 2007.

[43] Pamphilus, Eusebius. The Ecclesiastical History of Eusebius Pamphilus. Grand Rapids, Michigan: Baker Book House. 1984.

Beyond the Ordinary

1. There was very little about Philip's service that was impressive. He had little discerning vision, was pessimistic and lacked spiritual understanding and insight about preaching the Gospel. He needed to change his outlook on life and his source of motivation in ministry. What helped Philip to see his need to change? What was the thinking of Jesus toward Philip's attitude? What approach did Jesus use to reach out to Philip? Do you have a similar attitude to that of Philip?
2. Philip had difficulty adapting to new situations. Name some of them. Do you have challenges accepting new circumstances? To what degree does this hinder your ability to respond to people and uncertainties?
3. Philip was methodically reliable, but when circumstances required a different direction, he had no imagination to break his complacent routine. Do you find yourself desiring to think in ways that conflict with your normal reasoning patterns? How can Jesus redirect your actions?
4. Is your witness for Jesus lacking passion? You may be willing and capable of bringing someone to Jesus, but you are not motivated to do so. Why do you suppose that is true of yourself? Did anything about Philip's transformation impress you? What was it? Do you believe Jesus has the right and ability to change your attitude? Are you willing to let Jesus change you? Why or why not?
5. Philip suffered from self-deception about his mediocrity. This kind of self-deception is very dangerous and could be deadly to servanthood. Why is this true? Examine the attitude of Philip to answer this question. Why do think he could not escape his opinion of himself without help from Jesus?
6. Philip saw some unbelievable miracles, but they did not move him to trust Jesus more deeply. How can individuals experience the power and grace of Jesus Christ and not be moved to action?
7. What happened in Philip's life that proved he had moved **beyond the ordinary** characteristics of his former attitude and behavior? How could your answer relate to you?

Chapter Eight

THE APOSTLE MATTHEW, A TAX COLLECTOR, GOES BEYOND THE ORDINARY

The Apostle Matthew was a materialistic and short-sighted tax collector who was embraced by Jesus and suspiciously watched by the other disciples.

THE APOSTLE MATTHEW LIVED AND WORKED NEAR the Sea of Galilee, probably near the Cana and Capernaum region. (Mark 2:14) He was born the son of Alphaeus, a Syrian Jew. Tradition of the early church said he was married and had four children.[44] He was a man of reasonable wealth, a good business man, and not worried about his neighbor's opinions of his work. He was thirty-one-years old when he met Jesus.[45]

Matthew, by the nature of his occupation, was the only disciple of Jesus who declared himself as a vile sinner, an extortionist, social outcast and a publican. He was a Roman puppet, working directly for Herod Antipas, who was hired to collect taxes from the Jews to give to Rome, which caused the people to isolate him as a

---

[44] Allison, Dale C. <u>Studies in Matthew: Interpretation Past and Present</u>, Grand Rapids, MI: Baker Academic, 2005.

[45] Moir, Alfred and Michelangelo Merisi da Caravaggio. Caravaggio. <u>Masters of Art Series</u>. New York, NY: H.N. Adams, 1996.

traitor.⁴⁶ Remember, Herod was the Jewish tetrarch who ruled at the Roman's pleasure and was hated by the Jews for this. Matthew was the worst kind of tax collector because he paid for the right to extort the Jews. He paid the government for this privilege, and became wealthy off the common people.

Rome required a certain amount of tax to be collected, and any amount over that could be established and collected by Matthew. He used bribes and certain traveled roads to increase his bounty, sat tolls on roads, bridges and harbors, and was successful in pleasing Rome and his own selfish gain. Tax collectors were so hated that it was not a sin for the Jews to lie and deceive tax collectors. Tax collectors were banned from testifying in a court of law because of their reputation for lying and taking bribes and they were banished from worship in the synagogues and temples, which cut them off from access to God. Matthew lived the life of a foreigner in his own country and among his own people; no better than a pagan who worshipped the emperor of Rome as God.

Matthew held the most corrupt position in the tax collection business, that of a Mokhes. He could collect customs on everything: imports, exports, the roads an individual might travel, food, clothes, and any item he chose to tax. They were specialist in the profession, unlike the Gabbai, who only collected tax on property, income tax, and poll tax. Rome endorsed the Mokhes' system of revenue collection, and encouraged their initiative in business practices, such as segregating the workers: Little Mokhes and Great Mokhes.⁴⁷ The Great Mokhes hired a helper to do his tax collecting, and he would stay in the background and out of sight. The Little Mokhes, of whom Matthew is included, worked the trade themselves. They were too greedy to pay someone else to work for them, and they were not concerned about the social stigma placed on them by their peers. (Matthew 9:9)

Matthew was known by the name Levi. (Mark 2:14-22; Luke 5:27-38) The name Levi was a traditional religious Jewish name

---

[46] Goodspeed, Edgar J. Matthew, Apostle and Evangelist; A Study on the Authorship of the First Gospel. Philadelphia, PA, 1959.

[47] Allison, Dale C. Studies in Matthew: Interpretation Past and Present. Grand Rapids, MI: Baker Academic, 2005.

with rich Old Testament ties, so his choice to deny the teachings of the Law of Moses and the prophets was obvious and self-serving. He obeyed them when they did not cost him money. His practices as a tax collector and his phony connection to the Jewish religious practices ostracized him from the community.

Matthew, being a Jew, must have known the law of God to some degree, but his lifestyle showed no interest in spiritual things, and yet Jesus called him to ministry. Matthew was not an individual who fit the mold of someone chosen to represent the holiness and deity of God. There is no human logic that would excuse his past, and grant him an audience to preach the gospel, that Jesus was God's Son, who would die on a cross for the redemption on mankind, be buried and resurrected on the third day. (I Corinthians 15:1-4) Matthew, himself, would not seek to move **beyond the ordinary** lifestyle of cheating others without divine intervention.

Matthew must have been dissatisfied with his life, and this is evident because, at first opportunity, he immediately walked away from his career when Jesus met him and invited him to join His work. This was a major change in the life of Matthew, one that required more risks than that of the other disciples. Remember, Peter, James, John, Andrew and Philip were in the fishing business.[48] The fishing trade could be walked away from and returned to easily, when compared to the Matthew's business.

The Roman rulers replaced him immediately with another person who would sell their soul for financial gain. However, Matthew would have a long process of training and a major change to endure, before he would be suited to speak on the behalf of God. He was willing for this process to take place, and this was his first step to becoming a successful servant of Christ, who would later write his book, the Gospel of Matthew. He would have to overcome financial loss and face an angry religious crowd over his acceptance to follow Jesus. Remember, the scribes and Pharisees were not pleased with the uproar caused by Jesus, or anyone involved with Him.

---

[48] J. J. Scott. Josephus. Dictionary of Jesus and the Gospels, eds. Joel B. Green and Scott McKnight, Downers Grove, IL: Intervarsity Press, 1992.

The Christian experience, for Matthew, starts in Cana at a toll booth. (Matthew 9:9-13) Jesus met Matthew shortly after a controversial healing of paralytic man. He is accused of blasphemy by the scribes because He said the man's sins were forgiven. (Mark 2:5) Matthew, being at a public place, a tax office, overheard stories coming from the people about Jesus, and this particular account was appealing to him. Matthew's debauched life was tormenting him. He was intrigued by the thought that Jesus could forgive sins, the one debauchery that Matthew faced, his awful attitude and sinful thoughts. So, when Jesus asked him to follow Him, Matthew's heart was bursting with agony and hopelessness over a life wasted on the foolishness of greed. It is not unreasonable to think that Matthew, like the other Jews, was hoping for something better from religion, a Deliverer, a Messiah, and now he met Him, Jesus.

Imagine the scene for a moment. You are a merchant going to market, and you dread paying Matthew a tax for transporting your goods on his road. Everyone is pointing out Jesus, who is just in front of you in line to pay taxes. You are trying to deal with that confusion and you are about to be galled by a corrupt Roman official named Matthew. Then, that official does the unheard of; he gets up and leaves the collection table and goes after Jesus. You get off without paying taxes.

Now, think about the thoughts of Matthew as he makes this unpredictable change in his day's affairs.[49] Think about the fear of reprisal from the Roman authorities for Matthew's neglect to collect the taxes that day. He gave no retirement or a return to work notice. He just walked off the job. He could have been arrested and imprisoned, but he chose to face those risks and challenges. This was a great step of faith for him to leave everything behind and to acknowledge he was a sinner in need of salvation.

Shortly, Matthew held a public gathering for his fellow co-workers, and invited Jesus to join them. Sometimes the miraculous forgiveness of sin causes a person to do extraordinary things. Matthew acted impulsively by meeting with these men, who the

---

[49] Westerholm, Stephen. <u>Understanding Matthew: The Early Christian Worldview of the First Gospel</u>. Grand Rapids, MI: Baker Academic, 2006.

Pharisees noted were sinners and tax collectors, the scum of the earth. The Pharisees cornered the disciples to criticize Jesus about His dining with these publicans, but Jesus overheard the conversation and corrected these religious bigots.

Jesus faced them down with the purpose of His being there which was to save sinners from judgment, of which the Pharisees were numbered. Jesus said they were sin sick and needed mercy through deliverance by a gracious God. Matthew embraced this truth, but the Pharisees rejected the appeal. Matthew took a second step to defeating the reputation of corrupt living, and moved **beyond the ordinary** opinion that sin lasts forever with no chance of change. Matthew started to compare his life characterized by the love of money to that of being set free from the dictates of riches and power. He would soon learn that he was bought with a price, the shed blood of Jesus, and Matthew would never be the victim of money again.

Matthew's former occupation required him to be harsh and forthright in his demands for people to pay their taxes. This approach would not touch the ones who needed to hear the message of Jesus, so Matthew needed to change his thinking and communication skills. He had to learn humility, the most difficult task for a driven person to adopt. This is not an easy endeavor to undertake on one's own cognizance. The change does not come quickly. It took long periods of sitting at the feet of Jesus, appropriating His words into his heart, and observing the change in others, such as Peter and James, as they communed with God. This would be the testimony of Matthew's change, and it is obvious in his writings as he recalls the transforming power of Christ in the lives of others.

Matthew learned humility from the Sermon on the Mount. (Matthew 5:1-20) Jesus taught the disciples about the traits of a genuine believer in God. He masterfully unfolded the characteristics of a repentant heart, which was exactly the message Matthew, as well as the others, needed to hear. Matthew was eager to listen to the opposing side of his past attitude, how he should have treated people, and to grow in his awareness of Christ's forgiveness for his past sins. He had already learned of the meaning of being "born again." John had shared the conversation that

Jesus had with Nicodemus. (John 3:1-21) John would include this account in his gospel recordings.

Matthew heard John explain that Jesus said the rebirth of person was a spiritual affair, and was the work of God. John firmly shared that a new convert cannot fully understand this spiritual birth, but the believer has an internal witness of the birth, because the Holy Spirit indwells them. Matthew, like all believers, knew he was alright with God when he followed the call of Jesus. That was not his problem, but how he would share the love of Jesus was a challenge.

Matthew was secure in his relationship with Christ. He was saved, but Matthew had to allow this message and experience to season his heart. Remember, Matthew had to learn to operate in humility, to witness through love, a concept in which he was not experienced. He heard Jesus preach a stern message on morality, but in a fashion that humbled people not angered them. (Matthew 7:28-29) Humility cannot be bought and sold. It only comes to a person who drops his excuses for wrong decisions and accepts the consequences of those actions. Jesus gave Matthew the time he needed to work through his guilt and sensitivity of his wrongs done.

The Sermon on the Mount, preached by Jesus from a hillside northwest of Capernaum, overlooking the Sea of Galilee, implied the difference between an obstinate attitude compared to a humble demeanor, and Matthew was in perfect alignment with the message. He had followed Jesus for nearly a year, and was beginning to access the word of Jesus with spiritual ears. This message, for Matthew, would be different from any teaching of Jesus to date. Christ by-passed Matthew's physical limitations and pierced his heart, like the red-hot fires of the altars of sacrifice. (Exodus 30:28; 39:39; Leviticus 6:12-13)

The message of Jesus, like the eternal fires of sanctification, would burn in the heart of Matthew throughout his entire life. Matthew heard the divine commentary on practical morality, spirituality and the correct relationship between God and mankind. Jesus erased any false pretenses of Matthew's view of the perversions of Jewish immorality which might hinder his future service to Jesus.

Jesus said the poor in spirit would be blessed, implying the arrogant would suffer, and the boastful would be left behind in the end of time. Jesus shared that everyone who cried and anguished within their soul would be comforted. He said the meek would inherit the earth, not the manipulators within the world system of robbing other's security. (Mathew 5:2-12) Matthew had lived this horror and it had not worked. Now, his soul and spirit were resting in what he was hearing from the mouth of Jesus. His ideology was changing from one truth to another. His bosom was swelling with joy. He was being raised from an ordinary doctrine of the Judaism that taught joy only came from pleasing God through living in obedience to every law on the books—an impossible endeavor. Matthew was lifted **beyond the ordinary** understanding of grace that said performing to the best of your ability in fulfilled deeds is enough to earn God's forgiveness for sin, a deception that had not worked for him. (Matthew 5:1-7)

Matthew heard Jesus say that anyone searching for the truth of God, His knowledge and wisdom, would find it. Jesus said Matthew was clean because Jesus was his friend and Savior. Matthew recognized that merciful acts reaped mercy back, and no amount of money could influence this truth. Matthew heard Jesus declare that he was pure in God's eyes. There was no need to worry about his relationship with God being a lasting one; it was eternally safe through the love of Jesus! Matthew finally received the eternal revelation that Jesus is divine and is God's son, and anyone could live in peace and give this peace away to others who would listen. (Matthew 5:6-8)

The learning curve in Matthew's thinking continued at a steady pave. He would learn that persecution leveled at him and the other disciples was part of serving Jesus. Jesus shared a different view of suffering. Matthew heard Jesus say persecution was not necessarily the result of evil deeds, but may be the haters of God attacking God's people. Matthew realized that the attacks of the religious crowd against him was not a punishment from God because of his former sin, but was a sign that he was going to reign in the coming kingdom of God. (Matthew 5:10-12)

He was forever humbled by this revelation. Matthew truly climbed out of despair and was elevated ***beyond the ordinary*** plateau of service. It was his defining moment! Again, he could make this change in attitude and thought because he earnestly sought to be like Jesus. He made a conscious decision to remain in a Godly mindset of servanthood, not come upon by fate or accident. He would, like all Christians, be tempted to wander from serving Christ, but his choice to elevate his service never wandered.

Jesus continued to teach the necessary principles of the central tenants of Christian discipleship which the disciples and Matthew needed to learn. These lessons of servanthood would turn the known world upside down for Christ. Matthew, who had been part of the world system, heard Jesus dissect the problems facing the Jews and Gentiles. Serious problems ranging from the disciples exhibiting and publicly proclaiming Godly moral principles to a Godless society, to the proper reaction to anger and murder, to avoiding lust and adultery, to the dangers of divorce and re-marriage, to caring for the poor and the treatment of enemies, to fasting and prayer, to worry and judging others, to denouncing false teachers and the proper living of one's life. (Matthew 5:13-7:27) Matthew must have thought that Jesus was speaking directly to him, but isn't it that way when Jesus is elevating the faith of His believers?

Tradition says that Matthew preached in Parthia and Ethiopia, where he died a martyr's death. He was slain by a halberd in the city of Nadabah, in AD 60.[50] He was a true missionary who had left his former occupation and harsh attitude to become a faithful servant to Jesus Christ. He went ***beyond the ordinary***!

---

[50] Fox, John. <u>Foxe's Book of Martyrs</u>, 2007.

Beyond the Ordinary

1. The Apostle Matthew was an outcast, a traitor to his people, but his story is one of the most remarkable conversions to Christianity ever recorded. It proves no one is exempt from salvation through the atoning work of Jesus Christ on the Cross, in the grave and in the Resurrection from the dead. What is your story? Where would it rank in the annals of Christian history?
2. Matthew was hated by the Jews and despised by the Pharisees. They considered him to be morally corrupt, consumed by greed and willing to cheat, lie and steal to achieve his financial independence. Can you identify with his attitude, and if so, in what ways? How are you characterized by your family, loved ones, friends, co-workers and other Christians? What parts of Matthew's experience can you relate too and why?
3. Matthew became convinced of his sin, and jumped at the opportunity to have his slate cleansed by the grace of God. He received the gift of God referred to in Ephesians 2:8-10. Do you believe Matthew's immediate submission to the call of Jesus to follow Him was authentic or was it a way for Matthew to gain an inside examination of the financial worth of Jesus and his disciples, and report back to Herod? Do you believe in salvation at first encounters with Christ, or is time needed to truly believe in Jesus for the forgiveness of sins? Explain Ephesians 2:8-10 in comparison to Matthew and your experience with Jesus?
4. In what ways did Jesus teach Matthew about humility? Humility was the key to the change in Matthew that exalted him to a higher level of service. His adaptation of humility propelled him **beyond the ordinary** attitudes that sometimes encompasses believers and keeps them stuck in their old behaviors. What is divine humility, and how might you change your behavior considering your definition. Would you portray yourself as a humble person?
5. What about the life of Matthew most impressed you? Be specific.

Chapter Nine

THE APOSTLE THOMAS, THE QUESTIONER, GOES BEYOND THE ORDINARY

The Apostle Thomas is viewed as a natural doubter, a pessimist who must see events to believe they took place, but is that an honest and final appraisal of his approach to servanthood?

THE APOSTLE THOMAS, CALLED DIDYMUS, BECAUSE he probably had a twin sibling, is portrayed as being a skeptic, one who doubts everything.[51] He was the eighth disciple called to join Jesus at twenty-nine years-old, and had a family. He lived, according to undocumented traditions, in Tarichea on the west bank of the Jordon River where it flows out of the Sea of Galilee. He was a carpenter, a stone mason and a fisherman by trade, was well liked by all, and was a leading citizen of his community.[52] He had little education, but possessed a sharp mind, and he was extremely logical in making decisions.

Thomas would become known as a very loyal and courageous disciple for Christ, but not until he came to the point of no return in his faith. Thomas must forsake his philosophy of not being able

---

[51] Walker, Alexander. <u>Ante-Nicene Fathers</u>, Vol. 8. Edited by Alexander Roberts, James Donaldson, and A. Cleveland Coxe. Buffalo, NY: Christian Literature Publishing Co., 1886.

[52] "<u>The Apostle: Saint Thomas</u>." www.catholictradition.org

to know God without first knowing oneself. His reality of faith was found in the logic of a self-made awareness of God that exalts an innate virtuous soul to the conscious surface of thought.[53] He must learn that miraculous faith exceeds any form of logic and especially any expressions of faith fueled by doubt. Jesus would carry him **beyond the ordinary** the failures embedded within a skeptical attitude that originated from a faith based only on logical decisions.

No person is born a skeptic. Usually, an individual is exposed to negative or hurtful environments, such as a downtrodden culture, poor child-rearing, education that teaches doubt as a solution to problems or some religion that has no meaningful answers for troubling questions that one might face. The existence or non-existence of God is a good example. Certainty, the early life of Thomas could have been heavy influenced by a depressed culture, and a sense of abandonment from God, who had not spoken to the Jews for nearly four hundred years. Possibly, his parents struggled to provide him with an education or exposure to more positive role models, such as those found in synagogue settings. This could foster a skeptical response to the activities faced in life that normal assurances taught to a young person would avoid.

Thomas, for whatever the reasons, developed a disagreeable attitude toward other's opinions and a suspicious mind about the reality of surrounding circumstances. He would not accept the obvious until he had dissected every detail. Today, he would be known as philosophical skeptic, but he did not, to his favor, act condemning of other people, just their interpretation of current events, such as the disciples report in the Upper Room about the resurrection of Jesus. Thomas did not belittle them, just the information. (John 20:25) In fact, he was very truthful in his analysis of things and used the art of questioning to get at the facts, even the most buried details of situations. However, he was headstrong and found it nearly impossible to change his thinking once he decided on a matter.

Skeptics paraded their philosophy throughout the countryside during the time of Jesus' ministry. There are three descriptions for

---

[53] Snodgrass, Klyne R. "The Gospel of Thomas: A secondary Gospel," *Second Century* 7, 1989.

skepticism: commonsense, philosophical, and absolute. Common sense skepticism is a normal thought process for all people.[54] It is the realization that certain actions or thoughts have certain results. If a person jumps off a cliff, that individual will plunge to the ground beneath them, so it is normal to accept this reality. The sun will rise in the morning, and people will fall in love are other examples of facts that govern decisions.

Philosophical skepticism is grounded in human theories about the correctness, validity and soundness of acquired knowledge. A philosophical doubter will deny or argue against the information presented by consultants. These individuals claim that no knowledge is guaranteed, because it might be false assumptions and therefore, only opinions, thus, it cannot be reliable. If the information is unreliable, there is no basis for which to take actions or believe in the possibility of truth, apart from their individual theory. This could be more of the mindset of Thomas. Philosophical skepticism is inclusive and prejudice, and usually, denies the existence of God. Thomas did not challenge the existence of God. These skeptics can function in society, and have a somewhat normal existence.

The real problem lies within the theory of absolute skepticism. These skeptics practice a lifestyle based on no possibility of knowing anything, and no knowledge acclamation is afforded the human. So, what would be the motivation to live? What would be the foundation to even speak at all, since every word would be based on nothing? It seems this mind-set is impractical and impossible to sustain, and there are very few people who dare follow its ideas. There is no evidence to show Thomas ever camped there. Jesus defeated this practice in both word and deed. (John 14:5-6)

So, since Thomas is traditionally portrayed as a doubter, a skeptic, where does he fit in with the practice of skepticism? He had common sense skepticism and possibly some traits of philosophical skepticism, but it is more accurate to say he was a debater, a critical thinker, and more in the mold of a defender of observable behavior. He would never follow Jesus if this was not true. His

---

[54] Pojman, Louis P. and Vaughn, Lewis. The Moral Life. New York, NY: Oxford University Press, 2011.

challenge is and becomes, once he joins the missionary work with Jesus, to defeat his assumed characterization by the people around him, and the disciples. The question becomes, "Who would ever believe his testimony or salvation message, since he was suspicious and pessimistic of everything?" Jesus would have to bring him and others to a point of action, centered on non-judgmental presumptions. This would not be an easy acquisition to accomplish and would take time.

The journey of Thomas on the road of moving **beyond the ordinary** routine of irritating everyone around him with question after question started with his agreement to follow Jesus. (Matthew 10:2-4) His name is listed with the twelve apostles, but there is no record of his conversion to Christianity. However, an accurate picture can be surmised of his experience based on his testimony. He probably had heard about Jesus from the talk around town, Capernaum, and had questions to ask this man. Jesus was never opposed to sincere questions and would have entertained a meaningful dialect with Thomas. It is a recorded fact that Thomas became a follower of Jesus, and that he was influential in the work of the discipleship and expansion of the church.

Thomas was the kind of person who would impose his thoughts on others, and this is silently understood in the different sessions the disciples had with Jesus, those "teaching moments" found throughout the Bible. It is assumed that Thomas had been a member of the disciples from the beginning, and had witnessed several major events in their ministry with Jesus, events that challenge the basics of skepticism, such as the calming of the storm which arose on the Sea of Galilee. Jesus had fallen asleep in the back of the boat when the storm arose, threatening them with drowning. The disciples, in a panic and fear for their lives, awoke Jesus, heard Him speak to the wind and raging water, ordering them to stop.[55] Immediately, the storm stopped, and Jesus questioned their lack of faith in that desperate time. The disciples, assumingly led by Thomas, asked a question that would test the reality of such a phenomenon as this, "Who can do this?" The

---

[55] Nixon, R.E. Boanerges, The New Bible Dictionary. London, England: The Inter-Varsity Fellowship, 1963.

power of Jesus' voice defied nature. Thomas began to see an opposing side to assumed logic that no man has power over the natural elements, yet Jesus does.

Thomas took part in two impossible miracles, by man's standards, when Jesus multiplied the biscuits and fish, to feed the hungry crowds who were following His ministry. (John 6:3-14; Matthew 15:32-39) Jesus displayed supernatural power over the material confines of substances. No one can do this, but Jesus did. Then there was the time when Jesus defied gravity and walked on the waves of a violent sea, and empowered Peter to do likewise. (Matthew 14:28-33) He restored the hearing of a deaf man and gave sight to a man who was born blind. (Mark 7:31-37; John 9:1-34) These miracles helped curb the questions in the mind of Thomas to the deity of Jesus. Each of the miracles stimulated conversations that attested to the divine nature of Jesus, and Thomas gained strength in his faith through these extremely unusual and unimaginable events.

Many times, Thomas was engaged in the debate within the religious circles about the person of Jesus. The scribes, priests and Pharisees argued among themselves as to the identity of Jesus and to the source of His supernatural power. (Mark 8:11-21) Jesus discussed these issues with the disciples. Thomas was among those who questioned the complaints of these religious critics, but he also offered answers to these troubling debates. When Jesus warned them of the hypocrisy of the Pharisees, for example, Thomas was among those who were challenged by Jesus about his heart's condition. Did he have true faith or was his faith dependent on observable factors? Again, Thomas was involved in conversations concerning the appropriation of forgiveness, the relationship between husbands and wives, and the availability of redemption. (Matthew 18; 19:10, 25)

The change that Thomas needed to be an effective debater against those critics of Jesus and an effective servant, a "soul winner," came as he sought the answers to the most serious questions posed to him and the other disciples. (Mathew 7:3; 8:26; 9:28; 22:42; Luke 6:46; 18:41; John21:17) "Do you believe that I am able to do this?" "Why are you afraid, O you of little faith?"

"What do you think about the Christ?" "Do you love me?" "Why do you call me 'Lord, Lord', and not do what I tell you?" "What do you want Me to do for you?" "Why do you see the speck that is in your brother's eye, but not the log that is in your eye?" These questions challenged Thomas, and the answers pointed to Jesus, the giver of knowledge, wisdom and truth. (Proverbs 1:1-7; 12:1)

Every constructive answer to the skepticism of life is found here. Thomas reasoned through the questions and found his direction in life. He, over the course of his time with Jesus, chose to approach the affairs of life through constructive thinking, and looking for the assurance of faith, not the empty results of adverse questioning and expecting the worst conclusions. He forsook his idea of escaping the fears of death by knowing God through acquainting oneself with the innate virtuousness of one's own soul.

The first recorded account of the change in Thomas takes place during the events centered around Lazarus. (John 11:1-44) Jesus and his disciples were working around the Jordan River when word came that Lazarus, a close friend of Jesus, was sick back in Bethany. Jesus did a very strange thing. He did not immediately go to Lazarus, but He stayed in the Jordan area for two more days before traveling the two more days to Bethany. In the meantime, Lazarus died. The disciples argued against going to Bethany, near Jerusalem, because of the animosity toward Jesus by the religious leaders. They wanted Jesus dead, and the disciples thought it was foolish to go there. (John 11:1-15)

Jesus explained to the disciples that Lazarus's death was temporary, and that He would increase their faith in Him by going there. Thomas enters the discussion with what seems to be words of sarcasm, but expresses great faith in the resurrection of the dead.[56] He insisted that they stand firm with Jesus and should go with Him, even if they die with Him. (John 11:16) He believed it was better to die with Jesus than live without Him. It shows that Thomas believed Jesus. After all, Jesus had raised two other people from the dead, the son of the widow of Nain and the daughter of Jairus. (Luke 7:11-17; 8:51-56)

---

[56] The Apostle Saint Thomas. www.catholictradition.org

Mary and Martha, the sisters of Lazarus, met Jesus outside of town. Thomas watched as Jesus helped the sisters suffer through the pain of losing a brother. Thomas focused on Mary as she received hope from the words of Jesus. Thomas heard Jesus deliver Martha from her anguish by His acknowledging her remarks of His failure to arrive in time to heal Lazarus. Thomas recognized the honesty of Jesus in His empathy toward Martha by reminding her that He is the author and giver of life. Thomas does not question the invitation that Jesus gave to Martha to believe in Jesus. (John 11:17-27) The other disciples witnessed this and would have missed this faith-altering moment, had Thomas not pushed for their attending this occasion by his willingness to die with Jesus in Jerusalem. (John 11:16)

Jesus continued to teach the family and friends of Lazarus that "death" could not remain in His presence. Once everyone arrived at the home place, Thomas once again heard Jesus console Mary with the same admonition as He had given Martha. (John 11:32-35) Jesus joined her in her grief and cried, because of everyone's lack of faith in Him. Jesus' spirit was troubled, but He did not let that hinder His mission of raising His friend from the dead. Jesus asked to be taken to the tomb of their deceased brother. Thomas was not among those who questioned Jesus' sincerity over this unfolding drama. (John 11:37) Earlier in his life, he probably would have made a derogatory remark, but he had changed. He knew exactly what was about to take place. Lazarus would step out of death!

Jesus, at the tomb, shocked the crowd. He ordered the stone guarding the entrance of the grave to be removed, and called for Lazarus to come out of the tomb. Martha and Mary pleaded with Jesus to be merciful and conscious of their grief. They said the body of Lazarus was decaying and would smell awful. They were saying, in effect, leave their brother alone. Thomas would have jumped on this appraisal at earlier times in his life, but he remained silent, marveling at what was unfolding before their eyes.

Jesus prayed, not for His own benefit, but those around the tomb, that they might receive faith from this miracle, and realize Jesus had been given to them by God, the Father. Jesus calls

Lazarus by name, and he came forth wrapped in the graves clothes he had been buried in, and Jesus commanded Lazarus be loosened from them. (John 11:44) Thomas realized that nothing would stop Jesus from doing His work, not unbelief, not threats and attempts against His life, not appropriate or silly questions and not death itself. Thomas was bound to Jesus by a deep and enthusiastic love. He was becoming a leader.

During the farewell words of Jesus in the Upper Room, the love and admiration that Thomas felt for Jesus came through in his comments as he responded to Jesus telling the disciples about their future home in Heaven. Thomas reassured the disciples that they have no legitimate fear of not finding their way to eternal life. Thomas confronts their uncertainty about their trust of acting upon their faith. He does this through courageous, inquisitive and engaging comments with Jesus. He was not denouncing the instruction of Jesus; he simply affirmed the accuracy of Jesus' declaration that the disciples already knew the way to Heaven. Jesus would not tell them of a future home with Him and, at the same time, leave them in the dark as to how to get there. (John 14:1-4)

While Jesus spoke that final time in the Upper Room, Thomas remembered the many times that the disciples had questioned their faith, and he did not want this counseling time to rehearse those conversations. There was far too much revelation about the future being introduced by Jesus for Thomas to get hung up on less valuable instruction. (John 14:1-17:26) He was not willing to remain in the ordinary flow of things; he was **beyond the ordinary** basics of faith.

Thomas may have recalled the failed attempts of the disciples to act in faith. Attempts such as an unsuccessful effort of the disciples to heal the epileptic son of a certain man. (Matthew 17:14-21; Mark 9:14-29) The son's father told Jesus of their failure, and it greatly displeased Jesus. Jesus compares them to the perverse generation in which they were living, and tells them that He will not be with them forever, much like the current discussion He was having with them about Heaven.

Jesus had instructed them over and over about believing through faith in their abilities and calling from God to perform miracles, to trust in what He taught, and that Jesus would entrust His authority to them. Jesus scolded them, and wondered how much longer they would act in unbelief, and neglect meaningful prayer which defeats doubt. (James 1:6; Matthew 17:20; 21:21; Mark 11:23) Remember, later in the conversation, Philip asks about Jesus' father, but Thomas refrains from that encounter, because his attention was concentrated on kingdom business, and not on the other's doubtful nonsense.

The last episode between Jesus and Thomas would come after the death and resurrection of Jesus. (John 20:24-29) It is a classic illustration of how quickly a person can plunge backward in their thoughts and exhibitions of faith, and it reminds Christians of the gracious and merciful Savior who restores a person to their rightful place in the family of God. Thomas was absolutely devastated by the events of the last three days in the life of Jesus. His friend, Lord and Savior had been brutally murdered on a cross in plain daylight before the entire city of Jerusalem. Thousands had witnessed or heard about the execution.[57]

Thomas, in his weakened condition, felt deserted and horribly depressed. This is not unusual for people to temporary forget the lessons of forgone miracles and teachings in such a time as this. Thomas was hurt, he was wounded, and he did not want to be with people, so he stayed to himself. Many individuals behave this way. So, Thomas was not there when Jesus appeared to the disciples and women after the resurrection from the grave.

The disciples, out of respect for Thomas, told him that Jesus was alive and they had seen Him. Thomas, grief stricken, said he must see this for himself. The next time Thomas saw Jesus was the conclusive evidence he needed to stay above the norm, to go **beyond the ordinary**. It was his defining moment! Jesus came, after eight days, and appeared to Thomas. Jesus invited him to examine the nail prints in His hands and to put his hand in Jesus' wounded side. Thomas came to his senses and proclaimed that Jesus was his Lord and God. (John 20:28) Jesus solidified the faith of Thomas, and Jesus ended any crippling question by foretelling

---

[57] Schneemelcher, Wilhelm. ed., translation by R. McL. Wilson, <u>New Testament Apocrypha: Gospels and Related Writings</u>. Louisville: John Knox Press, 1992.

what Thomas must guard against in his future, potential downfalls caused by uncertainty. Jesus placed the emphasis of service on walking by faith, not on experiences which are seen. (John 20:29) Thomas would not forget, his future was rock solid.

Later, Thomas must have thought about all that had happened between himself and Jesus. Take the meeting between Thomas and Jesus after the resurrection. Have you ever pondered; for example, why Jesus miraculously appeared in the room where the disciples were gathering after the resurrection without opening the door to that room? Questioning the outcome of the episodes encountered in life builds faith. Thomas realized the body of Jesus was no longer bound by the laws of nature, and perhaps, it was to remind him that the philosophies of man are theories that try to excuse away the supernatural; the reality that there is a God, who is omniscient, omnipotent, omnipresent, immutable, eternal, "Love and Truth," and He is a personable God that is not ordinary. (Colossians 2:8)

Thomas would carry this reality into his ministry. He preached in India and died a martyr. He was run through by a spear, because of his gospel preaching. His fortitude to remain faithful to Jesus Christ, without question, brought a fitting end to his life, and like His Lord and Savior, he was pierced by a spear.[58] Thomas had overcome, gone **beyond the ordinary** scenario levied at him by all who testify of his service and relationship to Jesus! He was not a destructive doubter as so many proclaim.

---

[58] Fox, John. Foxe's Book of Martyrs, 2007.

Beyond the Ordinary

1. The Apostle Thomas is referred to as a doubter or skeptic. No person is born a skeptic. Usually, an individual is exposed to negative or hurtful environments, such as a downtrodden culture, poor child-rearing, education that teaches doubt as a solution to problems or some religion that has no meaningful answers for troubling questions that one might face. The existence or non-existence of God is a prime example. Would you define your attitude as that of a doubter? Why or why not? What in your background could have encouraged your skepticism, or what may have discouraged a doubting nature?
2. There are three divisions in the theory of skepticism: commonsense, philosophical, and absolute. Common sense skepticism is a normal thought process for all people. It is the realization that certain actions or thoughts have certain results. If a person jumps off a cliff, that individual will plunge to the ground beneath them, so it is normal to not doubt that reality. Philosophical skepticism is grounded in human theories about the correctness, validity and soundness of acquired knowledge. A philosophical doubter will deny or argue against the information presented by consultants. These individuals claim that no knowledge is guaranteed, because it might be false assumptions and therefore, only opinions, thus, it cannot be reliable. The absolute skeptic practices a lifestyle based on no possibility of knowing anything. No knowledge acclamation is afforded the human. Would you place yourself within one of these divisions of skepticism? Why or why not? What is the motivation of a skeptic or doubter to participate in daily activities? What would be their foundation to even speak at all, since every word would be based on nothing?
3. The journey of Thomas on the road to moving **beyond the ordinary** routine of irritating everyone around him with question after question started with his agreement to follow Jesus. Are you full of questions about everything? Do

you irritate people with your questioning? Do your questioning techniques lead others to see you as a doubter? Could you change your approach of conversation? How?
4. Thomas became a great help to Jesus in ministry. How did this take place? Be specific.
5. How could Jesus, in comparison to Thomas' contributions, use you more effectively in ministry?
6. Do you believe it is acceptable to question Jesus about such topics as His mission, assumed authority, activities, direction and motives, to the point of irritating those others who are engaged in conversation with Him? Why or why not, and be specific. In what ways did Jesus use these encounters with his disciples and Thomas to advance His plans?
7. What happened in the life of Thomas that moved him **beyond the ordinary** behavior that his former life was known to exhibit?

Chapter Ten

THE APOSTLE JAMES, THE SON OF ALPHAEUS, A MAMA'S BOY, GOES BEYOND THE ORDINARY

*The Apostle James, son of Alphaeus, called James the Lesser, was an obscure individual, one of the twelve disciples, with a reputation of being a mama's boy, yet he joined the honor role of faith, became a hero in the church, and went **beyond the ordinary**!*

THE APOSTLE JAMES, THE SON OF ALPHAEUS, IS one of three men known by the prominent name of James. The other two are James Zebedee and James, the brother of Jesus. Each of these men contributed to the Christian movement. James, the Son of Alphaeus, was from the Jewish tribe of Levi and a disciple of Jesus. (Matthew 10:3; Mark 16:1) James was from the City of Capernaum. Remember, it is located on the northwestern bank of the Sea of Galilee which meant he was acquainted with the other disciples from the region and probably grew up with them. Therefore, it can be assumed they were aware of his faults and shyness, and probably nagged him about them. Friends can be an individual's worst enemies!

James was an obscure servant for Jesus, and did not push himself on the other disciples, much like the Apostle Andrew. James did not bring attention to his low self-esteem, but it was a festering sore in his soul. James, because of the fame of the other two prominent men with his name, was trying to measure up to their standards. Every time someone told him to measure up to his name, the wounds deepened.[59] Neither Andrew nor James sought recognition or fame, and James received no glory or credit for his service to Jesus, but the fires of ministry, inconsideration and rudeness of others can still paralyze good intentions. James, like Andrew, also saw himself as the unknown member of his family and left out of his associate's relationship with Jesus, and if he were to go **beyond the ordinary** acceptance of this situation, he would need to re-evaluate his self-worth.

James' life was characterized by being overshadowed by those he valued the most, including his brother and John the Baptist. Jesus opened James's eyes to the truth that his inhibiting self-appraisal was the source of his agony, much like He did with Andrew. James and Andrew learned that the most important aspect of ministry is not public exposure and praise, it's winning people to Jesus. James, even though he faced a different kind of isolation and prejudice from the others, would grow **beyond the ordinary** expectation of his future by the other disciples, through the longsuffering and love of Jesus for him.

James had to live down three major problems in his life. First, he was compared to James, the son of Zebedee, who was one of the "Sons of Thunder," a larger man than James Alphaeus, and nicknamed "the Greater." James Alphaeus was nicknamed "the Lesser." (Mark 15:40) Second, the public and newer believers had a tendency to confuse him with James, the brother of Jesus, even though this was impossible, since the half-brothers of Jesus did not believe in Jesus until after His death. (John 7:25) James Alphaeus' mother, Mary, was a close relative of Mary the mother of Jesus, and for that reason, according to Jewish custom, he was sometimes called the brother of Jesus, which only added to his frustration. (Mark 16:1; Mark 6:3; Galatians 1:19) Third, his nickname indicated he was a small man in stature, and soft spoken when compared to James Zebedee, so he was prodded by everyone to

---

[59] Attridge, Harold W.; Hata, Gohei, eds. Eusebius, Christianity, and Judaism. Detroit MI: Wayne State Univ. Press, 1992.

man-up, and more hurtful yet, when everyone spoke of him, they included his mother in the conversation. Maybe his hardest plight was to overcome the stigma of being a "mama's boy."

The accumulative effect of partnering with Jesus brings James Alphaeus to a determination to make a difference in his sphere of influence. He aspired to be an ambassador for Christianity. This was his defining moment. Every disciple and follower of Jesus wants this.[60] No one seeks to live their entire life controlled by circumstances or other opinions, and no one wishes to be remembered as a failure or half-hearted Christian servant. Jesus surely did not desire this for His ambassadors, nor did James. (II Corinthians 5:18-20) James would go **beyond the ordinary**.

Ambassadors have an official responsibility to represent a nation on behalf of its rulers. They are sent to foreign lands to share the official position of the sovereign that gave them authority. The followers of Jesus are likened unto ambassadors with the authority to present the possibility of the reconciliation of sinners to God, once they acknowledge that Jesus is "the way, the truth and the life; King Jesus." (John 14:6; I Timothy 6:15) James was strengthened by the fact that ambassadors for Jesus are aliens in this world, but citizens of Heaven. (Hebrews 11:13-16; I Peter 2:11; John 15:18-19; Ephesians 6:20)

Remember, all the disciples had to make the walk of faith, to follow Jesus in all circumstances because they trusted Him. When they came to the crossroads in their commitment, to move forward or remain in place, they chose to move to a higher spiritual ranking in discipleship. There were no short-cuts to acquiring the change needed to move to the front lines of battle in the war against the enemies of God. The Apostles Paul, Peter, James and John Zebedee, and Andrew are noted as spiritual giants in the war between God and Satan, but the supply bearers are the real heroes, such as servants like Nathaniel, Philip, Matthew, Thomas, and James Alphaeus. Each one chose the right "fork in the road."

Front line soldiers need food, water, clothing, ammunition and emotional support from the rear guard. These rear-guard soldiers

---

[60] Marshall, I.H., ed. R. V. G. Tasker. <u>The Acts of the Apostles, The Tyndale New Testament Commentaries.</u> Grand Rapids, MI: Eerdmans, 1980.

face the same fears, frustration, mental and emotional wounds as front-line troops. It rains on them the same as the ones receiving the glory for being in battle; *all bleed red*. Jesus knows that all his fighters are irreplaceable. Jesus' challenge is convincing everyone of this reality.

The war James must fight was a spiritual war. (Ephesians 6:10-20) He did not take the "fork in the road" that birthed the demons of doubt, depression, prejudice and low self-esteem. He, with the help of Jesus, would fix his thoughts and actions on the things of God, the better "fork in the road." James would pre-fix his mindset, so to speak, so that his misled plans and expectations did not come to fruition, and he would continue to travel **beyond the ordinary** realms of existence. (Proverbs 19:21)

James would learn these principles while listening to the story of bravery shown by Jesus in the wilderness of temptation, and several other times where Jesus faced a "fork in the road," His will or God's will. (Matthew 4:1-11) It is noteworthy to remember that Andrew, with similar attitude challenges as James, was privileged to eventually participate in the inner-circle meetings, but not James Alphaeus. There is no Biblical account of his service for Jesus, but the testimony of history shows James died an exalted preacher.

Jesus went to war against Satan for His followers. It was a physical and spiritual battle that Satan brought to Jesus. Satan brought his ultimate temptation against Jesus, to take pre-eminence away from God, the Father. Satan wanted Jesus to take His future into His own hands.

James Alphaeus faced these same temptations, except he was tempted to ignore the plans of Jesus for his ministry, a ministry which left him in seclusion. James took Jesus' battle to heart. This experience spoke to the deep recesses of his soul. No one likes to go un-noticed. James faced the false ideas about his value to Jesus, and the power of Jesus to clean up these false thoughts. James associated his temptation to give credence to his desired prominence in kingdom work to the temptations of Satan for Jesus to deny God's plan for the salvation of mankind.

Satan wanted Jesus to take back His divine nature, to usurp His self-imposed limitation on His divine person, to take control away from God His Father, which would have cancelled the prophetic and sacrificial nature of the Messiah. Satan would have won and Jesus lost. (Philippians 2:6-11; John 14:10; Romans 11:36) Jesus only defeated the Devil by exercising His attributes by the will of His Father – never of His own initiative.[61] If James would have self-promoted himself to the forefront of popularity, if he had lobbied for self-gratification, and if he had accosted his mockers, Satan would have won.

James would be encouraged by the encounter between Jesus and Satan. Shortly after Jesus was baptized, he went into the wilderness to a desolate place to pray and fast. He prayed for forty days at which time Satan approached Him with the three most common temptations to everyone: the lust of the flesh or physical desires, the lust of the eyes or covetousness and the pride of life or lust for power. Satan, through these seductions, hoped to destroy the deity of Jesus Christ rendering Jesus unworthy to sacrifice Himself for mankind. Jesus faced these temptations to give Satan an opportunity to sever His relationship with God, and to prove that Satan is not able to derail any plans that God has put in place.

James faced the same strategies, just different avenues of attack were leveled at him. Satan wanted James to overcome his physical appearance through striking back at his mockers, proving he was more than a "mama's boy." He wanted James to concentrate on what might be, instead of what is reality, and Satan lured James toward an aggressive attitude. These were all the things that seemed warranted to James and the answer to changing his fellow comrade's perception of him, but they contradicted God's plan for him. James learned through the experience of Jesus to depend on the word of God to find favor with Jesus.

Satan is clever and deceptive. He attacked Jesus when Jesus was alone and isolated from any human contact. Sometimes, it feels like the assaults of the devil come during those lonely times in life, those long nights and empty days. The loneliness may be created by circumstances, others or the person's perception of the truth. James may have felt like the individual who is always

---

[61] Steward, Don. Blue Letter Bible, 2017.

picked last to play in a backyard ballgame or the one who is never asked their thoughts during a business discussion. A person can be present in the flesh but feel isolated from a group or action. People can be their worst enemy. (II Samuel 24:14) Jesus faced these self-righteous people. They chose Barabbas, a convicted criminal, over Jesus and Jesus would go to the Cross because of it. (John 18:38-41) Sometimes, circumstances seem unfair, like the crowd choosing Barabbas over Jesus, but this did not stop Jesus from staying focused on His purpose, and it is a lesson that James sensed in his spirit that he must do as well.

Nevertheless, hurt feelings from a simple misunderstanding between two people or arguments from life and death circumstances are equally real to those involved, and Jesus and James faced this challenge. It is during this time that one must answer the question, "Would I fulfill the role of God for myself according to God's will?" Regardless of one's answer, Satan is going to work to stop the guidance of God in the lives of believers. (I Thessalonians 2:18) Satan knows exactly how and when to apply human opposition, mental anguish and physical exhaustion to his advantage, to interfere with the spiritual directions of God for one's life. Satan wanted Jesus and James annihilated; Jesus because He is God's Son and James because he was associated with Jesus. Satan will use little foxes or major devastation to ruin lives, like a ravaging wolf. (Song of Solomon 2:15)

Satan tried to bait Jesus into a philosophical debate over the sovereignty of God and the love God has for "His Only Son, Jesus." However, Jesus would have no part in a useless argument with Satan. The philosophy of men in those times, skepticism, cynicism, epicureanism and stoicism, had no answers for sinful man.[62] Mankind cannot ignore their disobedience to God, nor can they hide from the reality of sin's consequences. They cannot find morality in a "live and let live" ideology, and an egoistic living style to please oneself leads to a failed attempt at finding happiness. Neither the Greeks nor Jews had answers to combat Satan's deception of true love and happiness, which he put into practice

---

[62] Pojman, Louis P. and Vaughn, Lewis. The Moral Life. New York, NY: Oxford University Press, 2011.

among unbelievers, declaring himself to be god of this world. (II Corinthians 4:4)

Suffering wrongly or rightly for an action or belief are realities of life, and there is no way to avoid the resulting pain or pleasure, other than through death, and even the Socratic approach to virtuous living, living to free the soul from evil, results in peaceful living. Jesus knew that peace and virtuous living would come to people only through His work on the Cross and the hope of the resurrection, and He was not going to allow the Devil to take that truth away. Jesus chose not to independently exercise His all-knowing, all powerful, all wise and all present relative attributes. He never forsook His moral attributes of love, holiness and truth, only His independent use of His mighty power.[63] Jesus worked under the will of His Heavenly Father, and James would learn the same truth while he walked with Jesus, thus seeing Jesus fulfill God's plan. James found acceptance, compassion, a listening ear and redemption from Jesus.

James heard about Jesus' response of quoting from the word of God to Satan's preposterous suggestions. James probably had many talks with Jesus about His responses to the Devil while in the wilderness, and would internalize the words of Jesus. Each response of Jesus was foundational building blocks for James to build his future. (Matthew 7:24-27) James would parallel these words with other sermons relating to establishing one's success in life and beneficial servanthood. James took to heart what Jesus taught about not judging others or you would be judged. He believed Jesus when Jesus said God would supply the vital necessities of life, and James was empowered by the words of Jesus to ask God for His provisions. (Matthew 6:9-15; Matthew 7:7) James learned that if he would pray, he would receive power from God to be a "winner," not a whiner. (James 5:16)

James was ever learning from Jesus, especially in the temptation lesson. When Satan urged Jesus to satisfy His hunger by turning the stones to bread, Jesus said, "It is written, 'Man shall not live by bread alone, but every word that proceeds from the mouth of God.'" (Matthew 4:4) Satan insisted that Jesus defy

---

[63] Steward, Don. Blue Letter Bible, 2017.

death by throwing Himself off the temple pinnacle, to which Jesus responded, "It is written again, 'You shall not tempt the Lord your God.'" (Matthew 4:7) Finally, Satan enticed Jesus with the idea that Jesus could rule the world, if He would worship Satan. Jesus silenced the Devil, "Away with you, Satan! For it written, 'You shall worship the Lord your God, and Him only you shall serve.'" (Matthew 4:10) The words of Jesus were to James like an apple in the eye of its beholder, both delicious and satisfying. (Proverbs 7:2; Psalm 17:8) James learned when he was tempted to step out of his pilgrimage, to take things into his own hands, to say, "No!"

The sermons and illustrations of Jesus continued to strengthen the resolve of James to live **beyond the ordinary** service of most believers. There was an account of Jesus, at the Pool of Bethesda, healing a man who had been sick for thirty-eight years that urged James to commit to a sincerer level of service to Jesus. (John 5:1-18) This was his defining moment!

Jesus did this miracle on the Sabbath day, which angered the Jews. They assaulted the healed man with many questions about the person who healed him and on which day it took place. The man could not answer their questions, and went to the temple for help. Jesus found him there and told him to sin no more or a worse illness may befall him. The man left the temple and told the Jews it was Jesus who had healed him. They hated Jesus and wanted to kill Him.

Jesus had also referred to Himself as God's Son, making Him equal with God.[64] The Jews could not stand this and would not listen to any more teaching from Jesus. However, James heard every word and it ministered to his heart. He heard Jesus explain that He did nothing apart from the will of His Heavenly Father and that the Jews were the ones emphasizing any self-willed desire on Jesus' part to act apart from God the Father. (John 5:30) James heard that all judgment and power had been given to Jesus by God. (John 5:18-22) This was marvelous news to James – to have hope and assurance for he was in a tightly knit family; the family of God.

---

[64] Eisenman, Robert. James the Brother of Jesus: The Key to Unlocking the Secrets of Early Christianity and the Dead Sea Scrolls. (Viking Penguin), 1997.

James believed Jesus when He taught that everyone who believed Jesus was saved and had passed from death into life. Great hope and peace entered James' understanding of his position with Jesus when he heard these words, and, suddenly, it made no difference what others thought of him. James had everlasting life with Jesus, even after he died. James saw with his spiritual eye that this temporal life has no hold on him. (John 5:23-30) He could be a "mama's boy" and it was all right. Jesus would make the necessary changes in James to make him a worthy servant, both now and forevermore!

The confirming of the faith of James in Jesus continued as he spent more time in ministry with Jesus. One day, James would take a giant leap forward in his awareness of his position in ministry and with the other disciples. He realized this as he listened to Jesus explain the dangers of speaking of one's own ability to succeed. This had been one of the problems that faced James early in his life. He questioned his perceptions of himself as noteworthy or not.

Some people were saying of Jesus that He was good and some were complaining that He had a demon, and was deceiving people with His doctrine. Just because Jesus said the Jews were trying to kill Him did not mean Jesus had a demon. James found solace in the words of Jesus that confirmed that anyone truly seeking God and His will, living a righteous life, has the promise of God that a relationship with Jesus assures that life. (John 7:10-24) No amount of education can alter that fact.

People can make false accusations against a person, but time with Jesus proves those statements to be wrong, and education has nothing to do with it. (John 7:14-15, 20) Jesus taught from authority given to Him by His Heavenly Father. James was not educated, yet he was taught by Jesus to trust Him in all things. This is exactly what was happening in the mind of James. His view of truth was in Jesus, and no one would be able to steal his peace, because he had been with Jesus. (Acts 4:13)

Remember, from what church tradition recited; James most likely would have labored with low self-esteem in early life, as anyone would.[65] It can be a festering sore in one's soul and every time a conflict arises, that sore is reopened. In the case of James, this scenario followed him into his walk with Jesus. His ego was wounded by others telling him to be more forthright with his testimony and preaching, but Jesus had given James a purpose, to sustain the Christian movement and each episode which Jesus faced only deepen James' commitment to that calling. James would grow stronger with every witness of the way Jesus handled confrontation over His calling. He watched and practiced the behavior of Jesus until it would become his lifestyle.

The opportunities for James to mature were numerous. Jesus would be tested, such as when a lawyer attempted to entrap Jesus with a narration concerning eternal life. (Luke 10:25-37) The lawyer wanted to know if obeying the great commandment to love God and neighbor, as you love yourself, with all your heart, soul, mind and strength would guaranteed a place in heaven, to which Jesus agreed. However, this was not good enough for the lawyer, so he pushed the issue by asking who is my neighbor? The answer Jesus gave blessed the heart of James and the other disciples. Jesus showed James and the others of His unfailing love that reaches out to all people. James especially, realized he was to help people regardless of who they are or what they have or have not done and voiced.

Jesus tells the lawyer a story about a person traveling from Jerusalem to Jericho. He is robbed, beaten and left half dead. Three people have an opportunity to help this person: a priest, a Levite and a Samaritan. The first two, religious men who should have helped, did not, but the most unlikely one did give the wounded man help. The Samaritan bandaged his wounds and took him to an inn. He paid his room and board while he healed and promised to return to pay the outstanding debt. Then Jesus asked the lawyer to acknowledge who was the neighbor? The lawyer said the one who helped, and Jesus told him to go and do the same.

---

[65] Schneemelcher, Wilhelm. <u>New Testament Apocrypha The Canon of the New Testament and Significance</u>. Louisville, KY: Westminster/ John Knox Press, 1987.

Immediately, James made the connection. He was a disciple and the one who should help others. He was not to be a figurehead, only seeking the glory of a position of leadership, like the priest and Levite. He must never be in too much of a hurry to help others or untouched by the hurting or blind to the abused of society. There would never be a place for prejudice in ministry. All people must be reached for Jesus; Jews, Gentiles and Samaritans. James must be a practicing servant, like his Master. After all, serving is what Jesus does!

James would learn that he should never be ashamed of his attitudes or actions. (Luke 10:10-13) Jesus taught this after healing a woman possessed for eighteen years with a spirit of infirmity. This miracle has a presenting problem, which was having the appearance of an illness, but a more serious underlying battle was present, devilish oppression. Jesus would teach James that his presenting problem was not how he was threatened by others, but the real challenge was recognizing the source behind such degrading of attitudes, spiritual war. The woman seemed to be hunched over because of an illness, but her physical condition was due to an evil spirit; the spirit of infirmity. Jesus exposed this and when Jesus laid hands on her the evil spirit left. (Luke 13:12) Now, once James was made aware of this Satanic oppression, he could guard against the Devil's attacks, and take charge. He learned that nothing happens by accident or bad luck, its spiritual warfare. (Ephesians 6:11-12)

This spiritual war was seen in the desire and plans of the chief priests and Pharisees to kill Jesus. (Luke 11:45-57) They used false predictions to create animosity against Jesus; lies that claimed Rome would take their land away if Jesus lived. (Luke 11:48) Lies of the Devil sway public opinion and set destinies. James saw through the religious leader's true motives and realized he would probably be lied about too, but he should never make decisions based on hearsay, ridicule of his weaknesses or any other hateful synopses. Sometimes a servant of God must avoid conflict for a better day. (Luke 11:54)

Again, this same lesson was emphasized during the trial of Jesus, when Pilate argued with the priests over the innocence of Jesus and then paraded Jesus before the crowds. These leaders lied about the crimes of Jesus, and persuaded the crowd to condemn Jesus. (John 18:28-40) This was a teaching moment for James and the other disciples, because Jesus did not defend Himself or call for an insurrection from His followers. (Luke 23:9; Matthew 26:53) He did not call the "angel army" from Heaven to release Him. He obeyed God and went to His death, proving that love never fails; the greatest lesson of His entire ministry. (I Corinthians 13:4-8)

The proof of the change in James' self-appraisal and resulting ministry is witnessed in his death. James underwent a dying process to not only physical death, but death from his inner demons of temptations: to move ahead of Jesus, to escape his pre-imposed, restricting obscureness of servanthood, to escape the lure of world philosophies and to not fear spiritual warfare. He overcame the emotional chains that bound him through the rude treatment of others. When he came to his "fork in the road" and had to choose the road of success through short-cutting the hard lessons of life or the road of becoming a member of God's family through faith and obedience to Jesus; James chose Jesus' way. He truly traveled **beyond the ordinary** in every sense of the concept.

He died not worrying about his name confusion with James Zebedee or the comparison of these two disciples' worth and ministry, nor did he feel devalued by his reputation of being a "mama's boy." He fulfilled God's will for his life and became a great ambassador for Christ. James did not need the approval of men as he had the commendation of Jesus. The walk of James with Jesus was seasoned by the frankness of Jesus to His accusers, by the compassion of Jesus for all people and by the endless energy and power through which Jesus spoke and loved all people. Jesus was not an ordinary man living in ordinary ways. He was God, and was **beyond the ordinary**!

The historians Josephus, Eusebius, and Jerome write about James Alphaeus. None of the other apostles received this much press. They tell of a horrendous time in Palestine among the Roman and religious representatives. Fetus, the governor of Judea, died and was replaced by Albinus. Meanwhile, Herod Agrippa II displaced the Jewish high priest, Joseph, with Ananus. Albinus had not arrived in the region when Ananus decided to force James to deny that Christ was the Messiah and the Son of God. He commanded James to stand on the temple wall and denounce Jesus to the crowds that were coming into Jerusalem for the preparation of the Passover celebration.

Suddenly this man, James Alphaeus, had his time in the sunlight. James surprised Ananus by preaching that Jesus was the Son of God who could forgive the people's sin and offered them eternal life through faith in Jesus. The religious leaders rushed him and threw him down from the temple wall. The fall did not kill James so they stoned him. He still did not die. An unnamed man fell upon him and beat him to death with a fuller's club. Great condemnation came to Ananus for ordering the death of James. The Romans were trying to keep peace with the Christians at this time in history. He was removed from the high priest role by Herod.

James Alphaeus, one of the twelve apostles, joined the honor role of faith, and became a hero among the apostles. He went **beyond the ordinary**!

Beyond the Ordinary

1. James started out in ministry as an obscure servant for Jesus; did not force himself on others, and suffered from low self-esteem. He had trouble seeing himself as measuring up to other's standards or expectations. His life was like a festering sore in his soul, and every time someone told him to measure up to his name, the wounds deepened. James sought no recognition or fame, and he received no glory or credit for his service to Jesus until after his death. This can have a paralyzing effect on a person. Have you been trapped by a mental picture of low self-esteem? Do you think that others look down on you? Why or why not?
2. James and Andrew have similar attitudes about themselves. Jesus opened Andrew's eyes to the truth that his inhibiting self-appraisal was the source of his agony. Andrew learned that the most important aspect of ministry is not public exposure and praise, its winning people to Jesus. James faced his own kind of isolation and prejudice from the others. Who are you isolated from? Is it your father or mother, children, other family members, friends, co-workers, recreational friends or spouse? Do they have a legitimate reason to ignore you? Why or why not?
3. What is your definition of an ordinary life? Is your understanding of ordinary living, success or failure, tied to the opinions of others? James would grow **beyond the ordinary** expectation he set for himself. Have you or are you willing too?
4. All the disciples had to decide to commit to servanthood **beyond the ordinary** expectations experienced by most Christians who walk in faith. When they came to the "fork in the road" in their commitment, making a choice to move forward or remain in place, they chose to move to a higher spiritual plateau in servanthood. Their testimonies show there were no short-cuts to obtaining their success in life, changes had to be accomplished. Have you come to a "fork in the road" in your relationship with Christ and

servanthood? What are the choices you must make to move you closer to fulfilling your purpose in life?
5. Jesus taught James to accept his position in life and ministry. Jesus exposed James to many situations that became "teaching moments" for him, such as the temptations in the wilderness, the healing at the Pool of Bethsaida, the death attempts against the life of Jesus and others. Go back through this chapter and identify those "teaching moments" that apply to your life.
6. A "rut in life" keeps people in the ditch of despair. Ruts come in many disguises, such as low self-esteem, depression, failures, un-forgiveness or a lack of desire to better oneself. They are the results of spiritual warfare. James could be characterized as living in a rut before he met Jesus. What specific principles do you believe helped change the opinion of James about himself, and that aided his move upward from his circumstances? What motivated his choices to climb out of his "rut in life?" Do these or other principles inspire you to become more involved in the spiritual warfare mentioned in this study? Why or why not?
7. What choices do you have to make to move **beyond the ordinary** in your life and ministry? Be specific. Are you willing to make those choices?

Chapter Eleven

THE APOSTLE THADDAEUS, SURNAMED LEBBAEUS, GOES BEYOND THE ORDINARY

*The Apostle Thaddaeus, surnamed Lebbaeus, was the baby of his family, who had a big heart for people. His friends knew him as a very courageous man, but he never lived **beyond the ordinary** obscurity of life, until he met Jesus!*

IT IS AMAZING TO CONSIDER THE MEN THAT JESUS called to follow Him, and entrusted into their hands the future of the church and Christianity. Jesus saved each one, understood their propensities to sin and molded their future service apart from their sin natures. Each disciple is unique in his own way. Some of the disciples had "in your face" attitudes. Paul was brilliant and highly educated; a devout defender of Judaism and a man determined to stop the Christian movement, yet Jesus chose him to start most of the early churches and write most of the New Testament books.[66]

Peter was bold, emotional and non-thinking in most of his endeavors with Jesus until he denied the Lord and was reinstated back into the discipleship by Jesus. Some of the disciples were easy going and behind the scenes individuals. Andrew was humble

---

[66] Dever, William G. <u>What Did the Biblical Writers Know and When Did They Know It?</u> Wm. B. Eerdmans Publishing Company, 2002.

and gentle who wanted no prominence, yet would courageously bring people to meet Jesus. Nathanael was a student of the Old Testament and a seeker of truth, honest and meditative, full of faith, yet a prejudice individual. Jesus used him to shape the future church.

There were explosive and very motivated personalities among the discipleship. James and John were given the name "Sons of Thunder" because of their fiery and uncontrollable tempers, yet Jesus moved in their lives and brought change in their attitudes that re-channeled their energy into great success as church leaders and evangelists. Matthew was hated by his people, the Jews, because he was a tax collector for hire by the Romans. Simon Zealot was a political fanatic who stopped at nothing, including the use of assassins, to force the Zealot ideology upon people, such as not paying taxes. Jesus brought these two men, enemies by occupations, into the discipleship, led them to change their futures and used them to win the lost to Jesus.

There were those disciples who needed to see physical consequences unfold so that they could accept servanthood on a higher plateau.[67] Thomas, a natural questioner and pessimist, became a powerful missionary who never waived from the message of salvation through Jesus. Philip, seen as an outsider to the Jewish people, had a Greek name, blended in with his culture, and yet was used by Jesus to connect with people. Obscure men such as James Alphaeus and Thaddaeus would evangelize the known world.

Jesus used men that were unqualified for spiritual understanding by their very depraved attitudes, unwanted by any other religious leaders, but who could be shaped into humbled, courageous, heart-felt servants of God. (I Corinthians 1:26-30) No sane spiritual giant would be seen with the ones Jesus picked to follow Him. Ironically, Jesus chose those Individuals who no one wanted to have as associates, and would be noticed by the populace as ignorant individuals. (Acts 4:12-14) Jesus used them under the banner of compassion, love and devotion to God, to prove nothing is impossible for Jesus. (Matthew 19:26) No other person but Jesus

---

[67] Clement, Alexander. Comments on the Epistle of Jude. Newadvent.org. Retrieved *24, 2015.*

the Son of God, could mold such a diverse group of men into such a powerful force for good. Jesus brought each one to a moment of decision where each one made a conscious commitment to never turn back from the sharing of the gospel message. Each one chose to move **beyond the ordinary** plans in their lives, to replace their desires for a walk in the spirit! (Romans 8:1-5)

The Apostle Judas, or Jude Thaddeus, the brother of James, was the next individual to accept the call of Jesus to follow Him. He fell within the same mold as the other disciples, a damaged individual who was willing to change to be an ambassador for Christ. Judas was known by the nicknames of Lebbaeus and Thaddaeus, and was identified as Judas; not Iscariot, to end any misunderstanding about his association with the traitor, Judas Iscariot. (Matthew 10:3; Mark 3:18; Luke 6:16; John 14:22) His given name, Judas, means "Jehovah leads" and was a very common name for boys.

He was the youngest of his family and this was probably the source of his two nicknames. Lebbaeus means a "heart child" and Thaddaeus means "breast child," which strapped him to the reputation of being his mother's baby boy. A picture is formed about this disciple, when you put the two meanings together. Typically, being the baby of the family meant he was dearly loved by his mother and family, and because he was known as a person with a big heart meant he was a strong courageous individual.[68] This seems to be a contradiction when nothing else is known of Thaddaeus until Jesus comes into his life, and leads him out of the shadows of an obscure life, to move **beyond the ordinary** daily routine of emptiness. Remember, this was a similar predicament as James Alphaeus faced.

Thaddaeus was born in the northern region of Galilee, in the town of Paneas which became Caesarea Philippi. His father was Clopas, brother of Joseph and his mother was Mary, a cousin of Mary, the mother of Jesus, making him a cousin of Jesus.[69] He was a farmer, a hard-working individual, and a law-abiding citizen. It is worth noting that Thaddaeus was given the name Jude by

---

[68] Roberts and Donaldson. <u>Preaching of the Apostle Thaddaeus at Edessa</u>. Ante Nicene Fathers.

[69] Matthew Henry Commentary

the New Testament writers to distinguish him from Judas Iscariot. Hegesippus, a historian of the early years of the church, tells of an incident involving two grandsons of Jude, so he was married with at least one child.[70]

Several illustrations taught by Jesus motivated Thaddaeus to change his negative thinking. Thaddaeus began to realize he needed a change in his obscure lifestyle when Jesus taught the disciples about Jonah. (Matthew 12:38-42) Thaddaeus must come out of seclusion and preach the gospel. The Pharisees had demanded Jesus to give them an astronomical sign from heaven, such as Samuel's thunder from a clear sky or Elijah's fire from heaven. (I Samuel 12:18; I Kings 18:38) Jesus told them only one sign would happen for their adulterous and evil generation, the Son of God would spend three days and nights in the heart of the earth, just as Jonah spent three days and nights in the belly of the great fish.

Jesus said that Nineveh had a revival and was secure in God, but the Pharisees were condemned for rejecting Jesus. Jesus condemned the generation of scribes and Pharisees for attempting to morally reform themselves apart from being indwelt by the Holy Spirit, and even if they temporarily walked a religious life, without true regeneration they would revert to their old behavior. They were spiritual adulterers. (Jeremiah 5:7-8)

Thaddaeus would learn two major lessons from Jesus' encounter with the Pharisees. One lesson was accepting that the salvation message is the key to having an everlasting relationship with Jesus. Two, even if an individual, such as Jonah, chooses to retreat into obscurity or has lived their entire life in obscurity, such as Thaddaeus; it is not the lifestyle that pleases Jesus. Thaddaeus knew that the prophet Jonah had gone into isolation so that he might not preach in Nineveh. Jonah was prejudiced against the citizens of Nineveh, and he knew the city was under the judgment of God as a penalty for their unrepentant sin. Jonah knew the Ninevites would repent and be saved if he preached there.

Thaddaeus, also, knew that God dealt harshly with Jonah for his decision to disobey the command of God to deliver the Ninevites. That is the reason he ended up in the belly of the fish

---

[70] Kirby, Peter. "Fragments of Hegesippus." Early Christian Writings, 2017

and Thaddaeus made the connection between his attitude of obscurity, and that of Jonah, even though the situation was somewhat different. Thaddaeus realized he must change his posture and commit to public ministry. This decision opened the door to his elevation **beyond the ordinary** ranks of service to Jesus.

Sometimes the opposite scenario takes place when an individual first learns to come out of hiding from the public. An individual may over react by being boisterous or pushy. Thaddaeus showed no signs of this behavior, and Jesus insured that Thaddaeus and the other disciples did not become over bearing in their approach to people by demonstrating the need to be private at times. Jesus went into private places to pray and seek directions from God. He did not gather crowds to hear him pray, as did the religious rulers, and He discouraged drawing attention to Himself after performing great miracles. (Matthew 6:5-6; Mark 1:43-44; Matthew 9:27-31)

Remember, Jesus cherished His "alone time" with God by retreating into desert places, mountain tops and the Garden of Gethsemane. (Matthew 14:13, 23; 26:36-46) He did not desire to motivate religious and governmental figures into pursuing Him beyond the point of not being able to conduct ministry. Jesus wanted limited fame; no sensationalism or political hazards to lessen His mobility in public. There is a fine line between managing potential hotspots and differing motives of interest of large crowds, and staying totally out of sight. Thaddaeus must stay in the eyes of the public while acting under the watchful eye of the Holy Spirit. He must learn to manage any newly found fame, and guard against being catapulted into the public arena without first praying for humility and wisdom. The actions of Jesus solidified this necessity in the mind of Thaddaeus.

The private lessons taught by Jesus to Thaddaeus and the other disciples did not damage the idea that Thaddaeus needed to be a public person. Jesus exercised restraint in teaching the disciples the deep things of God behind closed doors, but this did not mean the disciples were to be reclusive in nature. Jesus ingrained the emotions of gratitude, composure and enthusiasm into the hearts of the disciples. Thaddaeus was thankful to be included with the privileged of Jesus. (Luke 10:23-24) The great spiritual lessons of God are learned in private, but shared in public, and the decision of Thaddaeus to pursue ministry afforded him the ability to share divine attributes: love, joy, peace, longsuffering, kindness, goodness, faithfulness, gentleness and self-control. (Galatians 5:22) These would serve him well in the mission fields of Syria.

Thaddaeus grasped the seriousness of his choice to change his disposition during a discourse Jesus taught about the End Times. (Luke 17:20-37) The Pharisees wanted to know when the kingdom of God would come. They mockingly hinted that, if Jesus was the Messiah, He would overthrow Rome, and sit in triumph over the nations. Jesus refused to argue with them, but gave a frightening narration of the horrors of living when the end of time comes.

He spoke of fickle declarations of men claiming to be the Messiah: people eating, drinking, marrying, planting crops, building houses, selling and buying, and the destruction that would come suddenly upon all, the same as in Noah's day of the great flood and Sodom's day when fire and brimstone rained down from Heaven. (II Peter 3:10) Jesus spoke of the resurrection, with men and women being taken from sleep while others were left to suffer death. He prophesied that some would be taken from their work stations, but others left for judgment. People who struggled to hold onto life without faith would lose it and those who were focused on God would be safe. The Pharisees heard Jesus say their fixation should turn away from the false expectations of a political kingdom to spiritual rewards of the coming kingdom of the true Messiah.

Thaddaeus heard one very specific thought from this discourse that pertained to him. Everyone that was so consumed by their daily affairs were left behind, while those who were expecting the return of Christ were taken to Heaven. Especially, Thaddaeus remembered the lesson of Lot's wife. She was on the summit of delivery from the destruction of Sodom when she stopped and looked back, longing for the loss of the pleasures of a sinful city. She died there. Thaddaeus saw this as a warning to not return to a former habitude of existence. (Luke 17:32)

The lesson of the rich young ruler, who was not willing to forsake his wealth for a sure passage to eternity, flashed through Thaddaeus' mind, and Thaddaeus remembered the danger of holding onto the perishable things of life. (Matthew 19:16-26; Mark 10:17-27; Luke 18:18-27) He was struck anew by the proclamation of Jesus to leave tomorrow to itself and look for the righteousness of Jesus from where all the necessities of life would come. (Matthew 6:32-38) Thaddaeus chose to do whatever Jesus asked of him throughout all eternity. He left his good-natured engagement to mediocrity, to move **beyond the ordinary**. This was his defining moment!

The change in the attitude of Thaddaeus is seen in his conversation with Jesus on the night before Jesus would be tried before the priests and Pilate. (John 14:19-31) Jesus exclaimed to the disciples that anyone who truly loved Him would keep the commandments of God, He and the Father would love them, and Jesus would clearly speak to them. Jesus made it clear that talk is cheap and meaningless unless it is backed with obedience, so false claims of love without evidence is lying, and no liar can hear from God. Jesus reveals the reason those who do not know him are eternally lost because they cannot perceive the truth of divine love. Thaddaeus heard Jesus say first there is love toward God, and obedience out of a loving heart for God, and then comes the manifestation of outward service for Jesus; the world cannot know or understand this.

Jesus had to drive this point home to Thaddaeus. Thaddaeus was confused by what seemed to him to be a paradox – love produces works but those works are not seen by the populace. He asked Jesus, how this can happen? (John 14:23-24) He wanted to understand how only those who loved Jesus would be allowed to see and know Him. How would a lost individual ever be saved? How will you set up the earthly kingdom, overthrow Rome or be our Messiah without the world seeing it?

Thaddaeus was concentrating on the hopes and aspirations of the disciples to witness Jesus ruling from David's throne, the fulfilling of the Davidic Covenant which promised that King David would rule Israel again. Jesus answered Thaddaeus with a "mystery removing explanation." (II Corinthians 4:3-4) Jesus expounds on the truth of the gospel, the death, burial and resurrection being fulfilled. Jesus removes the blinders on the eyes of the disciples about preaching the saving message for which He really came to fulfill. Jesus tells the disciples and Thaddaeus that only those individuals who love Him will be saved. If an individual does not love Jesus, that individual cannot apprehend the gospel message. Jesus cleared the confusion in the minds of Thaddaeus and the others. (John14:24)

Jesus continues to teach and encourage the disciples by revealing to them that the Holy Spirit will be coming to help them with the work of the Savior, Jesus Christ. (John 14:25-29) Jesus confirms to them that the Holy Spirit will teach them in the future and they have nothing to worry about when it comes to succeeding in ministry. The Holy Spirit will bring to their minds everything that Jesus taught them while they were with Him for the past three and half years. Thaddaeus hears with "ears of understanding" that Jesus insures their peace and comfort is from God, not from impostors in the world. Jesus tells them He is leaving this earth, but He will come back, and for them to not be afraid. True love, Jesus says, rejoices over this truth, because the will of God the Father is done.

Thaddaeus sees with "eyes of understanding." (Matthew 11:15-16) He realizes he is in the family of God forever, like James Alphaeus, and he can proclaim that from the roof tops. Thaddaeus saw that divine love loosens the tongue! He had moved **beyond the ordinary** understanding of a non-believer in God, and had learned the gospel directly from Jesus. He would practice a great realization with all who gave him an audience, "Jesus saved him and Jesus will save them once they surrender to Christ!" (Romans 10:8-9, 13; Ephesians 2:8-10) Jesus removed the damaging thoughts entertained by Thaddaeus about himself, replaced them with a message of hope for all people, and healed his soul in the process. Nothing else matters!

Thaddaeus and Simon Zealot would go to Syria with the gospel message and a tremendous healing gift. Tradition says he approached the king of Syria, named Abgar, with the gospel message. Abgar was very ill so Thaddaeus healed him, and led him to the Lord Jesus Christ. The region rebelled against this action and Thaddaeus was captured and imprisoned by the king's apostate nephew. Thaddaeus was beheaded by an executioner using an ax, which Thaddaeus is shown holding in paintings depicting him. He was faithful to end, and this is seen through his statement, "But you, beloved, building up yourselves on the most holy faith, praying in the Holy Ghost, keep yourselves in the love of God, looking for the mercy of our Lord Jesus Christ unto eternal life." (Jude 1:20-21)

Beyond the Ordinary

1. Do you identify with Thaddaeus? Why or why not?
2. Thaddaeus was the youngest of his family, and this was probably the source of his two nicknames. Lebbaeus means "heart child" and Thaddaeus means "breast child," which strapped him to the reputation of being his mother's baby boy. It is difficult to live down a nickname especially when you do not like it. Do you have a nickname that aggravates you? How do you handle the irritation of being labeled by a name that you despise? Perhaps you have a nickname that you like. How has it helped you in life?
3. Thaddaeus was person who liked living an obscure life. He would learn two major lessons from Jesus' encounter with the Pharisees: accepting the salvation message is the key to having an everlasting relationship with Jesus, and even if an individual, such as Jonah, chooses to retreat into obscurity or has lived their entire life in obscurity, such as Thaddaeus, it is not the lifestyle that pleases Jesus. Why is this true? What must a person like Thaddaeus do to please Jesus? Are you such as person? How would you have to change to more fully succeed in ministry? What illustration did Jesus use to teach Thaddaeus about coming out of the shadows?
4. Did Jesus encourage a lifestyle that was totally public in its witness, or did He believe that a person needs both a public life and a private time of re-energizing one's spirituality? What examples did Jesus use to verify your answer?
5. What about the testimony of Lot's wife impressed Thaddaeus? Does this impress you, and if so, in what ways?
6. Jesus exclaimed to the disciples that anyone who truly loved Him would keep the commandments of God, He and God the Father would love them, and Jesus would clearly speak to them. Jesus made it clear that talk is cheap and meaningless unless it is backed with obedience, so false claims of love without evidence is lying, and no liar can hear from God. What is the lesson that Jesus is expressing

to the disciples and Thaddaeus with this exposition? What place does obedience and love hold in a person's walk with Jesus? What impact does obedience and love have on your service for Jesus? How could this improve?
7. How would you characterize your life as ordinary? What would it take to motivate you to move **beyond the ordinary** life of obscurity? Are you willing to change?

Chapter Twelve

THE APOSTLE SIMON, THE ZEALOT, AN ASSASSIN, GOES BEYOND THE ORDINARY

The Apostle Simon, the Zealot was a man zealous for the law, fiery, and open to acts of violence to obtain his goal of stamping out Roman dominance in his homeland, and might well have been a terrorist.

THE APOSTLE SIMON THE ZEALOT WAS A MEMBER of the Zealots. The Zealots political party was one of four major forces in Judea during the ministry of Jesus. The others were the Pharisees, Sadducees and Essences. The Zealots, founded by Judas of Galilee, were Judean Jews who sought to overthrow the Roman occupation of their homeland. (Acts 5:37) These fanatics were not limited by any method to accomplish their task, including murder, and they were relentless in defending the Law of Moses and the customs of the people. Often, they were called by the name "Sicarii" because they carried daggers under their clothing and would use them to stab those suspected of a sacrilegious act or any other behavior that was sympathetic to the Romans.

The Zealot movement against foreign rulers over the Jews traces back to the Maccabean revolt of 150 BC. This revolt, led by Judas Maccabeus, was an attempt to overthrow Greek oppression. The last Zealot rebellion was against the Romans and would end with the fall of Masada. The Zealots gained notoriety through their unorganized, but vicious attacks on foreign nations, particularly the Romans. These attacks eventually led to the destruction of the Jewish temple by the Romans in AD 70. Most of the Zealot members were born of the working class, which appealed to their peers. However, not all of them were totally devoted to their cause, and would take bribes from the Romans to "turn their heads" in the presence of Roman corruption. They would, on occasion, lie to their own people to incite riots and rebellions against the Roman government.

The atmosphere was very volatile during the time of Jesus. The populace was uneasy in their daily activities and in their relationship with God. They were fearful and depressed. They faced opposition from the Romans and the religious dictators who held them in bondage by unrealistic expectations placed on them. The Romans ruled through political puppets coupled with heavy taxation, while the religious leaders threatened them with excommunication from Judaism if they did not obey their desires. The peasants did not know which way to turn for help. Neither the government nor Judaism had any good answers to their dilemma of trying to please both factions. Judas of Galilee called Jews who payed taxes to Rome cowards, and worthy of death.[71] Where should their allegiance fall?

The Zealots, during this time, were staunch believers in the Torah, the Jewish sacred book, and attempted to force those teachings on everyone. They followed a strict adherence to YHWH's (Yahweh) as the only king of the Jews. They determined to establish YHWH's reign by defeating the Roman and religious yoke of tyranny and they separated themselves from the Gentile population, since Israel was God's chosen people in their minds. The Zealots dabbled in the moderate views of other established religious groups, such as the Pharisees and Sadducees, who were representatives of the upper class of wealth and aristocracy, but not the common person on the street.

Just imagine the scene. The Pharisees, legalist by nature, and Sadducees, liberal by nature, arguing over such things as the validity of a resurrection of the dead while parading around in their

---

[71] Josephus, Wars of the Jews, IV.

pompous religious dress, as opposed to the Zealots, who were acting like terrorists, going around looting, burning and conducting guerilla warfare. Jesus stepped into this picture and offered hope to all who would follow Him. Simon the Zealot, a potential terrorist and assassin, would become one of His followers.

Simon the Zealot was born in Cana of Galilee and lived in the Capernaum region. According to tradition he was a distant relative of Mary, the mother of Jesus. He was twenty-eight years old when he joined Jesus, leaving the merchant business.[72] He had a fiery reputation and was known to speak without thinking, much like Peter. Simon displayed a strong loyalty to the Zealot party and this loyalty trait would help him in his future ministry. However, he was very materialistic-minded and totally devoted to the Jewish nationalist movement.[73]

His strong sense of liberty for the Jewish nation would be transformed into a new passion of winning the lost to salvation in Jesus Christ. It was this fearless and damnable attitude, a firebrand of agitation, his ingrained tactic of terrorizing people that must change if Simon was to move **beyond the ordinary**. Jesus would have to subdue and transform Simon's actions if he was to become an effective preacher of "peace on earth and good will among men" instead of an insurrectionist. (Luke 2:14) Simon would need a transformational miracle. Jesus went about changing Simon through exerting a calm, poise and inexplicable composure during times of great controversy and the intimate moments of fellowship with the disciples.

It is obvious that a knife-toting terrorist would not be the best person to partner with in a ministry of grace and love, yet Jesus did just that. He took Simon under His wing. Jesus knew He could use the passion and zeal which Simon had illustrated in his desire to see social, economic and political change in Judea. Jesus did not argue with Simon over the need to have these changes, but Jesus motivated Simon to invest his energy in a different calling, to be a spiritual ambassador in the kingdom of God.

---

[72] Hippolytus, On the Twelve Apostles.

[73] Isaac, Lambertsen. The Lives of the Holy Apostles, Holy Apostles Convent Press, Buena Vista, CO, 1990.

Simon's change started with the marriage at Cana. (John 2:1-10) Remember this occasion in the life of John. Tradition says that Simon was the groom in the wedding and Mary was the host.[74] Jesus and His disciples came to the wedding at His mother's request. It was during the two-week celebration of the marriage of Simon to his bride that the wine ran out. Mary told the servants to do exactly what Jesus instructed them. Jesus told them to fill the jars to the brim with water at which time He turned water to wine.

This was a miracle of unprecedented magnitude. There were six water jars; about 180 gallons of water. The master of the wedding feast, after finding the new wine, announced to Simon that this wine impressed him, seeing that it was far better than the earlier drink. (John 2:9-10) Simon was so impressed by this power over the natural elements that he joined the disciples of Jesus and became a believer in Christ, along with his wife. He voluntarily gave up his plans as a married man to follow Jesus. (Matthew 19:29)

Simon and the other disciples would learn of the spiritual significance of this miracle. The jars were religious ceremonial water jars used in the Jewish rights of purification, and they were empty which symbolically said that the religion of the Jews was hollow, devoid of any possible connection to God. The new wine created by Jesus pointed to spiritual renewal, divine cleansing and the coming joyful peace through faith in Jesus, the Messiah. Simon would come to realize the changes he wanted for his world comes through companionship with Christ and not the advancement of social and governmental changes.

Simon's ideas were re-directed through observation of conflict management by Jesus. Simon was accustomed to violence as a tool for controversy with his enemies, but this was not the way Jesus took care of argumentative situations. Simon would see a true source of power in Jesus that motivated men to want to change without hateful and harmful coercion. One such incidence took place when Jesus heard about the death of John the Baptist.

Herod imprisoned John for reproving him for divorcing his wife, Phasaelis, and unlawfully taking Herodias, the wife of his brother

---

[74] Marshall, Taylor. <u>Thomas Aquinas in 50 Pages: A Layman's Quick Guide to Thomism</u>. Saint John Press, 2017.

Herold Philip I. Herodias' daughter, Salome, danced before Herod on his birthday and schemed with her mother to have the head of John the Baptist on a platter.[75] Herod, in a drunken stupor, agreed to give Salome anything she requested, so he had John beheaded. (Matthew 14:1-12) Herod claimed he killed John because John may cause a rebellion against Herod's evil jurisdiction, a rebellion that Simon would have wanted to transpire. Simon watched and listened to see what Jesus would do and say.

Jesus did not respond to the news of the death of John the Baptist as Simon expected. (Matthew 14:13-14) Simon may have looked for someone to kill, but instead Jesus retired to a boat, a solitude place to pray. Jesus found peace and direction from His Father in Heaven. Jesus always acted at the edict of His Father, and Simon would learn to act according the directives of Jesus. Simon needed to learn compassion, something he lacked in his past. Simon also needed to know that Jesus prayed about everything, including the loss of a good friend.

The death of John the Baptist gave Jesus to opportunity to impress Simon with a true demonstration of compassion. Jesus wanted to be alone, but the crowds that hounded Him daily found Him and Jesus could not turn them away. Simon saw Jesus, in His time of grief, choose to stay focused on people, healing the sick and feeding the hungry, not exactly what Simon expected to witness under the circumstances. (Matthew 14:13-21) This is exactly what Simon needed to experience because it was the very opposite of his nature. Simon heard and saw a divine love in Jesus and it drew Simon even closer to moving **beyond the ordinary** hateful attitude of his past actions!

The next major episode in the remaking of Simon's distorted attitude takes place during a conflict between Jesus, the scribes and Pharisees over the traditions of men. (Matthew 15:1) These religious leaders came to Jesus from Jerusalem with complaints that the disciples did not wash their hands before a meal. The Pharisees were arguing a tradition that was not based on the Law of Moses to condemn Jesus. Jesus countered the Pharisees by

---

[75] Isaac Lambertson. <u>The Lives of the Holy Apostles</u>. Buena Vista, CO: Holy Apostles Convent Press, 1990.

asking them why they dishonored fathers and mothers, a Law of Moses, by claiming they could not financially care for them and pay tithes to God at the same time. The holy men approved this practice which nullified God's law. (Exodus 20:12; 21:17; Deuteronomy 5:16) Simon heard Jesus call them "Hypocrites" and his blood ran hot with anticipation of a fight, but none came. This was the very type of thing that infuriated the Zealots. Instead, Jesus spoke of the heart condition of man.

Simon listened as Jesus taught that words reflect the innermost consciousness of a person; a person's soul, referenced by Jesus as the heart of man. (Matthew 15:7-20) Simon understood the power of words. He had used them to bully and strike fear into the hearts of Roman supporters and religious imposters. Now, he encountered a different influence which words reveal; the morality or immorality of a person. Simon started to realize that compassion was expressed through words originating in the heart and resulting in action.

A person may dirty oneself by ceremonially eating without washing their hands, but a person tars oneself morally by evil speaking: evil thoughts, murders, adulteries, fornications, thefts, false witness and blasphemies, many of which Simon had done. Moral defilement corrupts the soul. Jesus said to leave such persons alone – leave them to God's judgment. This triggers a mind-altering connection; he was guilty of word assassination, but he was forgiven. (Romans 3:23; 6:23) God's grace covered his past sins and would offer forgiveness for his future sins. How could he not live under and offer to others the same mercy? This mindset is **beyond the ordinary** posture of most people.

Remember, taxes were a big source of confrontation for the Zealots. Simon would learn that taxes are not to be a source of aggravation to him or the work of the ministry. (Matthew 17:24-27) Simon was growing in his faith, but there were still issues to be dealt with and government opposition was one of those issues. Simon felt that paying taxes was sinful and it was still a major stumbling block for him; such prejudices hold on. Remember, the leader of the Zealots, Judas Galilee, felt the same hatred. Jesus would shock Simon into a more logical approach of paying your fair taxes, whether to the religious establishment or the government.

The Apostle Peter asked Jesus if paying the temple tax was necessary, and Jesus answered, "Yes." Then He added not to offend those who were collecting it. Usually, kings did not pay taxes, and since Jesus was, technically a king, He was exempt from taxation, but Jesus wanted the disciples to be aware that this should not be an issue. Jesus could have made it an issue, but surprised the disciples by teaching a lesson on it. The taxes were used to keep the temple expenses paid and the temple available to the Jews for worship. Simon heard this explanation, but when Jesus took the time to perform a miracle because of it; Simon was touched in his spirit.

Jesus told Peter to go fishing in the sea, take the first fish he caught and look in its mouth. There Peter found money enough to pay the taxes. Suddenly, Simon realized the depth to which Jesus was referring when Jesus did not want to offend. This would not have been Simon's choice, but he learned the importance of doing the right thing. Jesus could have walked away without paying the tax, but He thought it important enough to pay it, that He performed a great miracle to do so. (Romans 13:1-7; I Peter 2:13-17)

The next tax encounter came when the Pharisees, in partnership with the Herodians, tried to entrap Jesus over paying a poll tax, which Rome had imposed on everyone. (Matthew 22:17-22) Remember, the Romans backed the Herodian dynasty and this infuriated the Zealots. The Herodians were a politically motivated party who had strong ties to the Sadducees, but were not religiously connected with the Pharisees until now. The enemies of Christ have strange bed partners and these three natural adversaries to each other united for the sole purpose of destroying Jesus.

The poll tax was especially grievous to the Jews because the revenue from this tax financed the Roman army, and it suggested the Jews were owned by Rome. The Jews were proud people and considered themselves as property of God, not an evil emperor who lived hundreds of miles away from them in a pagan city. The accusers of Jesus were sure they had entrapped Him. He would be disloyal to the Jews and lose their support if Jesus said pay the tax, and then if Jesus said do not pay the tax; He would be charged with treason to Rome by the Herodians. Simon was incensed by this cleverly designed trap.

Simon, who was mellowing in his political views, still faced strong temptations to revert to his old ways of dealing with tax people. He, again, waited anxiously to spring into action against these evil doers, but once again his mind was renewed with Godly principles taught by Jesus. This was not easy for Simon to swallow, but it was vital to his future success as a preacher of the gospel. Simon had to learn Godly compassion supersedes personal conviction to right a wrong, by committing a wrong. (Romans 1:32) His heart had to be purged of wrong reasoning, enraged thoughts, and false justification for his acts. Simon had to learn to defuse any threats to his new-found purpose for living, even if he desperately wanted to avenge the wicked practices of ignorant people. (Romans 12:19)

Jesus magnificently defused the tax issue by turning the tables on His accusers. (Matthew 22:18-22) He faced them down with strong words that characterized their motives. He called them, "Hypocrites!" However, He did it in a way that neutralized them instead of empowering them, and Jesus got their full attention. Simon saw Jesus kill their scheme without killing them. Jesus left the door open for their potential opportunity to turn to Him for forgiveness and redemption. Jesus asked these religious know-it-alls, "'Whose image and inscription is on a denarius?' They answered, 'Caesars.' Jesus said, 'Give to Caesar the things that belong to him and to God the things that belong to Him.'" (Luke 20:24)

Jesus took away their fire. They knew Jesus was comparing the natural world to the spiritual world. Jesus referred to Caesar as having a right to collect taxes because Caesar ruled the world, but the things of God belong to God, because God alone owns the souls of men. These accusers knew that Jesus was saying, ultimately God owns everything, but they could say nothing. This was brilliant! (Romans 11:36; II Corinthians 5:18; Revelation 4:11) Simon was eternally impressed by the power of properly spoken words; no dagger was needed. Simon would remember later what Jesus taught the disciple. He understood that Jesus would give him the needed words to say to answer his future accusers and what to say to bring conviction to the hearts of those living without Christ. (Luke 12:11-12; I Corinthians 9:19-23)

Simon would continue to change his thinking for the better. Jesus forced him to confront his ill-felt emotions toward those who oppressed Israel. Perhaps the most noted illustration of this was having Simon and Matthew on the same team. Remember, Matthew was a former tax collector and one of the individuals Simon and his crowd hated. Matthew, to Simon, was like having a sore that continued oozing pus, but that infection would heal as Simon experienced the words and actions of compassion shown to him by Jesus. Jesus transcends political causes, governmental oppression and turmoil created by everyday problems. Simon latched onto this truth and moved to higher ground, out of the black hole of failing to change the world's system, and began winning one person at a time to Jesus.

The final instruction from Jesus that changed Simon forever came while Jesus taught on the Mount of Olives. (Matthew 24:4-14) Jesus told the disciples that they would be delivered into the hands of evil people who would persecute and kill them. Simon could understand the seriousness of this tactic by opposing factions of the Gospel. It was the same strategy of the Zealots. The Zealots used inhumane punishment of people to stop their opposition. Jesus continued to express that many false leaders would surface as imposters to the cause of God. These false messiahs would cry that the end of the world was at hand due the wars and rumors of wars in the world. These evil teachers would try to convince the people that the future famines, pestilences and earthquakes were proof of an angry God who would destroy the world. Jesus expressed that great offenses would come against them, and nations would hate them because they believed in Him. This persecution must happen, but it does not mean the end of time is imminent. The world will attack all of God's servants.

Simon's fortitude was strengthened by the reality of the fight ahead for him and the other disciples. He invited it as a way to prove his allegiances to Jesus. Jesus spared no words in telling the disciples that lawlessness and love for people would grow cold as time unfolded, but they were to steadfastly preach the good news of the gospel of the kingdom. (Matthew 24:11-14; Mark 13:5-13; Luke 21:8-19) Simon decided to commit whole heartedly to that task, and he would move **beyond the ordinary** in his witnessing for Jesus. It was his defining moment!

Satan would attack with his deception through false teachers, the wars, persecutions, natural disasters, defections from Jesus, and every obstacle he could present, but Simon and the other disciples held true to the call of Jesus upon their hearts. (I Peter 1:5; Hebrews 10:23; Revelation 3:11; John 10:28-29) Simon and the other disciples would penetrate the world with the message that Jesus saves.

The ministry of Simon the Zealot testifies to his change in thought and action. He believed the work of Jesus was to save souls from hell and not to defeat tyranny. Simon heard over and over of the miraculous change that comes into people's lives when they receive compassion. Jesus said His kingdom was not of this world and if it were, His servants would fight. (John 18:36) Simon carried this thought into his mission's work. Simon remained full of zeal for the Lord Jesus, but his zeal was seasoned with compassion and truth.

The Roman historian, Jerome, refers to the zeal of Simon as fiery, yet salted with Godly compassion, denouncing of devilish doctrine and false preaching, much like that of Elijah, Peter and Paul. Jerome compares Simon to the harsh preaching of Elijah, the unwavering decision of Peter to have Ananias and Sapphira put to death and Paul's lasting punishment of blindness placed on Elymas the sorcerer for withstanding the ways of the Lord. (II Kings 1:9-15; Acts 5:1-11; Acts 13:6-12)[76] Simon became strong yet sensitive, like Jesus.

Simon's work was honored in the lyrics of many early church hymns. Simon enforced the Law of Moses, which he had honored his entire life, laws which called for the shedding of blood. (Deuteronomy 13:6-11) However, the major difference between Simon's old ministry and his new service for Jesus was his

---

[76] The Lives of the Saints in the Russian Language, According to the Menology of St. Dimitri of Rostov, Moscow, Synodal Press, 1908.

willingness to spare the life of sinners, and to show compassion. He preferred grace and mercy to killing, and become a great evangelist.

Simon traveled to many places, spreading the message of the good news of Jesus Christ. His message countered the madness of idolatry, and proclaimed the truth of the Holy Trinity, one God in three persons; God the Father, God the Son and God the Holy Spirit. His work carried him through the northern coast of Africa, Egypt, Mauritania, Libya, Numidia, Cyrenia and Abkhazia, on the northwestern side of the Black Sea.[77] Church tradition says he went to Britain in AD 60, during the time of the Boadicean War, where he was crucified by the Roman, Catus Decianus, at Caistor, for refusing to stop sharing Jesus with the people.[78] Simon's life and ministry was anything but ordinary, it was ***beyond the ordinary***!

---

[77] Stichera for Vespers of the Commemoration of the Holy Apostle Simon the Zealot, May 10th, Russian Menaion, St. John of Kronstadt Press, Liberty, TN.

[78] Isaac Lambertsen, The Lives of the Holy Apostles, Holy Apostles Convent Press, Buena Vista, CO, 1990.

Beyond the Ordinary

1. Do you identify with Simon the Zealot? Why or why not?
2. The atmosphere was very volatile during the time of Jesus. The populace was uneasy in their daily activities, and in their relationship with God. They were fearful and depressed. They faced opposition from the Romans and the religious leaders who held them in bondage by unrealistic expectations placed on them. The Romans ruled through political puppets coupled with heavy taxation, while the religious system threatened them with excommunication from Judaism if they did not obey their desires. The peasants did not know which way to turn for help. Do you see any similarities from the time of Jesus to today? What are these similarities? Be specific.
3. Simon the Zealot displayed a strong loyalty to the Zealot party and this loyalty trait would help him in his future ministry. However, he was very materialistic and totally devoted to the Jewish nationalist movement.[79] His strong sense of liberty for the Jewish nation would be transformed into a new passion of winning the lost to salvation in Jesus Christ. Would you compare Simon's passion and loyalty to any current political movements of today? Which ones and why? Do you think these movements need to take a different direction? What would that direction be? Are you a Simon type of person? Can you name anyone else who has a Simon approach to life?
4. Simon had a fearless and damnable attitude, a firebrand of agitation, which must change if he was to move **beyond the ordinary** acts of his ingrained attitude of harmful aggression. He would stop at nothing to convince people to support his ideas. Do you have such tendencies? Do you have such tendencies and how effective are they? What could you change in your approach to people that would better serve your passion for change in the world?

---

[79] Isaac, Lambertsen. <u>The Lives of the Holy Apostles</u>, Holy Apostles Convent Press, Buena Vista, CO, 1990.

5. Simon's attitude was re-directed through observation of conflict management displayed by Jesus. Simon was accustomed to violence as a tool for controversy with those who opposed his ideology, but this was not the way Jesus took care of argumentative circumstances. Simon would see a true source of power in Jesus that motivated men to want to change without hateful and harmful coercion. Jesus worked through compassion in argumentative confrontations, and He kept to the mission of bringing people to a salvation decision, not a political debacle. Review these accounts in his life. What is it about the love of Jesus for Simon that impressed you? Can you understand the importance of showing compassion and love in confrontational circumstances? Would your answer have changed the outcome of any former situations in your life? How?
6. You may be a person with a Simon attitude. Do you want to change and move **beyond the ordinary** hurtful mindset of your past? What do you think Jesus could do that would bring a change in your thinking? Are you willing to allow this change to take place? Why or why not?

Chapter Thirteen

THE APOSTLE JUDAS ISCARIOT, A TRAITOR, FAILS TO GO BEYOND THE ORDINARY

The Apostle Judas Iscariot was a personal choice of Jesus to be a disciple, yet he was possessed by his ideology and greed, to the point he would betray Jesus with a "kiss of death," and he would never move **beyond the ordinary** *evilness of bad decisions.*

THE APOSTLE JUDAS ISCARIOT HAS A COMMON first name, and is a simple form of the name Judah, meaning either Jehovah leads or one who is praised. His name certainly did not characterize his life. Judas Iscariot was the opposite of a person led by God or worthy of praise. His last name, Iscariot, comes from two meanings: "ish" meaning man and "kerioth" meaning town. He was probably named after his home town of Kerioth. Kerioth was a small Jewish town in the southern section of Judea and had the reputation of not associating with the Jews of the Galilean region. They felt superior to the rural Jews of the north, and looked down on the southern dwellers.

The town of Kerioth was located twenty-three miles south of Jerusalem and only seven miles from Hebron. It is consisted of smaller dwellings characterized by many farms. It is mentioned in the Book of Joshua, but has no significance other than being the home of Judas Iscariot. Certainly, its citizens would be shocked that one of its own would become the worst traitor of all times. Even the ill feelings that existed between them and the northern Jews should not have produced an atmosphere that would birth a traitor such as Judas, and unlike some of the environments which altered the behavior of a few of the disciples, did not foster the evil attitude of Judas. Judas had an evil heart that no town, culture, family, peer group or religion could have ripened or changed for the better.

The personalities and character of the disciples varied greatly. Remember, Jesus handpicked each one with a specific purpose in mind, re-molded the attitude of each one to fit the purpose for which Jesus called them to follow Him, and taught them how to preach, teach, heal and cast out demons. Each disciple came to a point of decision and committed to move **beyond the ordinary** lifestyles from where they came, everyone except Judas Iscariot. He was a loner, vile, evil and a walking insult to humanity.

Judas was never a spiritual man, but concentrated on attempting to force Jesus into a political endeavor to overthrow Rome. He was selfish and believed he had the power and persuasion to infiltrate the inner-circle of the discipleship: Peter, James, John and Andrew. Judas Iscariot was driven by greed and manipulation.[80] It is a mystery as to why Jesus chose Judas, except to say that God's ways are not the way of man, and God, knowing all things, uses all things to control His creation. Remember, Jesus liked bewildering the establishment by asking such men as Peter, a denier, Matthew, an extortioner, and Simon Zealot, an assassin, to follow Him. Jesus chose many disciples, but only a few stayed the course, and ironically, Judas Iscariot was one of those who associated with Jesus until he denied Jesus, the final denial. (John 6:12; Luke 6:16)

Judas Iscariot was the fulfillment of the Old Testament. The book says that the betrayer of Christ would be a friend: a confidant; someone who would walk, eat, serve Jesus, yet would have venom in his heart, an asp in disguise. This person would be a

---

[80] Ehrman, Bart D. The Lost Gospel of Judas Iscariot: A New Look at Betrayer and Betrayed. Oxford University Press, USA, 2008.

master deceiver and an aid to Satan. (Psalm 41:9) Jesus, being omniscient, would use this knowledge to bring the plan of God to a conclusion. Jesus would have Judas play a major role in His arrest and death.

A person may ask, "Why would Jesus condemn a person to such a fate?" Remember, everyone has a choice about their faith and to what level they will serve Jesus. Jesus never forces anyone to sin or act outside of their will, but He will use every person and circumstance to His good pleasure. Judas had many chances to change, but refused to bow down to the desire of Jesus for him. Therefore, Judas Iscariot became a sinful, non-repentant individual in the hands of a sovereign God. Judas was not lost by Jesus, nor was he saved and lost; he was a lost soul from the onset of his time with Jesus. Jesus lost none of the disciples, but the lost one; Judas Iscariot who never left the state of lostness in the first place. (John 17:12) You cannot lose what is already lost. Jesus chose Judas because He knew Judas Iscariot was the fulfillment of Scripture, and a devil. (John 6:70)

Judas had the same opportunities as the other disciples. Perhaps he had a greater avenue to salvation than the others since he was the treasurer of the ministry of Jesus, and spent private times with Jesus discussing their financial status. (John 12:6) Instead of using this time to draw closer to Jesus, Judas stole money from the ministry to satisfy his pleasures. He was a thief and an opportunist who would make a profit anyway he could manage, including accepting a bribe from the chief priest to betray Jesus. (Matthew 26:14-16)

Judas Iscariot had ample chances to commit to Jesus as Lord. He witnessed many healing miracles of Jesus: a man's hand on the Sabbath, a demon-possessed man, two blind men, a mute demoniac, and a deaf man, a man with dropsy, a blind man in Bethsaida and many other miracles. (Matthew 4:23-25; 9:27-34; 12:1-8, 22-23; 15:29-31; 20:29-34; Mark 7:31-37; 8:22-26; Luke 14:2-6) He saw Jesus overpower the demons; a legion of demons cast out of a violent man and the demons ordered to enter a herd of pigs. (Matthew 8:28-34; 17:14-18) He was there when Jesus took authority over the natural elements by walking on the water and calming the storm. (Matthew 14:22-36; Mark 4:35-41) Judas witnessed Jesus rescue people from sickness, job loss, marriage problems and death itself, and still was not touched with Godly sorrow that leads to repentance. (I Corinthians 15:55; II Corinthians 7:10)

None of the things he saw produced any eagerness to clear his conscience, nor did they send an alarm to his heart that he was in deep trouble with God. Judas Iscariot displayed no sadness over his depraved condition as all the other disciples had done. His wretchedness within his spirit grew bolder and more pronounced, displaying itself in his displeasure over the way ministry was transpiring, such as when he protested Mary wasting costly perfume to wash the feet of Jesus. (John 12:3-7) Judas is a perfect portrait of a person living in darkness, an individual willfully blinded by Satan and the presence of his old sin nature. Judas Iscariot never allowed the Holy Spirit to enter him and transform his sinful nature. He enacted the "sin unto death!" (Mark 3:27-30)

Judas Iscariot heard Jesus proclaim He was the "light of the world" during the Feast of the Tabernacles. (John 8:12-18) He told the crowd that He was the reason for the feast celebration; He was the Messiah. Jesus used the lighting ritual of the feast to illustrate that He was the divine personage of God. Four large lamps in the court of the women were lit and a great worship service followed with torches held high while dancing and singing. The Leviticus orchestras played and people praised God. The allusion was that these practices set forth were in expectation of the Messiah's return. Jesus would be a light for His people. (Isaiah 60:19-22; Zechariah 14:5-8) Judas Iscariot should have been able to connect the dots, but he did not.

Judas Iscariot should have immediately recognized that Jesus was the Messiah, but chose not to appropriate this vital truth. The problem with Judas was he did not want to totally surrender to the mission of Jesus as a Savior of mankind from their sin. (Matthew 8:18-22; 10:38-39) Judas Iscariot looked for higher rewards that would come if Jesus rose as an earthly king. Judas Iscariot had convinced his mind that Jesus would eventually do as he wished. He did hear Jesus reveal the eternal consequences of denying Him, that of spiritual death. Judas never paralleled the example that

Jesus used to expose a spiritual dead person to himself. He was self-righteous, earthbound, unbelieving and willfully ignorant! (John 8:20-29)

Judas Iscariot not only did not learn from the miracles of Jesus, he did not listen to the teachings of Jesus. Judas needed spiritual light, which he should have received from the teachings of Jesus, the truth that would lead to a change in his thinking. Truth about oneself regarding the punishment or forgiveness of sin is a tough pill to swallow, especially when he was not motivated to recant his position of self-righteousness. Jesus taught that He had provided the necessary spiritual insight to cause deliverance from evil thoughts and actions. Jesus instructed the disciples, and Judas Iscariot, that "good eyes" come from heeding the Word of God and Jesus, the "lamp," is the source. Metaphorically, Jesus told them that "good eyes" testified of a good person and "bad eyes" exposed an evil individual, the same as when a bright light expels darkness. Judas Iscariot ignored this revelation. (Luke 11:33-36)

Jesus warns the disciples and thus, Judas Iscariot, about being too ambitious. (Luke 14:7-14) Judas Iscariot was full of pride, and his desire to be prominent in the coming kingdom dictated to his lack of sense for fair play. He wanted the best of everything Jesus had to offer, except salvation. Jesus countered this errant ambitious behavior with an illustration of people being invited to a wedding. Those people came in and sat in the best seats at the front of the room, instead of sitting in the lesser seats in the back, until they were invited to move forward. Jesus said this would be very embarrassing to them and to avoid such pompous attitudes. Jesus said it was far better to humble oneself over exalting oneself.

Jesus continued to explain it would be more rewarding for the host of the wedding to invite the less fortunate instead of the rich, indicating that an invitation to your family, friends and the rich is not a spiritual act of true charity. Judas Iscariot did not embrace the idea because how could the poor, in comparison to the rich, ever return any owed favors for the prize seats in the house? (Deuteronomy 14:28-29) He also failed to see the magnitude of attending a wedding when an invitation had been given, which aggrandized his insincerity. (Luke 14:15-24)

Judas was a person who believed he could buy his way to success. Jesus gave him a golden opportunity to reverse his views and find true fortune in a relationship with God, but Judas declined the invitation. (Luke 18:18-27; Proverbs 2:4; Acts 3:6) Jesus made it very clear in an interview with a rich young ruler, that money and fame will not buy the way into every lasting life. Jesus told this ruler that he must sell all his goods and give it to the poor. Then he would have treasure in Heaven, but the rich young ruler would not do this. Thus, he lost his opportunity to be saved, even though he knew Jesus was a good teacher; he had not committed adultery, murder, lying or stealing. This young man had honored his father and mother and was, by all intent and purposes, a good person. He was better off than Judas Iscariot ever was, but Judas missed the comparison between his status and the rich young man.[81] Jesus was saddened by the rich ruler and Judas Iscariot's rejection of the gospel. If only Judas had accepted the truth of sacrifice which Jesus taught, he would have had all he sought! (Matthew 19:27-30; Mark 10:28-31; Luke 18:28-30)

The Pharisees attacked the concept that good acts are not substantial enough to secure a lasting fellowship with God. (Luke 16:14-16) Jesus denounced their attempts to persuade Him to change His stance, and suggested that the behavior of the Pharisees was no more than a forgery of some great portrait. Jesus condemned the Pharisaical behavior of trying to please men with phony masks of righteous behavior and insisted they stop preaching a false representation of the Law. (Matthew 23:27-33) Remember, John the Baptist had condemned such savagery. Thus, the Pharisees and Judas never joined the masses of sinners entering the kingdom of God through repentance. (Matthew 3:2; 11:12; Mark 1:15; Luke 19:1-10)

The crowds continued to come to see Jesus and hear His message. (John 12:9; Matthew 21) The disciples and Judas Iscariot had followed Jesus throughout His three years of public ministry, and now it was time for Jesus to enter Jerusalem for the last time. It is unfathomable that Judas would unite with the chief priests to

---

[81] Fitzmyer, Joseph. The Gospel according to Luke: Introduction, Translation, and Notes. Garden City, NY: Doubleday, 1985.

have Jesus arrested and crucified, especially when considering the hatred and disdain shown to Jesus by these wicked religious bigots. There were obvious times when these scribes and priests conspired to have Jesus killed, and yet Judas, who wanted Jesus to rise to authority, joined their evil plot to murder Him.[82] Perhaps Judas Iscariot thought, in his evil perception of things, that if he forced Jesus into a corner; Jesus would come out fighting and overthrow the ruling authorities. Several encounters with the chief priest to kill Jesus took place during the Passion Week. (Matthew 21:1-46) Jesus cleansed the temple for a second time and was confronted by the priests with several questions concerning His actions. They were angered by the actions of Jesus and wanted to know by what authority he was acting. Jesus, without answering them, left them and went to Bethany for the night.

Jesus returned to Jerusalem the next day and went back to the temple to teach. The elders and chief priests argued with Him again, but Jesus bewildered them with answers that would turn the crowds against them if they responded. Jesus, by His answers, proclaimed to be worthy of the praise only God deserved. He set them at odds with the populace when He drew them into a dialog concerning John the Baptist and his preaching. Jesus forced them to authenticate John's ministry, which they despised, or not answer for fear of the people, who revered John the Baptist. Jesus referred to Himself as being a stumbling stone to Israel, avowed the upcoming killing of the Messiah and confirmed the fruitlessness of Judaism. His imagery of messianic forth telling infuriated the religious leaders.

The religious establishment desperately wanted to rid themselves of Jesus, just as they had tried to do earlier in His ministry, but they were powerless against the Son of God. (John 5:18; 10:31-33) The Pharisees and Sadducees plotted to kill Jesus and were incensed when Jesus condemned them. (Matthew 22:23) These religious hypocrites found it frustrating to not have the crowds on their side of the public conflict with Jesus, but the people saw Jesus as a prophet leaving their hands tied. These religious leaders

---

[82] Towns, Elmer. Bible Answers for All Your Questions. Nashville, TN: Thomas Nelson Publishers, 2003.

viewed Jesus as a thorn in their side and Judas Iscariot saw Him as a source of his prosperity. This mind-set would be the final nail in his coffin, and he would ally with the disciples of the Devil to have Jesus captured and murdered.

Jesus reached out to Judas Iscariot one more time in the upper room. (John 13:21-30) It was Thursday evening of the week of Passover. Jesus and the disciples were sharing a last meal together. Jesus was giving them their final marching orders before He would be crucified on the Cross, buried and rise on the third day, as He had predicted. (Matthew 26:1-2) He washed the disciple's feet as an indictment to them to be servants to God and others. Jesus uses this foot washing to demonstrate their need to be spiritually clean, especially Judas Iscariot who had just returned from making his deal with the chief priests to betray Jesus. Then, Jesus shocks them with His announcement that one of them would betray Him. They could not believe their ears and were bewildered at the news that someone would do such a dastardly deed. Jesus said the one he gave a sop would be the one. (Psalm 41:9; John 13:10)

Peter, who inclined next to John, asked John to ask Jesus who it is, for fear he may act impulsively once again and make a terrible mistake – he feared he was the traitor. Remember, John was the beloved disciple so he knew he would not be the one. The others, still discussing this dilemma and not fully attentive to Jesus, did not hear Jesus' announcement about the sop or they would have attacked Judas Iscariot on the spot, so the meal continued undisturbed.

The sop that Jesus mentions was a piece of bread that was dipped in a paste-like jam made of fruit and nuts. It was given to the honored guest at a meal. The host would dip it and give to the honored guest as a sign of respect, love and encouragement. Jesus reached out to Judas with divine love, but Judas Iscariot was incapable of receiving this act of friendship. Judas could have righted the ship at that very moment by confessing his plans to turn Jesus over to the priests, but he just could not bring himself to surrender his hidden agenda. How sad! Judas was empowered by Satan to finish the deal he had already negotiated with the chief priests, and would be paid thirty pieces of silver–the price of a slave for his treacherous act. (Matthew 26:14-15; Mark 14:1-2; Luke 22:1-2; Zechariah 11) His action must be carried out or he would be exposed as a traitor.

Every disciple had started their walk with Jesus in the same vein, on level ground. All of them, except Judas Iscariot, had been elevated **beyond the ordinary** by the acceptance of change in their understanding of servanthood, but not Judas Iscariot. He never moved beyond the earthly prison of disillusionment. The others had worldliness, selfishness, greed, power struggles and enormous prejudices, but they chose to love Jesus, and in that love for Jesus, they were lifted out of the filth of worldly opinions and philosophies.[83] Their misguided passions were channeled to preaching Jesus as the answer for the evils of the world, but Judas never abandoned his wicked passion. He could have!

Jesus was troubled in His spirit over evil and non-repentant people. (John 13:21) He knew He was about to die an agonizing death on the Cross, and he was burdened and upset with Judas Iscariot for not accepting the offer of forgiveness and chance to change his destiny. Jesus agonized in His soul for Judas because He knew the horrors of Hell that were awaiting Judas. Jesus knew the terror of facing an angry God and He did not desire Judas Iscariot to have this future meeting with God. Jesus knew the eternal judgment that would be handed down to Judas at the Great White Throne of Judgment and it grieved Him to know Judas Iscariot was entering a period of hopelessness. (Hebrew 10:26-31; Revelation 20:11-15; John 11:35; Isaiah 53:3) Jesus was sickened in His spirit over the lostness of mankind; He was a man of sorrows! (Matthew 27:46; Luke 19:41; John 11:33-34; Hebrews 2:17; 5:7)

The drama continued with Judas Iscariot. Jesus, after giving Judas Iscariot the sop, ordered him to go quickly and do what he must. (Matthew 26:16; Mark 14:11; Luke 22:6) Judas went back to the chief priest and pledged with them to sell out Jesus. The selling price for Jesus was a testimony against Judas and the chief priests, and the price of thirty pieces of silver showed a greedy and evil attitude towards Judas. Judas was a traitor and the chief priests,

---

[83] Roberts and Donaldson. Copy of Five Letters from Agar; Memoirs of Edessa of Edessa and Other Ancient Syriac Documents. Ante Nicene Fathers.

even though they needed him to fulfill their plot to kill Jesus, had no respect for Judas. Judas Iscariot desecrated the Passover with blood money and he stained his fellowship with Jesus by revealing the most secret place of prayer for Jesus; the Garden of Gethsemane. Judas gathered together an arresting band of soldiers, temple guards and priests to go and capture Jesus; about two hundred in all. He would kiss Jesus on the cheek so the authorities could identify Him. (John 18:1)

Jesus and the other disciples prayed and sang a song, left the upper room, walked across the Brook Kidron, and up the Mount of Olives to the garden. (Matthew 26:30; John 14:31; 18:1) Jesus left the disciples at the entrance and went inside the garden to pray. Remember, Peter, John and James were asked by Jesus to pray with Him, but they fell asleep. (Matthew 26:36-46) The prayer time ended with the appearance of Judas Iscariot. Judas led the band of soldiers carrying torches and weapons to the spot where he knew Jesus would be and kissed Jesus.

Imagine the early morning silence being broken with the noise, confusion and show of Roman soldiers barking orders. Judas must have felt really important as he carried out his damnable act. The kiss would have been unnecessary because Jesus approached them and asked who they wanted, but Judas Iscariot had to act surprised at this, as part of his hypocritical deception; no one was to know of his pact with the Devil. The fact that Judas kissed Jesus on the cheek was Satan's highest mockery of Jesus to date; one of Jesus' own disciples could be bought. (Matthew 26:48) A kiss on the cheek, unlike a kiss on the back of the hand, the hem of a robe or the feet, was the greatest show of an intimate relationship. Judas was bad to the bone!

The scene became ugly with Peter pulling a dagger and cutting off the ear of Malcus, the high priest's servant, and then Jesus having to miraculously restore the ear. (Matthew 26:10; Mark 14:46-47; Luke 22:11; 49-50; John 18:10-11) Roman soldiers looked for a fight in every circumstance and this was a prime opportunity for things to explode into a blood bath. Perhaps, Judas Iscariot thought, for a fleeing moment, that Jesus might exert His power and start a rebellion against Rome, but Jesus ordered his disciples to back down, allowed His arrest and motioned for them to leave the area.[84] The disciples fled and went into hiding, much to the delight of Jesus' enemies. (Matthew 26:55-56; Mark 14:48-52; Luke 22:52-54; John 18:12)

What better show of Satan's power than to watch the disciples of Jesus cowering away into the dawn light, like sheep without a shepherd. Jesus quickly regained control. The sound of Jesus' voice drove the arresting mob backward and they fell on the ground. Stupidly, they rose to their feet and bound Jesus. Could not Judas Iscariot see that to bind the hands of Jesus, the One who had authority over death, was ridiculous? (Matthew 10:7-8) Satan had convinced him that he was in control.

It was before dawn. Jesus was led away to Annas, father-in-law to Caiaphas who was the high priest, where he was examined about His doctrine and asked who were His disciples? (John 18:6-23) Jesus simply said He spoke publicly and had no secrets. Jesus was struck in the face by one of the officials for speaking against Annas. (John 18:22) Annas did not find any charges worthy of the death penalty, so he kept Jesus bound and sent Him to Caiaphas, who was the only one who could ask for a civil trial. (Matthew 26:22-24) Remember, Peter denied Jesus during this time and John was nearby. (Matthew 26:69-72; Mark 14:66-77; John 18:17-27)

The next hours would prove to be the defining time for the future of Judas Iscariot. He stood by and watched Jesus suffer an agonizing horror of lies, torture and crucifixion. Jesus was taken to the house of Caiaphas, who was waiting for Jesus with the other scribes and elders. They had pre-planned the meeting and had witnesses who would lie against Jesus. The roosters had not yet crowed, which was an indictment against them for breaking Jewish law—no one could be tried in darkness, and the proceedings must take place in the temple and in public.

Caiaphas found two witnesses who claimed Jesus spoke against the temple of God by saying He could destroy it and rebuild it in three days. (Matthew 26:59-61; Mark 14:55-59) Jesus was

---

[84] Brown, Raymond. The Death of the Messiah, From Gethsemane to the Grave, A Commentary on the Passion Narratives in the Four Gospels. New Haven, CT: Yale University Press, 1998.

speaking of the death, burial and resurrection of Himself, the true Son of God. Caiaphas exploded in a fit of anger and questioned Jesus about His claim of being the Son of God, for which Jesus affirmed. Caiaphas, in a show of disgust, tore his clothes as sign of grief over this acquisition when, in fact, he was wallowing in his supposedly success of power and control. The accusers of Jesus heard this as blasphemy against Judaism and called for the death of Jesus. They spat on Jesus, covered His face with a blindfold, beat Him in the face and mocked Him unmercifully. Then, the attackers challenged Jesus to identify who assaulted Him, while Judas Iscariot did nothing. (Matthew 26:59-68; Mark 14:65)

Jesus was pronounced guilty by the Sanhedrin at first full daybreak, and was taken from Caiaphas to the Praetorium, the headquarters for the Roman military governor, Pontus Pilate. (Matthew 26:62-66; Mark 14:60-64; Luke 22:66-71; John 18:28) The accusers of Jesus refused to enter the Roman hall because this was viewed as an unclean act against their ceremonial practice; Jews did not go before Gentiles.[85] This would be the first of two meetings with Pilate. Pilate questioned them about the charges brought before him concerning Jesus, and was hesitant to proceed with the meeting. The chief priests charged Jesus with perverting the nation, forbidding the payment of taxes to Caesar and saying He was the Christ, a King. The chief priests insisted that Pilate hand down a death penalty, but would not involve themselves in this demanded verdict.

Pilate asked Jesus if He was a king fearing an uprising from the hundreds of Jews entering Jerusalem for the Passover, and if Jesus was guilty of this crime against Rome. (Luke 23:1-3, 5) Pilate was not ignorant of this problem with Jesus since he had to give permission for the Roman guards to assist in the arrest of Jesus. Jesus answered that His kingdom was not of this world and, if it happened to be so, His servants would fight. Jesus continued the conversation by bewildering Pilate about the meaning of truth. Pilate decided there was no sufficient cause for indicting Jesus and sought to release Him. (John 18:28-38)

---

[85] Barnes, Timothy D. Constantine and Eusebius. Cambridge, MA: Harvard University Press, 1981.

Judas Iscariot, like Satan who had entered him, lingered around the fringes of these interrogations hoping to witness the anger of Jesus. Judas had to be careful because he no longer had a connection to these scribes and priests. Satan had used him and now, he was unknowingly left to himself.

Pilate decided to send Jesus to Herod, the ruler of Galilee, who was visiting Jerusalem for the Passover festivities. Some of the priests were telling Pilate that Jesus was causing uprisings in Galilee, so Pilate figured he would pass this Galilean problem, Jesus, off to Herold. (Luke 23:5-12) Herod had a history with the Christians. He had John the Baptist beheaded and had threatened to kill Jesus. (Luke 9:7-9; 13:31-33) However, Jesus was not in Galilee now, and he saw no reason to endanger his pleasurable time in Jerusalem by upsetting the Jews, but he was curious about Jesus, and ironically, was excited to meet Him.

Herod enticed Jesus to perform miracles, and cross-examined Him in front of the scribes and chief priests, but Jesus remained silent. Herod's anger was kindled against Jesus. His soldiers, men of war, made fun of Jesus and arrayed Jesus with one of Herod's old robes. (Luke 23:11-12) He would send Jesus back to Pilate. Once again, common enemies, Herod and Pilate, became friends. (Luke 23:12) Judas Iscariot was following all this drama as it unfolded, and maybe he was starting to see that Jesus was not going to cause an insurrection against Rome. He would never become a wealthy man by holding onto the coattails of Jesus, and worse yet; he was digging a grave of which he would never escape.

The sun had risen, and Herod sent Jesus back to Pilate, who immediately summoned the chief priests and scribes and declared that Jesus was innocent of the charges brought against Him. Pilate agreed with Herod that Jesus was no danger to the Roman Empire and should go free. He tells the scribes he will chastise Jesus and let the crowd choose a prisoner to liberate, in hopes they would choose Jesus. Pilate attempted to appease the priests by offering a criminal, named Barabbas, to take the place of Jesus, but the priest would not hear of this action.

Everyone cried out for the release of Barabbas. Pilate had Jesus whipped with a "cat of nine tails." This was a Roman flagellum, a three-foot-long leather wipe with sharp pieces of lamb bones, small hooks and glass material attached to it every three inches. The Jews only scourged a person with thirty-nine lashes, but the Romans whipped a person forty times or more because that would usually bring death. Satan hoped for this death for Jesus, so the death on the Cross would not take place, thus spoiling God's redemptive plan for humankind. Jesus did not die, but His body was lacerated by deep wounds and stripes. (Isaiah 53:5; Deuteronomy 25:1-3; John 19:1) Soon, Judas Iscariot would look upon the body of Jesus as He carried His Cross through the streets of Jerusalem!

Pilate desperately wanted to free Jesus, but he was weakened by his political behavior of past crimes committed against the Jews. He had alienated himself from the Jews by introducing, in Jerusalem, certain ensigns engraved with the image of Caesar, and he slaughtered Galilean Jews and mingled their blood with their sacrifices. He stole, assaulted the populace and executed untried prisoners. His oppressive, greedy, stubborn and cruel acts separated him from any loyalty from the Jews.[86] The scribes and priests used this against him when they shouted he was no friend of Caesar when he insisted on freeing Jesus. So, after three attempts to release Jesus and against his wife's warning; Pilate set Barabbas, a thief and a murderer, free in the place of Jesus. (Matthew 27:15-26; Mark 15:6-15; Luke 23:8-25; John 19:12) He did not want to displease Rome and bring condemnation on himself if a religious rebellion occurred.

Pilate washed his hands of Jesus before the people while they screamed that Jesus' blood would be on their hands and the hands of their children. The crowd in Jerusalem had been persuaded to turn on Jesus, whom they had praised earlier in the week when He entered Jerusalem, shouting "Hosanna: blessed is the King of Israel." (John 12:12-19) Now, they shouted for His death!

The power of words, energized by the Devil, has great swaying influence on people, and the chief priests had filled the people's head with evil. They shouted to crucify Jesus so Pilate delivered Jesus to his soldiers. (John 19:15-16; Matthew 27:27-30) Judas

---

[86] Josephus

Iscariot was in that mob, and could not believe his ears. His plans had failed and now it appeared that Jesus would die that day. There was nothing he could do, except repent of his betrayal and sins, but he would not. He could have moved **beyond the ordinary** failure of ungodly individuals.

The soldiers of Pilate took Jesus into the common hall and gathered the entire garrison. (Matthew 27:27-30) They totally humiliated Jesus, stripping Him of His clothes and replacing them with a scarlet robe, to cover the deep wounds from His whipping. They pushed a crown of thorns into his head, put a reed in His right hand and bowed before Him in mockery, proclaiming Him to be a King of the Jews. They drove the long sharp thorns of the crown into His brow with a rod, plucked His beard and spat in His face. (Isaiah 50:4-9; Micah 5:1; Mark 15:16-19) Then, Pilate brought Jesus to the judgment seat that is called Pavement, and presented His mangled body to the crowd. It had no resemblance or form of a human body. Jesus had been beaten beyond the appearance of a man. (Isaiah 52:14; 53:3) They continued to cry for Jesus' crucifixion and threatened Pilate that they would go to Rome to testify against him if Jesus walked free. Jesus would be crucified!

The soldiers dressed Jesus in His own clothes and forced Him into the streets of Jerusalem. Jesus was exhausted and weak from the loss of blood. He could hardly carry the over one hundred and ten pound cross that the soldiers had lain on Him, so the soldiers forced a member of the crowd, Simon a Cyrenian, the father of Alexander and Rufus, to bear it. Imagine, if only Judas Iscariot would have stepped up to help Jesus in His agony. He could have found forgiveness, but Judas remained hidden from sight, and watched as they hounded Jesus through the streets of Jerusalem and up Calvary. (Matthew 27:31-34; Mark 15:20-21; Luke 23:26)

The scene that the dangerous and boisterous mob, scribes and priests, followers of Jesus, men and women, and Judas Iscariot would see next would cause a person to vomit. (Matthew 27:33-58; Mark 15:22-41; Luke 23:32-49; John 19:17-37) The Roman soldiers had to forcibly restrain the crowd as they pressed toward Simon and Jesus. Everyone wanted a closer look at the supposedly Savior of the world. They would have plenty of time to run ahead of Jesus as He stumbled over six hundred and fifty yards of walkways, the Via Dolorosa, from the Praetorium upward on the way to the top of Calvary's hill. The disciples, except for John, were in hiding.

Judas Iscariot stayed in the shadows, but he must have wondered, "What in this world have I done?" He must have battled within his soul, agonized in his mind, yet glassed over his emotions to survive the next six hours while Jesus hung on the cross. There is no possible way he could not have realized Jesus was there for his potential salvation, but the truth of what was really happening slivered away from him like a snake. (Genesis 3:1) He was so confused by the schemes of Satan that he could not pull himself out of Satan's dark deception and delusion.

Crucifixion was slow torture for the individual hanging on the cross. It was perfected by the Persians, Carthaginians and Phoenicians. The Romans adopted the crucifixion and delighted in the victims of crucifixion living for days until they died from exhaustion or dehydration. Some died from lingering fevers that caused them to shake violently from their bodies shutting down. Many times, birds of prey or wild animals would come and tear at their bodies or pluck their eyes out while they hung defenseless from the cross. The weight of the body pulling down on the body's diaphragm would cause the crucified to drown in their own bodily fluids which would collect in their lungs. They died gasping for one more breath.

The Romans would allow the criminals to suffer on the cross for days or they may hurry the death along by smashing the legs of the crucified, so they could not push up with their legs to breathe. That way the victims of crucifixion would suffocate more quickly. That was the case on the day that Jesus was crucified, since the Jews would be offended if Jesus, a Jew, remained on the Cross during the Passover. However, Jesus died before the soldiers had the pleasure of breaking His legs. (John 19:31-33; Galatians 3:13; 5:11; Hebrews 12:2)

Jesus was stripped of His clothes and nailed to the cross, one nail through each wrist and one nail driven through the Achilles tendon of both feet. (Psalm 22:14-16; Zechariah 12:10) This caused excruciating pain as the hours dragged, but this practice would not speed up death. The Roman soldiers simply enjoyed driving the nails. (Isaiah 53:12) Jesus and two other prisoners were lifted up on the Cross before all who chose to watch. (Matthew 27:38) The stigma of being crucified was the height of disgrace for any person, but especially for the Son of God who had committed no wrong.

The Romans added humiliation to the crucifixion of Jesus by attaching a placard to His Cross which read, "This is Jesus the King of the Jews." (Matthew 27:37) This, even to a traitor such as Judas Iscariot, had to stir animosity within his heart for the Romans. Judas watched as Jesus was maligned at the amusement of the infidels. He probably stiffened when he heard the Jews betray Jesus with swelling words of hatred, and still his heart was so cemented in evil that even this mistreatment of Jesus did not propel him to repentance. (Matthew 27:39; Mark 15:29-32; Luke 35:35) Amazing!

The four soldiers in charge of the crucifixion that morning cast lots for the coat without a seam that Jesus wore. (Psalm 22:18; John 19:23) They joined the chief priests, scribes and others who reviled Jesus. The mob mockingly cried out with gestures which echoed throughout the crowd. Shouts of ridicule rang out over and over, "Jesus saved others let Him save Himself," or "You are a King so come down off the cross", or "Let God save you." (Psalm 22:7-8; Matthew 27:39-43; Mark 15:29-32; Luke 23:37; John 19:21) The soldiers offered Jesus a drink of vinegar, but Jesus refused it. He must suffer the penalty of sin without any human aid. (Luke 23:36) Satan gloated in this affair through possessing Judas Iscariot. He had a premier seat!

If things did not seem terrible enough, they would escalate as the minutes passed. The crowds began to thin. It became more difficult for Judas Iscariot to blend in with everyone else. His identity as a traitor had not yet been exposed. The blood ran out of his face as he listened to Jesus speak from the Cross. Judas Iscariot expected to hear insults and demands coming from Jesus, but only love flowed from the lips of Jesus. Judas was impotent to intercede in the unfolding events of the next hours. Once again, he would fail to move **beyond the ordinary** view of love.

Jesus repeatedly asked God to forgive the sin of humankind. (Luke 23:34; I Corinthians 2:8) He said they did not understand the purpose for which they were killing Him. He bade His mother, Mary, to look upon Him and solidify her faith in Him, and then asked John to care for His mother. (John 20:26-27) He accepted the plea of the thief hanging to his right, and instilled in him a belief that he would be with Him in paradise. That thief had believed in Jesus as the Son of God while the other one rebuked him and Jesus. (Luke 23:43) Judas Iscariot could not believe his ears. Jesus was still more interested in others than Himself. (II Corinthians 24:4) Satan's deception was so strong in Judas Iscariot that neither Mary nor John recognized the evil presence of Judas. (Luke 23:34; John 19:26-27; Luke 23:39-43)

Jesus had been nailed to the Cross for three hours when Judas Iscariot and the others heard Him cry out, "My God, my God why have You forsaken Me?" (Psalm 22:1) Satan leaped within Judas when he heard this. Judas was torn between ideation and disgust. His unrepentant heart was tugging him toward Jesus, but his mind was pulled away by Satan. He warred within himself, while the Devil celebrated a victory that would not happen.

The remaining few people questioned among themselves if Jesus was calling for Elijah. Jesus said He was thirsty, so the guards offered Him a second drink of vinegar, a form of pain killer, but Jesus refused. He suffered the full penalty for man's sin without the help of any aids. The people wanted to see if Elias would come, and harassed the soldiers for offering Jesus a drink. The sky turned darker than the deepest cave as Jesus accepted the sin of the world into His being. (Matthew 27:45-49; Mark 15:33-36; John 19:28-30) A fearful and deadly silence fell on the place.

The daylight returned and Jesus called out, "It is finished." (John 20:30) He had fulfilled the eternal plan of salvation. Jesus had removed the curse placed on all of creation due to the fall of Adam and Eve in the Garden of Eden. The sin debt was forgiven for all who placed their faith in Jesus. Now, every person could rise **beyond the ordinary** scenes of life and choose to serve Jesus.

Then, Jesus graciously bowed His head. The people heard Him tenderly say, "Father, into Your hands I commend My spirit." And

Jesus willingly gave up His spirit. (Luke 23:46) The earth shook and spilt. Thunder filled the heavens. The graves were opened and many of the saints rose. The chief priests reported that the temple curtain, a two-inch-thick veil, which blocked the Most Holy Place was torn into from top to bottom. (Matthew 27:51) God had removed His separation from all people through a new and living way. Satan's celebration turned to repulsion. Jesus had snatched the Devil's victory over God away from him. Fear fell on Judas as he started to see the dastardly deed that he had done. He and the others ran a short way from Calvary, but continued to watch from a distance. (Matthew 27:55-56; Mark 15:40-41; Luke 23:49)

One of the Roman soldiers, possibly all four soldiers, surrendered themselves to Jesus. (Matthew 27:54; Mark 15:39) They believed Jesus was the Son of God. Judas Iscariot, in disbelief, strained to hear this soldier's testimony. How could one of the enemies of Jesus become a believer? Judas would never experience this miracle. Word came from Pilate to kill Jesus and the other two thieves with Him. They were surprised to see Jesus was dead and so they did not break His legs, but one of the soldiers did pierce His side with a spear. The wound open Jesus' heart and blood and water flowed out. The Scripture was fulfilled that day—not a bone of the Messiah would be broken and the Jews would look upon Him whom they pierced. (Numbers 9:12; Psalm 34:20; Zechariah 12:10; John 19:37)

The soldiers took an iron mallet and broke the legs of the other two and they soon died. Mary and John, Mary Magdalene, Mary the mother of James and Joses and the mother of Zebedee's children left and joined the other disciples in hiding. (Mark 15:40)

The soldiers took Jesus and the other two off the crosses, and reported to Pilate that they were dead. Joseph of Arimathaea, a rich man, had requested the body of Jesus from Pilate. (Isaiah 53:9; Zechariah 12:10; John 19:37) He and his friend, Nicodemus, who had visited Jesus at night, took it and wrapped it in linen and laid it in Joseph's tomb, a new tomb hewn in stone. Mary Magdalene and another Mary joined them and witnessed the burial, later to return with spices and ointments, a sticky resin, to temporarily beautify the corpse and help adhere his clothes to his body. A stone was rolled across the entrance and Pilate ordered guards to stand watch in fear that the followers of Jesus may steal the body. (Matthew 27:57-61; Mark 15:42-47; Luke 23:50-55; John 19:31-42) Judas Iscariot had joined the others in hiding, and was still unexposed for what he had done.

The atmosphere in Jerusalem was very unsettled. Everyone was talking about the crucifixion and the strange phenomena of events. The Jews and visitors in Jerusalem were cautious in speaking publicly. The Roman officials were on edge and expected trouble from the followers of Jesus. Roman soldiers patrolled the streets looking for trouble makers and the disciples. Great fear engulfed the homes of Jerusalem. The grave yards had open graves and the bodies were gone. An eerie feeling was in the air and a sense of the unknown prevailed. It seemed that danger lurked around every corner.

Unanswered questions dominated the conversations. Was Jesus who He said He was, the Son of God? Was God angry with the world? What would happen next, another earthquake, deafening thunder from Heaven as though God was angry, or worse? The chief priests and scribes, including Annas and Caiaphas, had no answers for the Jews. The temple was a mess with the torn fragments from the split veil laying on the floor and the Most Holy Place being exposed to commoners. The Levites hurried the people through the temple services and scolded those who asked questions. What would the next day bring?

Three days passed. It was the first day of the week, and the women were determined to go to the grave of Jesus to pay proper respects and to anoint His body with spices and ointments. Very early on the first day of the week, Mary Magdalene and the other Mary headed for the tomb. Nearing the tomb, a great earthquake shook the ground. The guards at the tomb were frozen in their place by the appearance of a mighty angel who rolled the stone guarding the entrance of the tomb away and sat on it. (Matthew 28:1-7) The angel eased the women's fear and announced that Jesus had risen. They cautiously entered the tomb and were greeted by two men in shining clothes, obviously angels. They told them to not look for the living among the dead. One young man dressed in white exclaimed to them that Jesus of Nazareth had risen from the dead and was not there. The frightened women hurried from the tomb, but were resolved to tell Peter and the others what the man had instructed them to say. (Matthew 28:1-8; Mark 16:1-8; Luke 23:56-24:12; John 20:1-2)

The women announced to Peter that Jesus had risen from the dead. The eleven disciples, not including Thomas who was missing, had trouble believing these women because they really did not think Jesus would come back from the dead. (Luke 24:9) The disciples were in a state of shock and confused. They treated this news as a joke. Jesus was dead, they did not know the whereabouts of Thomas, and Judas Iscariot was acting withdrawn. He was trembling at the thought of being exposed if Jesus was alive. Just in case Mary was telling the truth, Peter and John raced from the place toward Joseph Arimathaea's tomb, John arriving there first.

John stooped and looked inside. Once Peter arrived they did not hesitate in entering the tomb. They found the burial wrappings on the burial bed and the napkin which covered the face of Jesus lying in a separate place. Peter and John, still perplexed by the awful death of Jesus on the Cross and their wavering faith, decided to go to their homes, only to join the others shortly. (Luke 24:12; John 20:3-10)

Mary Magdalene wandered back to the tomb and stood outside weeping. She stooped down and looked inside out of desperation to see Jesus. Jesus had delivered her from seven demons, and she could not bear not finding Him. Again, two angels spoke to her and asked why all the tears. She was hurt and frustrated, and turned away from them only to see a figure through the midst of the morning. Supposing him to be a gardener, and in her desperation, she begged for an answer. This person asked her why she was crying? She emphatically asked him if he had seen Jesus. Jesus called her by name and her heart nearly stopped. It was Jesus, He was alive! Jesus banished her fears but forbade her to touch Him. He had to appear at the throne of His Father before anyone could embrace His body. Mary, once again, hurried to tell the others. (John 20:11-17)

Jesus appeared to the other women shortly thereafter, and they too rushed and reported their encounter with Jesus. This meeting was observed by some others who reported the meeting to the chief priests. The elders considered this to be a trick of the followers of Jesus, but they decided to pay off the guards at the tomb, if they would say the body of Jesus was stolen during the night. This became a common story throughout Jerusalem. (Matthew 28:9-15; Mark 16:10-11; John 20:18) A deepening sickness had started to grip Judas Iscariot, and he realized that everything Jesus had predicted was coming true. The Devil left him to his own demise. This is a common practice for Satan. He moves people for his purposes; just as a chess player moves pawns on a chest board. (Ephesians 2:1-3)

Later, the disciples were together behind locked doors. Two of the disciples of Jesus, possibly two of the five disciples He called after the twelve, Joseph of Arimathaea, Nicodemus, Justus, Barabbas or Matthias had returned to the eleven disciples after meeting Jesus on the way to Emmaus. (Mark 16:12-13; Luke 24:13-32; Acts 1:23) Once there, they told how Jesus had opened the scripture to them, fellowshipped with them and was about to eat with them when He vanished. They explained that Jesus disappeared right before them after blessing some food. Each exclaimed how their hearts burned in His presence. They testified that Jesus said He had met with Peter. (Luke 24:34; I Corinthians 15:5) Judas Iscariot continued to be bewildered in the presence of these disciples who had encountered Jesus. He wondered if Jesus had mentioned him in any way?

Then it happened; Jesus came into the room where the eleven disciples and the others were eating a meal. Again, Thomas was missing. Jesus did not knock or open the door, He just appeared. Everyone was scared to death at this sudden meeting with Jesus. (Luke 24:36-46; John 20:19-24) Jesus upbraided them for not believing the resurrection or the witness of those who had seen him. Peter had not spoken about his meeting with Jesus; perhaps because of his shame for denying Jesus and not being sure of his future. Jesus bestowed peace on them and reassured them it was Him. He showed them the nail prints in His hands and feet, and shared a meal with them. Jesus told them to receive the Holy Spirit who would soon come, and they would have authority to bring conviction upon sinners. (John 20:23) Judas Iscariot reached his breaking point. He agonized within himself. Most likely it was a suspenseful time for everyone. One can only imagine how Judas Iscariot could hardly swallow his food, and could not look at Jesus.

Jesus came back to speak with the disciples again in a week. He eased the meeting by encouraging them to be at peace and not to be troubled in their spirits. Everyone but Judas Iscariot took His encouragement to heart. Judas Iscariot was petrified with fear. Would this be the time that Jesus denounced him? He had escaped detection thus far. His sorrow for his actions swelled in his heart, but he had gone too far. His heart was hardened beyond repair. Every time he moved the thirty pieces of silver jingled in his pocket. Thomas had joined the discipleship at this meeting, and met Jesus face to face. Jesus commanded him to put his fingers in the nail prints of His hands and feet, and Thomas immediately exclaimed that Jesus was his Lord and God. Jesus announced that everyone who saw and believed was less blessed than those who had not seen Him and yet believed. Judas Iscariot had seen Jesus and not believed, so where did that leave him? Lost! The hopelessness that Jesus feared for Judas Iscariot had come upon him.

Judas Iscariot would not see Jesus face to face again. He could no longer live with the horrible act of treason against Jesus, the Son of God. Matthew reported in his gospel that Judas Iscariot found the elders and chief priests and threw the thirty pieces of silver down in the temple in front of them, went out and hung himself. (Matthew 27:3-10) Matthew's report seemed to place this event prior to the crucifixion and resurrection of Jesus, but his report was not a chronological report. Matthew simply told of what would take place with Judas Iscariot.

Mark and Luke spoke of the fact that eleven disciples, minus one, Thomas, were present in a private meeting after the resurrection of Jesus proving Judas Iscariot was there. (Mark 16:14; Luke 24:33) John spoke of Thomas's absence in this meeting with the eleven. (John 20:24) If Thomas had been there, all twelve disciples, including Judas Iscariot would have been present. The

Apostle Paul testified that all twelve disciples saw the resurrected Jesus. (I Corinthians 15:5) Indeed, Judas Iscariot had numerous chances to confess his crime and ask forgiveness from a resurrected Christ! It would have been better if he had never been born. (Matthew 26:24)

Judas Iscariot did admit he had sinned against innocent blood. It was the only right thing Judas accomplished in his life. It was **beyond the ordinary** act of a greedy person, but it was not an act of repentance. (II Corinthians 7:10) He never let Jesus bring him to repentance and forgiveness for his sins. He never had his old sin nature reshaped into a useful vessel; his evil thinking blockaded any hope for change. Judas Iscariot never arrived at a moment of decision to further his ability to serve Jesus in a pure ministry. Ironically, the only credit he achieved was providing a grave yard for the dead with the betrayal money.

The hypocritical elders and chief priests refused the silver under the pretense that it was the price of blood and unlawful for them to handle. They took the silver and bought a potter's field. (Matthew 27:3-10) Satan had finished with Judas Iscariot and left him to deal with his emotions, terror and guilt. Judas should have turned to his friend, Jesus Christ, but instead he did what he always had done, he took the fool's way and hung himself outside of Jerusalem. It was a gruesome act as He hung himself in the heat of the day. His dead body swelled to the point that when the limb from which he hung himself broke, and his body hit the ground, it burst spilling his internal organs on the ground. The field, which the elders bought with the silver, was called "Akeldama, the field of blood!" (Acts 1:15-20)

Beyond the Ordinary

1. What is your most vivid image of Judas Iscariot? When you think of him, what is the image that first comes to mind?
2. Judas Iscariot is a lesson against living an evil life. What does living such a life teach us? Is it to never betray your friends or not to despair? Is it to never commit suicide? Be specific in your answer.
3. What difference does it make if Judas Iscariot dies immediately after the betrayal or lives longer? Think of the events before the betrayal and after the crucifixion before you answer. Be detailed in your answer. It will help you understand the depth of which Satan can control an unbeliever and the length to which Jesus will go to save a believer.
4. Define and discuss your understanding of repentance and regret. Did Judas Iscariot repent or just regret what he did? What difference would this have made in his future?
5. ZDefine the gospel. Discuss God's plan of salvation. If Jesus died for your sins, and for all sins, did he die for Judas's sin? If he did, is it possible that Judas Iscariot could have been saved after the betrayal? Why or why not and be specific in your answer.
6. Define the doctrine of free will, sometimes known as freedom of choice. Define the doctrine of predestination. Did Judas Iscariot have free will or was he predestined to be lost? If not how are the following passages to be explained: Mt 26:25; Jn. 13:27-30; 17:11-12; Psa. 41:9; Acts 1:16?" What verses support the doctrine of free will? How is this supposedly contradiction in scripture reconciled?
7. According Matthew 26:20, during the Passover supper, Christ informed the disciples that one of them would betray him. Each of them began to question the Savior, "Is it I, Lord?" It is amazing that each one could doubt his decision to follow Jesus, wondering if he could be a traitor. What can make a person betray his best friend? What could make you betray a friend? Can you imagine betraying Jesus Christ? Why and be specific.

9. Which episode in the life of Judas Iscariot could have moved him *beyond the ordinary*? Was there only one time in his life where a different choice on his part could have changed his outcome or were there many? What does this say about Jesus?

Chapter Fourteen

BEYOND THE ORDINARY SUMMARY

*Are you ready to move beyond the ordinary? Identify with the disciple that reflects your behavior, learn of his change, adopt that change for yourself, that you might fulfill your life's purpose, and move **beyond the ordinary**!*

EACH DISCIPLE ACCEPTED THE CALL OF JESUS AND were saved to everlasting life, but they still had to deal with their limitations to potential success in ministry. They had to constantly deny their old sin nature, not unlike all believers in Christ, but they had victory through the indwelling Holy Spirit who set them aside for service to Jesus. Jesus spent forty days with the disciples and those He loved after the Resurrection. Jesus, during this time, solidified all that the disciples had witnessed and learned over their previous three and half years with Him, and their point of decision, to move **beyond the ordinary**. They believed God had better things for them than an ordinary life of mediocrity. (Ephesians 3:20-21) Each one would need a change in their approach to servanthood.

Jesus summarized how each had chosen to elevate their love, friendship, and service to Him, and Jesus did this by defining divine love through which He called them, and through which they sought a meaningful ministry. "This is my commandment, that you love one another as I have loved you." (John 13:34-35) Then, he told them what this love is, "Greater love has no one that this, than to lay down one's life for his friends." (John 15:13) The disciple's eternal choice to follow Jesus in ministry came as they appropriated the life of Jesus, "You are my friends if you do whatever I command you." (John 12:12-14) The Apostle Paul and each disciple, except Judas Iscariot believed this, were friends with Jesus, and did great things for God! (John 14:12-14)

Each disciple of Jesus had a specific defining moment when their attitude toward themselves and others changed, before they could totally fulfill their purpose in ministry. Every Christian will identify with one or more of the disciples. Each disciple's life will mirror every believer since Adam and Eve, and are illustrations for the need of change in every person's weakness to move beyond their former attitudes of addressing issues in life and work. Everyone must ask themselves a gut-wrenching question. **What makes the difference in their life that raises their service to extraordinary heights or cast them down to unbearable failure in ministry?**

Now, let's review the disciples starting with the Apostle Paul. Try to identify the disciple that pictures your need for change. Paul was driven, a highly-educated enemy of Christianity, and would not change easily. He was prejudiced against Gentiles and dogmatic about his beliefs in Judaism. His major challenge, once he met Jesus and embraced grace, was trying to reconcile his quest for inner-peace which he knew came from grace, but that his subconscious would not accept. Peace seemed to elude him over his war between his conscious belief in a grace walk and the unconscious demands to work out his salvation. It was hard for Paul to let go of his relationship to God based solely on a Jewish work ethic verses a friendship with God through grace provided by the sole work of Jesus.

Paul lacked inner-peace because he was unable to control his thoughts, words and actions until he accepted the change necessary to move him *beyond the ordinary,* thought that peace of mind comes from self-righteousness acquired through works, even though he preached salvation through grace. Paul exposed his weakness of the flesh to prepare to receive God's provision for Godly living. His life changed when he appropriated Christ's wisdom and power to offer him peace that his accomplishments did not provide. Paul consciously chose to think in like manner as Jesus. He would become a decisive and strong leader, an encourager through his writings. He learned that the "righteous live by faith," and "the peace that surpasses all our understanding!" (Romans 1:17; Philippians 4:7)

The Apostle Peter had followed Jesus at a distance. He distanced himself from Jesus in thought and action by being consumed in his own desires. He was emotional, bold and a risk taker who must learn to listen to others and submit to Jesus. He needed to come closer to Jesus by letting Jesus speak to him and by denying his desires. Peter failed Jesus and cursed Him, yet Jesus immersed Peter's heart in love which removed Peter's guilt, shame, and focus upon himself. Peter's choice to submit to God's plan for him moved him **beyond the ordinary** position of following Jesus from a distance, a self-absorbed attitude. He reached the summit of service. He would develop into a warm hearted, spontaneous to the words of Jesus, and flexible disciple.

The Apostle Andrew was subdued and a behind the scenes type of person. He was a man of faith and was willing to obey Jesus, but viewed himself as a second-class disciple. Andrew would grow into realizing that Jesus loved him equally with the other disciples. He must learn to listen to Jesus in every place and circumstances. Jesus did allow him into the inner-circle of disciples, but he first had to learn that everyone is important to the success of ministry. He made a choice to allow his thought life to be in harmony with his deeds. He learned that he did not have to be acknowledged by men to be joyous.

The lesson Andrew applied to his mindset was to be satisfied in his relationship with the other disciples and to accept his role in ministry. He learned those who follow can also lead. This propelled him **beyond the ordinary** self-imposed thought limitations that rob the joy and fulfillment of knowing Jesus! He continued his warm-hearted approach to people, became a team player in small matters and was a strong contributor to the ministry.

The Apostle James Zebedee was fiery tempered, religious and a strong defender of the Jewish nation. He was brave, industrious and spontaneous. James' reputation as a "hothead" must be overcome if he was to become the leader that Jesus needed in the early church. He must follow the example set by Jesus. James must change his attitude toward modeling the compassion and calmness of Jesus during controversy. He must learn to not push a personal agenda through an angry spirit. James embraced the idea of preaching the gospel in a level-headed fashion while loving everyone equally: the rich and poor, healthy and sick, great and small and enemy and friend. The words of Jesus escalated him to higher ground, **beyond the ordinary** posture of angrily pushing an agenda. He heard, believed and accepted his new service. He became a realistic, practical problem solver in the church by getting things done in an efficient way while subduing his forceful attitude.

The Apostle John, brother of James Zebedee, was also fiery and inherited, to a lesser degree, the same attitude as his older brother. He was a man of justice and fair play. This allowed him to enact the justice of Jesus, once he chose to allow Jesus to draw out his hidden quality, a quality of extraordinary love. He had attempted to be like his brother which had dampened his ability to share compassion. John was moved to change while watching Jesus restore Peter to the ministry. The great love of which Jesus showed Peter moved John **beyond the ordinary** bounds of over simplifying and self-acknowledgment of love, and eternally changed him from a "Son of Thunder" to the "Beloved Disciple!" He learned to share love and develop fellowship in the church.

The Apostle Nathanael was a scholar and searcher of Scripture, and this aided him in recognizing the Messiah. His thinking changed, in a moment, from having a pious approach to the understanding of Scripture, which had brought him into alliance with other religious students who belittled everyone from Nazareth, the home of Jesus. He was a blind student looking for a hidden treasure, the Messiah. Jesus said he was a sincere and honest person but filled with pride. This pride must die if he was to move **beyond the ordinary** attitude of being better than everyone else.

Jesus, in His first encounter with Nathanael, challenged his life of segregation from the under privileged people, and his mislead opinion of the Law of Moses and the Prophets. Nathanael saw in Jesus a Savior who knew all things about people, yet offered acceptance to all who followed Him. Immediately, Nathanael chose to open his mind and heart to the words of Jesus. He did not hesitate for a moment. His change came the instant Jesus spoke to Him. He developed a high standard of competence and performance in the church.

The Apostle Philip was always being mischaracterized as being Greek even though he was a Jew. He grew up looking and acting like a Greek, and was somewhat gullible and shy. This attitude of blending in with the crowd was a major weakness in him, and must be overcome. He lacked imagination to overcome the everyday hassles of life, and this lack of vision would, if not reshaped, bring defeat during the drudgeries of ministry. Philip's change came in his realization that Jesus was a man of vision and purpose. Jesus was uninhibited by circumstances or people. Philip made a conscious decision to examine things through spiritual eyes which meant he committed to follow Jesus without reservation. Philip would dream big and move on to a ministry **beyond the ordinary** commonplace drudgery of life. He learned to socially interact with the public and to follow the faith exerted by Jesus.

The Apostle Matthew was a social outcast, a traitor to his people. He was a tax collector and hated by the Jews for this reason. He was an extortionist and a publican. He proved to be self-serving through his denial of the Law of Moses and the prophets by cheating the people for monetary gain. Matthew became a vital testimony to the truth that Jesus would save anyone who confessed their sins, repented of them and accepted forgiveness from Jesus Christ. Once Matthew was saved, he would still need a major change in his thoughts of unforgiveable sin, if he was to move **beyond the ordinary** opinion that the consequences of sin lasts forever.

He was parallelized by the thought that he was useless due to his public reputation of being a lover of money and a fraud. He was ignored and persecuted by everyone. Jesus would teach him of a better love, the love of God. Matthew changed his defeatist attitude of himself when he realized that hatred comes upon a person because of wrong and right deeds. He made a conscious decision to be like Jesus, accept whatever comes his way and stay focused on the greater picture, evangelizing the non-believer in Christ with a message of eternal forgiveness of sins and ever-lasting life. He became tolerate, flexible, and willing to share his faith without expecting monetary gain. He expanded his energy into sharing the gospel.

The Apostle Thomas was a natural critical thinker and pessimist who wanted to see everything from a "naked eye" perspective. He had little education, but a sharp mind, was a questioner of all things and needed to be convinced of the truth. Thomas was the one who was accused of doubting the resurrection of Jesus from the dead, and he brought attention to the other disciples of their skeptical behavior concerning the resurrected Christ. He was a logical thinker throughout his life and his salvation experience did not change that pattern. He needed to go **beyond the ordinary** boundaries of logical thinking. He moved to a higher ground of faith when he chose to follow Jesus and his faith was eternally solidified when he saw the resurrected body of Jesus. Thomas threw logic out the window, reasoned on a spiritual plain and never sought physical evidence again. He learned to avoid logical determinations without having faith. Faith became his governing key factor in ministry.

The Apostle James Alphaeus was a student of Scripture, a pious Jew and a rigorous observer of the Law. However, he suffered from low self-esteem which was magnified by others who nagged him over being less aggressive in demeanor than the major players of the discipleship, particularly those who shared his first name; James Zebedee and James, the brother of Jesus. He received no fame for his service to Jesus, and this had a potentially damaging effect on his success of future ministry.

Jesus would teach him that he must get **beyond the ordinary** evaluations of others if he truly loved Jesus and wanted a powerful ministry. James would learn that behaviors and ministry are not judged on people appraisals but on a relationship with Jesus, who judges righteously. True authority comes by being appointed by God to represent Christ. James learned this as he listened to Jesus teach. He learned that loyalty to values and to people are the main elements to attract people to Jesus which meant one must share the knowledge of God to be a true servant to Jesus.

The Apostle Thaddaeus was a momma's boy. He grew up living an obscure life and carried this practice into his walk with Jesus. Jesus wanted him to come out of this seclusion and preach the gospel, but a change would have to take place in his isolated approach to thinking. Jesus reminded him of several hard lessons about withdrawing from the public or not stepping up to follow God's directives in the illustrations of Jonah's withdrawal from obedience to the call of Christ to preach to the Ninevites. Thaddaeus saw in Jonah a possible scenario for his life if he did not step up, a visit inside a fish's belly was possible, like when Jonah found himself in a difficult place in life, a place that could happen to the future end of times participants because of their refusal to follow instructions. Thaddaeus saw he must avoid the harshness of God toward disobedient servants, even if they were by nature, antisocial. He would grow **beyond the ordinary** routine of living a reclusive daily life. He overcame his standoffish position in life, his engagement with mediocrity, to become a forerunner of Christianity. He learned to focus on immediate truth and the straightway exercise of solving problems that arise.

The Apostle Simon Zealot was a political and militant rebel rouser. He was opposed to the Greek culture and Roman occupation of Jerusalem. Simon had a fiery reputation, spoke without thinking and was materialistic by practice. His loyalties fell between the Zealot Movement and the Jewish Nationalist Group. Simon, after he met Jesus, would come to a major decision in his life. He would choose to forsake his firebrand and damnable opinions for a relationship with Jesus.

He climbed out of the insurrectionist movement to advance **beyond the ordinary** ingrained practice of terrorizing people to winning souls to Christ. Jesus would subdue his erroneous thinking through a consistent granting of miracles to people which displayed compassion and love. This chipped away, like a sculptor chiseling a statue, at Simon's misguided sense of pride and prejudice. Simon received mercy from Jesus and this turned his heart from being cruel and non-accepting of people to forgiving others and witnessing to them about the grace of God. He learned to control his leadership qualities and forego aggressive and divisive methods of reaching one's goals.

Judas Iscariot was a personal choice of Jesus to be a disciple, yet he was possessed by his ideology and greed, to the point he would betray Jesus with a "kiss of death." He would never move **beyond the ordinary** evilness of bad decisions. He was entrapped by an earthly prison of disillusionment. Judas Iscariot believed, through the deceptive Satanic interpretation of the nature of Jesus, that he could control the Son of God, Jesus Christ. He would not submit his desire to the will of God, and remained, by choice, in lostness. He is a sad illustration of an individual who hears the truth, feels regret over their actions, yet will not repent, confess and ask Jesus Christ for forgiveness. Judas was guilty of blaspheming the Holy Spirit. (Mark 3:28-29) He did things his way and died an eternal death, forever separated from a loving Heavenly Father. He learned nothing!

Do you have an idea of which disciple fits your personality? Can you write a one sentence description of your attitude and possibility for service to Jesus? The disciples would quickly tell you who they were before they chose to be saved and follow Jesus Christ, and they could describe the process through which Jesus took them to elevate their service opportunities. They could explain their need to move **beyond the ordinary** excuses and actions of most followers of Jesus for not serving Jesus at a high level of success. Each disciple can give testimony to the events leading up to their elevation to higher servanthood. They knew how Jesus changed them! Do you?

So, what makes the difference in their life that raises their service to extraordinary heights or cast them down to unbearable failure in ministry? Remember, the first step to reaching extraordinary heights in life is acknowledgment and acceptance of Jesus Christ as the only Son of God and your Lord and Savior. (You may want to read the 'Introduction' again.) God's plan for salvation is seen in Ephesians 2:8-10, "For by grace you have been saved through faith, and that not of yourselves; *it is* the gift of God, not of works, lest anyone should boast. For we are His workmanship, created in Christ Jesus for good works, which God prepared beforehand that we should walk in them."

John 3:16 declares, "For God so loved the world that He gave His only begotten Son, that whoever believes in Him should not perish but have everlasting life." Believe by faith in Jesus Christ as God's Son and receive Jesus' gift of forgiveness from sin. Romans 10:9-10 confirms faith, "That if you confess with your mouth the Lord Jesus and believe in your heart that God has raised Him from the dead, you will be saved. For with the heart one believes unto righteousness, and with the mouth confession is made unto salvation."

A decision to follow Jesus starts once you realize you are a sinner and in need of a Savior, admit to God that you are a sinner. Romans 3:23 says, "For all have sinned and fall short of the glory of God." Admitting that you are a sinner and separated from God is the first step of repentance, which is turning from sin and self, and turning toward God. Matthew 4:17 reminds us, "From that time Jesus began to preach and to say, "Repent, for the kingdom of heaven is at hand."

Then, confess your need to be forgiven and to forsake your self-desire to govern your own life. Proverbs 28:16 confirms, "He who covers his sins will not prosper, but whoever confesses and forsakes them will have mercy." You choose to repent, to turn away from your sin of erroneous self-evaluation of righteous living. The decision to be saved requires asking Jesus for forgiveness and receiving Him into your heart; your desires are forsaken and replaced by God's desire for your life. (Romans 3:10-18, 23; 6:23; Ephesians 2:8-10, Romans 10:13; 10:8-9) Remember, in the death of Jesus on the cross, God provided salvation for all who would repent of their sins and believe in Jesus. Confess your faith in Jesus Christ as Savior and Lord to others. Romans 10:13 says, "For whoever calls on the name of the LORD SHALL BE SAVED."

After you have received Jesus Christ into your life, share your decision with another person. Tell your pastor or a Christian friend about your decision, and follow Christ's example by asking for baptism by immersion, in your local church as a public expression of your faith. Acts 2:38, "Then Peter said to them, 'Repent, and let every one of you be baptized in the name of Jesus Christ for the remission of sins; and you shall receive the gift of the Holy Spirit."

Baptism is a dramatic show of faith. Jews were excommunicated from their family when they accepted Jesus by faith and were baptized as a testimony of their decision.[87] Don't follow the example of many new believers by refusing to be baptized nor joining a Bible believing church. Matthew 10:32-33 warns us, "Therefore whoever confesses Me before men, him I will also confess before My Father who is in heaven. But whoever denies Me before men, him I will also deny before My Father who is in heaven."

Sometimes, like the Apostle Nathanael, surrendering our self-imposed knowledge for determining how to succeed happens the moment we receive Jesus, but for most believers it takes time and is a process of events. Remember II Corinthians 5:17 teaches us, "Therefore, if anyone *is* in Christ, he is a new creation; old things have passed away; behold, all things have become new." This is the testimony of the disciples. Two questions must be answered by you and every person. Are you saved and are you willing to be molded into a miracle working servant of Jesus Christ? Are you ready to move ***beyond the ordinary***?"

---

[87] Tenney, Merrill C. <u>New Testament Survey</u>. Grand Rapids, MI: Wm. B. Eerdmans Publishing Company, 1961.

BIBLIOGRAPHY FOR ADVANCED STUDY

(Each of these authors and works contributed to the overall understanding of the background and lives of the apostles in this work. I am grateful for their enormous insight.)

Allison, Dale C. <u>Studies in Matthew: Interpretation Past and Present</u>. Grand Rapids, MI: Baker Academic, 2005.

Attridge, Harold W.; Hata, Gohei, eds. <u>Eusebius, Christianity, and Judaism</u>. Detroit MI: Wayne State Univ. Press, 1992.

Attwater, Donald and Catherine Rachel John. <u>The Penguin Dictionary of Saints</u>. 3rd edition. New York, NY: Penguin Books, 1993.

Ayers. Philip E. <u>When Anger Strikes</u>. www.XulonPress.com, 2016.

Barnes, Timothy D. <u>Constantine and Eusebius</u>. Cambridge, MA: Harvard University Press, 1981.

Barclay, William. <u>The Letters of John and Jude – The Daily Bible Series</u>, Revised Edition. Philadelphia, PA: Westminster Press, 1935.

Batten, Alicia J. "<u>Fishing Economy in the Sea of Galilee</u>", n.p. [cited 14 Sep 2017].

BiblePath.com, 6921 D Carnation St., Richmond, VA 23225.

BiblePath.com. <u>Ministry of the Twelve Apostles</u>. Richmond, VA., 2017.

Bock, Darrell L. Recovering the Lost Gospel: Reclaiming the Gospel as Good News. B & H Academic, 2010.

Brainerd, David. (n.d.) AZQuotes.com, 2017.

Brown, Raymond. The Death of the Messiah, From Gethsemane to the Grave, A Commentary on the Passion Narratives in the Four Gospels. New Haven, CT: Yale University Press, 1998.

Campbell, Joseph. Papers from the Eranos Yearbooks. Princeton University Press, 1981.

Cavendish, Richard. London's Last Bartholomew Fair. History Today, Vol.55, Issue 9, 2005.

Clement, Alexander. Comments on the Epistle of Jude. Newadvent.org. Retrieved 24, 2015.

Cross, F. L. The Oxford Dictionary of the Christian Church. New York, N.Y: Oxford University Press, 2005.

Dever, William G. What Did the Biblical Writers Know and When Did They Know It? Wm. B. Eerdmans Publishing Company, 2002.

Dr. Valadimir Antonov, Edition and Commentaries: Translated by Anton Teplyy, Dr. Mikhail Nikolenko and Hiero Nori, Antonov V.V., 2002.

Dunn, James D.G. Jesus, Paul, and the Gospels. Grand Rapids, MI: Wm. B. Eerdmans, 2011.

Eisenman, Robert. James the Brother of Jesus: The Key to Unlocking the Secrets of Early Christianity and the Dead Sea Scrolls. (Viking Penguin), 1997.

Ehrman, Bart. Peter, Paul, and Mary Magdalene: The Followers of Jesus in History and Legend. Oxford University Press, USA, 2006.

Ehrman, Bart D. The Lost Gospel of Judas Iscariot: A New Look at Betrayer and Betrayed. Oxford University Press, USA, 2008.

Eusebius. The History of the Church from Christ to Constantine. G.A. Williams, trans. New York, NY: Dorset Press, 1989.

Fitzmyer, Joseph. The Gospel according to Luke: Introduction, Translation, and Notes. Garden City, NY: Doubleday, 1985.

Bibliography For Advanced Study

Fox, John. Foxe's Book of Martyrs. Peabody, MA: Hendrickson Publishers, 2004.

Goodspeed, Edgar J. Matthew, Apostle and Evangelist; A Study on the Authorship of the First Gospel. Philadelphia, PA, 1959.

EL Sukenik. Ancient Synagogues of Palestine and Greece, (London, 1934).

Frend, William Hugh Clifford. The Archaeology of Early Christianity, A History. Geoffrey Chapman, 1997.

Halton, Thomas Patrick. On Illustrious Men, The Fathers of the Church. CUA Press, 1999.

Isaac Lambertson. The Lives of the Holy Apostles. Buena Vista, CO: Holy Apostles Convent Press, 1990.

Hippolytus, On the Twelve Apostles.com.

Isaac Lambertsen, The Lives of the Holy Apostles, Holy Apostles Convent Press, Buena Vista, CO, 1990.

Jedin, Hubert. Papal Legate at The Council of Trent. St Louis, MO: B. Herder Book Co, 1947.

Jeffrey, David Lyle. Fishers of Men: A Dictionary of Biblical Tradition in English Literature. Grand Rapids, MI: W.B. Eerdmans, 1992.

Jensen, Irving. Jensen's Survey of the New Testament. Chicago, IL: Moody Press, 1981.

J. J. Scott. Josephus. Dictionary of Jesus and the Gospels, eds. Joel B. Green and Scott McKnight, Downers Grove, IL: Intervarsity Press, 1992.

Josephus. Wars of the Jews, IV.

Kirby, Peter. "Fragments of Hegesippus." Early Christian Writings, 2017.

Kirby, Peter. Hippolytus of Rome. Early Christian Writings, 2017.

Kirby, Peter. Historical Jesus Theories. Early Christian Writings, 2017.

Kruse, Colin G. The Gospel According to John: An Introduction and Commentary. Grand Rapids, MI: Wm. B. Eerdmans, 2004.

Langton, Daniel R. The Apostle Paul in the Jewish Imagination. Cambridge, UK: Cambridge University Press, 2010.

Longenecker, Richard N., ed. Frank E. Gaebelein. The Acts of the Apostles, The Expositors Bible Commentary. Grand Rapids, MI: Zondervan Books, 1981.

Louth, Andrew. Eusebius and the Birth of Church History. Cambridge, MA: Cambridge Univ. Press, 2004.

MacArthur, John. MacArthur Study Bible, New King James Version. Nashville, TN: Nelson/Word Publishing, 1997.

Maccoby, Hyam. The Mythmaker: Paul and the Invention of Christianity. New York, NY: Harper & Row, 1986.

Mancini, Ignazio. Archaeological Discoveries Relative to the Judaeo-Christians: Historical Survey, trans. [from Italian] by G. Bushnell [as] updated by the author. In series, Publications of the Studium Biblicum Franciscanum: Collectio minor. Jerusalem: Franciscan Printing Press, 1970.

Marshall, I.H., ed. R. V. G. Tasker. The Acts of the Apostles, The Tyndale New Testament Commentaries. Grand Rapids, MI: Eerdmans, 1980.

Marshall, Taylor. Thomas Aquinas in 50 Pages: A Layman's Quick Guide to Thomism. Saint John Press, 2017.

Mason, Steve. Josephus and the New Testament. Peabody, MA: Hendrickson Press, 1992.

Metzger, Bruce. An Introduction to the Apocrypha. New York, NY: Oxford, 1957.

Metzger, Bruce M. The Canon of the New Testament: Its Origin, Development, and Significance. Clarendon Press. Oxford, 1987.

Moir, Alfred and Michelangelo Mersisi da Caravaggio. Caravaggio. Master of Art Series. New York, NY: H.N. Abrams, 1989.

Most, Glenn W. Doubting Thomas. Cambridge, Mass., London: Harvard University Press, 2005.

Murphy-O'Connor, Jerome. Paul the Letter-Writer: His World, His Options, His Skills. Collegeville, MN: Liturgical Press, 1995.

Mykytiuk, Lawrence J. (2004). <u>Identifying Biblical Persons in Northwest Semitic Inscriptions of 1200–539 B.C.E</u>. SBL Academia Biblica series, no. 12. Atlanta, Ga.: Society of Biblical Literature.

Nixon, R.E. <u>Boanerges, The New Bible Dictionary</u>. London, England: The Inter-Varsity Fellowship, 1963.

O'Day, Gail R. <u>Introduction to the Gospel of John in New Revised Standard Translation of the Bible</u>. Abingdon Press, Nashville, 2003.

Pamphilus, Eusebius. <u>The Ecclesiastical History of Eusebius Pamphilus</u>. Grand Rapids, MI: Baker Book House, 1984.

Pearlman, Meyer. <u>Through the Bible Book by Book – Part IV New Testament Epistles and Revelation</u>. Springfield, MI: Gospel Publishing House, 1935.

Pojman, Louis P. and Vaughn, Lewis. <u>The Moral Life</u>. New York, NY: Oxford University Press, 2011.

Robinson, James M. ed., <u>The Nag Hammadi Library in English</u>. San Francisco, CA: HarperCollins, 1990.

Roberts and Donaldson. <u>Copy of Five Letters from Agar; Memoirs of Edessa of Edessa and Other Ancient Syriac Documents</u>. Ante Nicene Fathers.

Roberts and Donaldson. <u>Preaching of the Apostle Thaddaeus at Edessa</u>. Ante Nicene Fathers.

Robertson, J.C. <u>Sketches of Church History: The Age of the Apostles</u>. New York, NY: Crosswalk Publishing Company, 2001.

Ryle, <u>Charles Caldwell</u>. <u>Basic Theology</u>. Chicago, IL: Moody Press, 1999.

Schneemelcher, Wilhelm. <u>New Testament Apocrypha The Canon of the New Testament and Significance</u>. Louisville, KY: Westminster/ John Knox Press, *1987.*

Schneemelcher, Wilhelm. ed., translation by R. McL. Wilson, <u>New Testament Apocrypha: Gospels and Related Writings</u>. Louisville: John Knox Press, 1992.

Smith, William and Cheetham, Samuel. A Dictionary of Christian Antiquities, 1875.

Snodgrass, Klyne R. The Gospel of Thomas: A Secondary Gospel, Second Century 7, 1989.

Spurgeon, Charles. Christianquotes.info, 2017.

Steward, Don. Blue Letter Bible, 2017.

Stichera for Vespers of the Commemoration of the Holy Apostle Simon the Zealot, May 10th, Russian Menaion, St. John of Kronstadt Press, Liberty, TN.

Tenney, Merrill C. New Testament Survey. Grand Rapids, MI: Wm. B. Eerdmans Publishing Company, 1961.

The Apostle Saint Thomas. www.catholictradition.org

The Lives of the Saints in the Russian Language, According to the Menology of St. Dimitri of Rostov. Moscow, Synod Press, 1908.

Towns, Elmer. Bible Answers for All Your Questions. Nashville, TN: Thomas Nelson Publishers, 2003.

Towns, Elmer. Theology for Today. Dubuque, IO: Kendal/Hunt Publishing Company, 1989.

Utley, Bob. The Study Bible Commentaries Series, New Testament. Bible.org, 2012.

Vaugh, Lewis. Doing Ethics. New York, NY: W.W. Norton & Company, 2017.

Walter Kaiser, Jr. and Duane Garrett. Archaeological Study Bible: An Illustrated Walk. Grand Rapids, MI: Zondervan Books, 2005.

Wasson, Donald L. "Pliny the Elder." Ancient History Encyclopedia. Ancient History Encyclopedia, 12 Jun 2014. Web. 14 Sep 2017.

Westerholm, Stephen. Understanding Matthew: The Early Christian Worldview of the First Gospel. Grand Rapids, MI: Baker Academic, 2006.

Wuellner, Wilhelm H. The Meaning of Fishers of Men. Louisville, KY: Westminster Press, 1967.

DR. PHIL AYERS BIO

EDUCATION:

A.S., Virginia Western Community College, 1973.
D.S.Th., Colonial Baptist College, 1980.
B.R.ED., Trinity College of the Bible, 1982.
M.Min., Trinity Theological Seminary, 1985.
M.A. (Counseling), Liberty University, 1991.
D.MIN., Liberty Theological Seminary, 2005.

OTHER PUBLICATIONS:

A Proverb a Day Keeps the Devil Away
ISBN: 978-1-60647-844-8

What Ever Happened to Respect? America's Loss of Respect for Pastors
ISBN: 1-4208-6623-0 (sc)

In Jail Once, Imprisoned for Life
Registration: TXu-1-733-031

MARINE Featuring: The Battle of Hickory May 1967
ISBN: 978-1-6241-9556-3

Traveling Upward
ISBN: 978-1-4984-2183-6

When Anger Strikes (Me and My Stupid Behavior)
ISBN: 978-1-4984-8197-7

CPSIA information can be obtained
at www.ICGtesting.com
Printed in the USA
FFOW03n2300190118
44601613-44525FF